Intuitionism

BLOOMSBURY ETHICS SERIES

Bloomsbury Ethics is a series of books written to help students explore, engage with, and master key topics in contemporary ethics and moral philosophy.

Available now:

Reasons, Eric Wiland

Forthcoming in the series:

Moral Motivation, Leonard Kahn
Moral Realism, Kevin DeLapp
Trust, Ethics and Human Reason, Olli Lagerspetz
Virtue Ethics, Nafsika Athanassoulis

Series Editors:

Thom Brooks is Reader in Political and Legal Philosophy at the University of Newcastle, UK. He is the founding editor of the *Journal of Moral Philosophy* and runs a popular Political Philosophy blog called The Brooks Blog.

Simon Kirchin is Senior Lecturer in Philosophy at the University of Kent, UK. He is President of the British Society for Ethical Theory and co-editor of *Arguing About Metaethics* (Routledge, 2006).

BLOOMSBURY ETHICS

Intuitionism

DAVID KASPAR

BLOOMSBURY

LONDON • NEW DELHI • NEW YORK • SYDNEY

Bloomsbury Academic

An imprint of Bloomsbury Publishing Plc

50 Bedford Square
London
WC1B 3DP
UK

175 Fifth Avenue
New York
NY 10010
USA

www.bloomsbury.com

First published 2012

British Library Cataloguing-in-Publication Data
A catalogue record for this book is available from the British Library.

ISBN: HB: 978-1-4411-1446-4
PB: 978-1-4411-7954-8

Library of Congress Cataloging-in-Publication Data
Kaspar, David.
Intuitionism / David Kaspar.
p. cm. – (Continuum ethics)
Includes bibliographical references and index.
ISBN 978-1-4411-1446-4 (alk. paper) – ISBN 978-1-4411-7954-8
(pbk. : alk. paper) – ISBN 978-1-4411-9625-5 (ebook epub : alk. paper) –
ISBN 978-1-4411-5986-1 (ebook pdf : alk. paper)   1. Ethical intuitionism.
2. Ethics.   3. Intuition.   I. Title.
BJ1472.K37 2012
171'.2–dc23
2012004676

Typeset by Newgen Imaging Systems, Pvt Ltd, Chennai, India
Printed and bound in India

For my mother

CONTENTS

ACKNOWLEDGMENTS

I am grateful to many people for their assistance in writing this book. Mike Huemer, Tom Carson, and Michael Cholbi provided valuable comments and suggestions on earlier material that was included in the book. Three students at the University of Nevada, Reno—Jonathan Kanzelmeyer, Andrew Ross, and Kara Hammer gave helpful feedback on one half of a book draft for a seminar I taught there. Four friends and former UNR colleagues assisted me greatly by discussing the book with me at weekly meetings in June 2011: Tom Nickles, Jack Kelly, Jose Martin, and Chris Williams. Chris also provided constructive suggestions and comments on my book proposal and on different chapters. I thank Rob Talisse for his sound advice on the book production process. Barry Smith provided valuable feedback on Chapter 3. Denise Vigani's comments on Chapter 7 helped improve it. The book benefited from comments on the entire manuscript from Tom Nickles and from Dena Davidson. Many thanks to Robert Delfino for his extensive, detailed, and valuable comments and discussions on the entire manuscript. I appreciate the Series Editors, Thom Brooks and Simon Kirchin for their encouragement and suggestions. Simon's chapter-by-chapter recommendations helped me to better structure the book. Lastly, I would like to thank my family and friends for their support.

Introduction

Imagine a world much like ours. It is inhabited by people much like us. Most of the time they go about their business, generally leaving others alone. Here and there they might tell little lies, and sometimes tell big ones. Rarely does one of them try to kill another. But it happens. There is, however, one key difference between their world and ours among the following few things we have in common:

> The people in this world can know with certainty fundamental moral truths. These truths are true no matter how people feel about them.

> Morality in this world is neither based on personal emotions, on cultural norms, nor on the social evolution of the species. Instead, morality is based on the fact that certain acts are by their very nature right and others are similarly wrong.

> Lastly, the people in this world believe that they have knowledge of fundamental moral truths.

So what's that one thing that sets them apart from us? According to intuitionism, what distinguishes the inhabitants of this other world from us is that *they believe* they know what's right, many of us don't. Everything else is the same. If this picture is true, that means that our moral thinking is in error today. You might say, then, that many of us are living in moral perplexity. Our perplexity is partly explained by our awareness of the extreme complexity of morality itself. But a better part of it is due to factors which are not primarily moral. Since society's mores are less uniform than they once were it doesn't assure us in our moral beliefs as it once did. Perhaps more importantly, science, with its technological offshoots, has vastly increased our knowledge of everything but morality. Even if we know very little science we are sure that morality is not a scientific matter, and sense that ethics cannot

legitimately be called a science. Against this background, most of
us see our moral beliefs merely as a product of our personal histories. We think that if we were raised differently we would have
different morals.

At the same time, we are often confident we know what's right.
When someone lies to us, we don't merely think that they have low-
ered our enjoyment of life. We don't just think that liars are not to
be trusted in the same way that unreliable people are untrustwor-
thy. We think they've *wronged* us. We think liars are *bad* people.
And our moral confidence is not limited to matters which affect us
personally. We get into heated arguments about events occurring
outside of our neighborhood. For example, opponents and support-
ers of the Iraq War argued about whether invading Iraq was *morally justified*. While such discussions rarely change minds, often
each side is convinced they are on the side of morality. However, at
other times we are unsure of our moral beliefs. We might feel that
something is immoral about eating animals or abortion without
being confident about it.

Beliefs reflecting our moral positions are not all there is to
morality. There are our beliefs *about* morality and what morality *is*. This is the point at which our current perplexity arises, and
where the impact of science is felt. Generally, in today's world,
we have serious doubts about morality. We say, "Not everything
is black and white. There's a lot of gray," "Moral beliefs cannot
be proved," "Morality is subjective," "Killing and stealing are not
always wrong," and so on. Many ethical theories reflect these quite
common doubts about morality.

So a certain tension has emerged. We are individually confident
in some of our moral beliefs. But we are less sure that morality
is an objective affair. But doesn't it seem strange to be so confident of something we believe to be an inherently nonobjective
matter?

Intuitionism is a book about morality from the standpoint of
moral intuitionism. Intuitionism is the moral theory which claims
that *you know what's right*. We know, for example, that murdering, breaking promises, and lying are wrong. The extent and nature
of this knowledge will be addressed later. One attractive feature of
intuitionism is that, on my account, it makes the most sense of
our moral beliefs and of our beliefs about morality, including the
skeptical beliefs presented above. At different points in the book,

I'll show how intuitionism explains the following common beliefs we have about morality:

(a) You know what's right.

(b) Not everything is black and white.

(c) Sometimes, in extreme cases, it is morally permissible to lie, steal, and so on.

(d) We each feel more confident claiming that *we* have a duty to keep our promises, for example, than claiming that other people do.

(e) There are emergencies in which a cold cost-benefit assessment makes the most moral sense.

(f) There is no way to prove that, for instance, harming others is wrong.

(g) Ethics is not a hard science.

(h) Supreme principle moral theories, such as utilitarianism or Kantianism, are not initially convincing, and are often not ultimately convincing.

(i) There is no satisfactory way to resolve some moral disagreements at certain times.

(j) Most of our duties are based on particular relations we have to other people.

(k) Moral absolutism was more plausible before the twentieth century, and less plausible during and after the twentieth century.

(l) Moral disagreement is common.

1. The search for a supreme principle

Ethicists harbor doubts about morality just like everyone else. Some have left doubt and arrived at outright skepticism. Moral nihilists think that everything we believe or say about morality is false. Expressivists hold that morality is merely an expression of one's subjective feelings. However, despite having doubts about morality, most ethicists who try to explain what is moral develop objective theories of morality. Often such theories rest on a supreme principle of morality. A supreme principle of morality is a single moral principle which is variously claimed to have one or more of these functions: to prove, to justify, to explain, or to guide us in deciding what is right in every possible case.

Agreeing that there is something objective to morality, you might turn to ethics for answers. What will you find? An ethics class will often cover many theories, many of which claim that a supreme principle of morality can tell us what is morally right. Here are some such principles that have been offered:

Always act so as to maximize pleasure (utilitarianism).

Act only on that principle of action that you can simultaneously will as a universal law (Kantianism).

Do not do what any agent motivated to find general principles of social regulation could reasonably reject (Scanlon's contractarianism).

Each of these principles has able defenders and detractors. But a student facing them for the first time is likely to be bewildered by their number and variety. It may be that exposure to such a parade of moral theories only contributes to doubts about morality.[1]

Intuitionism differs from other objectivist moral theories by claiming that there is no need for a supreme principle of morality. We know what's right, and thus have no need to deduce, derive, or justify our moral knowledge by means of a supreme principle. The challenge of figuring out what is right in an actual moral situation is a problem of application, not of deduction or derivation. Intuitionists notice that supreme principle theories try to argue their case by showing that their principle implies or justifies a number of moral rules, such as "do not murder," "do not steal," "do not lie," and so forth. Intuitionism begins by claiming we are certain of such rules, and so there is no need for a principle which supposedly implies or justifies them. One task of this book is to show that there is little reason for confidence that there is a supreme principle of morality.

2. We know what's right

We may err in our believing in two ways. We can believe we know what we do not, in fact, know. And we can believe we don't know what we really do know. Philosophers have understandably been most concerned with the first kind of error. For any given issue, out of innumerable possibilities, there is only one belief that is true. Considering matters abstractly it is more likely that we mistakenly believe what we don't know. And the common beliefs of past civilizations, most philosophical works, even the history of science, show us that error is the norm in human inquiry.

Intuitionism claims that morality is one area in which we know the truth. If that is correct, that means that widely divergent positions in ethical inquiry have a common source: the error of not believing what we know. Ordinary people's mistaken beliefs about morality too have the same basis. One feature of this work is to explain how different moral theories make errors of this kind, by diverging from moral knowledge. So different "error theories" must be introduced to explain why different theories disagree with intuitionism.

But, it might be asked, if we know what is right, why do we think otherwise? My hypothesis is that we do not think we know what's right because we do not know how to *explain* what's right, or how we know it. In my view, all general mistakes about moral knowledge rest on the matter of explanation. And this is where the issue of science comes in. People's beliefs about morality are based on what they think is the best explanation for moral phenomena. Lay people tend to believe a *causal explanation* of our moral beliefs is what is in order. If we think that a social explanation of our different moral beliefs makes the most sense, then we will believe cultural relativism—that each morality is relative to a distinct culture. If we think personal history best explains our moral beliefs, then a psychological explanation will suit us best. We will be subjectivists and believe that morality is a subjective matter, differing in content from person to person.

Ethicists also disagree based on what they think is the promising explanation. Since some philosophers are less interested in causal explanations of our moral beliefs, and more interested in what moral beliefs we ought to have, they concentrate on the most plausible *normative explanations* of them. Ethicists, once more, often agree on the "moral rules." In my view, their agreement is based on their knowledge of them. So such philosophers disagree about the promising explanation of moral rules: the greatest good, the maximum pleasure, reason itself, or a hypothetical agreement among agents. Other ethicists, such as expressivists and nihilists, begin with the model of scientific knowledge, argue that objective moral facts do not fit into the scientific worldview, and explain morality by individual emotions, or simply claim moral notions are null and void. So both laymen and philosophers form their distinctive moral views based on what they believe to be the most promising explanation of morality.

Where does intuitionism stand on the matter of moral explanation? If you were to ask the critics of intuitionism, their answer would come in a chorus: nowhere. All of the major alleged weaknesses of intuitionism can be boiled down to one thing. Intuitionism does not explain moral matters very well, if it explains them at all. "Intuitionism doesn't explain morality" might be the slogan of all anti-intuitionists. Some of the things intuitionism has been accused of not explaining are: how we know what is moral, how we come to have moral knowledge, how we ought to decide what's right in concrete moral situations, and how moral facts fit into natural facts. Lastly, intuitionism has no way to explain our moral disagreement. It is thought that, if there really were objective moral facts, if we really do know what's right, then why is there so much moral disagreement?

The core of the case for intuitionism made in this book is this. Other ethical theories seem to have greater explanatory promise than intuitionism. But the promise is one thing, the deed another. Intuitionism only has less explanatory promise according to *the standards* of *other theories*. I argue that, when we give the explanatory resources of intuitionism a more careful look, and recognize they are just of a different kind than those offered by other theories, then we will see its explanatory power. I claim that intuitionism is most capable of explaining all the 12 listed common beliefs, from (a) to (l). And I would bet that no other theory can explain them as effortlessly or as naturally.

3. The approach of *intuitionism*

Intuitionism, in my view, is the most promising research program in ethics. *Intuitionism* is something of an introduction to the intuitionist outlook. The approach usually taken in books like this is to examine and compare the thought of many thinkers who hold the theory being studied. There are several merits to this approach. To get a clearer understanding and overview of several thinkers, it is quite helpful. But this approach has one flaw. Where several thinkers are introduced, compared, and their conflicts highlighted it suggests that philosophy is merely a discussion of different views. My view is that philosophy is the search for the whole truth, and that while discussion is an indispensable means in our search, we must never lose sight of that goal. This book reflects that standpoint.

The question guiding my approach is, what if intuitionism is true? I am seeking to find out what a completed intuitionist moral theory would be like. Consider how science builds on the thought of many thinkers and incorporates their different thoughts based on their individual discoveries. Take physics, for example. Newton's laws cover macroscopic objects; Maxwell's laws cover electromagnetic fields; Einstein's laws cover gravitational fields; Bohr's laws cover quantum events. So working scientists, unlike philosophers, do not spend time comparing Newton and Einstein's views of gravity.

Philosophers interested in the whole truth of some matter would do well to follow the scientists' lead here. A completed intuitionist moral theory will likely incorporate the distinct strengths of different intuitionists and other ethicists. In this book, I will combine W. D. Ross's theory of duty, H. A. Prichard's case against moral proofs, G. E. Moore's theory of good, Robert Audi's account of self-evidence, Michael Huemer's theory of intuitions, Russ Shafer-Landau's case for nonnaturalist moral supervenience, and A. C. Ewing's partners-in-crime defense of the use of intuitions. I will also consult the work of some unsung intuitionist heroes. Oliver Johnson's unjustly neglected argument for synthetic a priori truths and, most importantly, Adolf Reinach's theory of intelligible, abstract moral kinds will be critical for making the case for intuitionism. *Intuitionism* combines all of these theories, as well as some of my own, into a comprehensive synthesis. Now I am certainly aware that this is not the only plausible synthesis of intuitionist theories. However, it is the one that I think is the strongest and most defensible.

One of the original contributions I make is to provide a theory which explains the existence and nature of moral facts and how we know them. This is one part of the book that is metaphysically speculative, and consequently takes big epistemological risks. Some intuitionists might say these risks are unnecessary. But the main reason I nonetheless proceed with them is to provide that part of intuitionism whose absence has been most keenly felt: a way to connect our moral intuitions with the physical facts of the world. The result is what may be called a *stout nonnaturalism*. Even if it turns out that my moral metaphysics is mistaken, I hope to convince some readers that some such work needs to be carried out to round out intuitionism and demonstrate its explanatory force. Hopefully, the steps I take will lead to a better intuitionist synthesis in the future.

4. Overview

In Chapter 1, I give an outline of intuitionism and provide an opportunity for testing our moral intuitions. Chapter 2 relates the fortunes of intuitionism in the past hundred years, explaining both its downfall in the middle of the twentieth century and its recent revitalization. Chapter 3 makes the case for the intuitionist position on moral knowledge and shows why a number of objections to intuitionism do not pass muster. In Chapter 4, I review recent attacks on intuitionism, provide some intuitionist responses, and pinpoint some of the major metaethical challenges intuitionism must overcome, chief among them being the problem of moral supervenience. Chapter 5 outlines a theory of the grounds of intuitionism, a much neglected topic. In my view, explaining moral rightness requires providing a theory of moral relations and a theory of moral kinds. In Chapter 6, I show that Prichard and Ross gave us more reasons to believe than not to believe that morally right actions are also intrinsically good. I then take this result, combine it with the theory of moral kinds, and provide an outline of moral explanation which overcomes the problem of moral supervenience. Chapter 7 examines normative rivals to intuition-ism, Kantianism, New Kantianism, utilitarianism, and one recent variety of virtue ethics I call "exemplarism." I show why each of them is lacking. Finally, Chapter 8 both brings things down to the practical level to explain how we act on the principles of intuition-ism and touches upon some of the ultimate issues of ethics, such as whether God must exist for there to be moral truth.

CHAPTER ONE

Thinking about morality

Introduction

Intuitionism is an old view that has only recently been revived. What is especially exciting about it is that, despite its age, intuitionism has a wide range of promising yet unexplored theoretical possibilities. Its explanatory power covers a surprising number of areas. That power is firmly rooted in its foundational knowledge. The first order of business, then, is to bring you into the kind of basic moral reflection that establishes intuitionism's foundations. Since many who oppose it go astray right at the initial stage of moral inquiry, such elementary reflections form an important part of the case for intuitionism.

This chapter outlines a big picture perspective of intuitionism and provides an opportunity to test our moral intuitions. What I will establish here are intuitionism's foundations, the methods by which they are secured, as well as its basic doctrines. Beyond that I do not present the main arguments to support it or vigorously defend it from any of many attacks. All that will come later. I do, however, clear up a number of prevalent misunderstandings of the view. My purpose in all this is to give both novice and expert ethicists the best opportunity to understand intuitionism.

One previously unexplored topic is explored here. Intuitionism explains why we have the moral beliefs we do, in fact, have. More specifically, it explains why each of us has our moral beliefs, as well as why civilizations over millennia have consistently adhered to certain moral principles. The task of explaining our actual moral beliefs is one philosophers previously relinquished to psychologists. And many moral theories have good reason for not taking a position on the matter. But if moral knowledge is genuinely within the reach of all of us, as intuitionism asserts, then our psychological histories are only one part, and a less important part, of the explanation for why we have the moral beliefs we have. I will conclude this chapter by reviewing some of the many things that intuitionism explains.

1. Moral beliefs and intuitionism

We all have moral beliefs. We tend to think that assaulting others is wrong and that helping others in need is right. As we seriously reflect on such beliefs, we also think of potential complications, especially in extraordinary circumstances. Although assaulting a stranger sitting on a park bench seems obviously wrong to us, assaulting the guard of a terrorist haven to stop a terrorist attack seems right. We believe we have a duty to help others in need, but recognize limitations to that duty. We are certainly free to donate so much to the needy that we have to sell our house. But we don't believe it's our duty to do so.

Intuitionism begins by looking at our moral thought and moral experience. What we *really think* about morality is something to be investigated, not dismissed.[1] On the basis of our genuine moral thoughts, intuitionism holds that, in general, *we know what's right*. That means that moral knowledge is something we bring with us to ethics, not something born whole from ethical inquiry. Our knowledge that lying is wrong, for example, is explained as follows. The proposition that lying is wrong is self-evidently true, and we grasp that truth. Just as we do not believe that the chair we are sitting on exists on the basis of a particular metaphysical theory of material objects, so we do not believe that lying is wrong because of a moral theory called intuitionism. Rather, intuitionism strives to explain what we already know.

Many reading this book, I am sure, believe they know what's right, but do not know *how* they know it. Also, they might think they know certain acts are wrong, but be unsure about others. Other readers, I am equally sure, are surprised to learn that they have moral knowledge, for they are not aware of having any! Since the basis of intuitionism is what we really think about morality, and since we obviously have very different beliefs about morality, it seems best to start our investigation with each reader's personal beliefs. So let us start with what *you* believe about morality.

Let us think carefully together about the moral statements listed below. As you think about each one, try to determine, first, whether or not you believe it. Having done that, ask how strongly you hold your belief. Do you feel certain of it? Are you only somewhat convinced? Or is your confidence in a particular judgment weak? Later I will assess these moral statements. Here is the list:

Depriving others of liberty is wrong.

Morality is subjective.

Abortion is morally permissible.

There are moral facts.

Keeping promises is required.

Harming others is wrong.

Animals have no right to life.

Thinking about these claims provides material for moral reflection. But there are other reasons for each of us to examine what seems to us to be true in morality. By beginning with the truths, and providing theoretical support later, I begin with what intuitionists regard as most important, giving you the best opportunity to take on the intuitionist perspective.

Intuitionists and their critics have often been working from different sets of data. As I aim to show, intuitionism is able to account for all of the data moral theorists must deal with. But the data intuitionists consider most important, what we really think about morality, are ignored or devalued by many critics. So by considering our genuine moral thoughts we open the prospect of taking into account all data relevant to moral inquiry. And besides, can you think of any good reason *not* to consider how moral matters appear to you?

2. Methods of intuitionism

An intuition is an intellectual appearance. It is how things really seem to our minds concerning a given abstract subject or about an abstract feature of a particular concrete situation. We have intuitions about geometry, logic, arithmetic, and their applications. And we have intuitions of moral principles and of the moral situations in which they find application. A moral intuition is what we really think about a moral issue. That genuine moral thought is the basis of intuitionism will strike many as unpromising. Given our widely divergent personal moral beliefs, how can it be asserted that by starting with what we *think* about morality we can ever arrive at secure moral *knowledge*?

Regard this entire book as an answer to that question. But the initial response is that intuitionism deals with moral thoughts that survive critical reflection. We are primarily reflecting on three things: the *moral content* of moral propositions, the *logical relations* between them, and their *practical applications*. Any method of reflection that makes what we really think about morality of the first importance and by which we can determine whether one of our moral thoughts should be considered an instance of moral knowledge may be called a *method of intuitionism*.

Reflection on morality must begin in our moral experience. To know what our moral intuitions are requires beginning where morality really counts: in *actual moral situations*. Actual moral situations are the primary context of moral knowledge. Think of the following circumstances:

> We make promises to others. When the time comes to make good on one, we should reflect on what thoughts we have about keeping it. At other times we find ourselves in situations in which, to avoid an inconvenience, we are tempted to lie. Observing how we actually think about lying will give us useful information for our inquiry. Drawing from such experiences and reflecting on what we think is right will provide the first data of ethics: what we think our actual duties are.

Most works in ethics begin by plunging into theory immediately. Intuitionism holds that both the starting-point and the end-point of moral theory is what we really think about morality. This is not to say that intuitionism eschews theory for mere moral self-reflection. Rather, intuitionism recognizes that if we do not have some moral knowledge to start with, theorizing will, in the final analysis, be futile, and that there is no alternative ultimate touchstone for accepting or rejecting abstract moral principles to what we really think about morality.

Why is initial moral reflection so crucial to intuitionism? It holds that the basic moral principles like "Lying is wrong" are self-evident truths.[2] If we start by making the theoretical case for self-evident truths, we will eventually reach the following impasse. Suppose we have somehow shown that there are self-evident truths. That would certainly be a coup for intuitionism. But just because there are self-evident truths does not show that there are any self-evident *moral* truths. And even if it were recognized that there are self-evident moral truths, that would not by any means show *which* moral principles are self-evidently true. That is why we must first attempt to establish which moral thoughts appear true through moral reflection.

3. The first data of ethics

An effective way to determine the first data of ethics is by way of contrasts, through what is called *epistemic appraisal.*[3] Consider the situation in which you are tempted to lie. As you are experiencing the situation, or soon after, give some thought to the following judgments: (1) You should not lie, (2) You should lie, (3) You may lie. Reflecting on these contrasting judgments will help you to determine what you really think concerning what is moral in the situation. To make sure that we are dealing with what we really think, after we have made our initial judgment concerning propositions (1), (2), and (3), we should double-check all our options. So if we have determined, say, that we should not lie in this case, we should ask, "Do I really think that I should not lie in this situation? Am I certain of it?"

Considered thoughts of *what* we should do in actual moral situations are the first data of ethics. The next thing to determine is *why* we believe we should so act. Whatever answers the question of why we should perform a certain moral act, which we experience as having some authority, is a *moral reason.* Initial inquiry on our moral reasons will, as previously, be aimed at determining what we really think. And it will continue to be crucial that we think about what our moral reasons are in the context of actual moral situations.

Contrasting various moral reasons in thought will help us to assess their relative epistemic strengths. If, given the situation you just considered, you thought it was your duty not to lie, then why was it? One straightforward answer might have been that "It's just wrong to lie" gave you sufficient reason not to lie. An alternative reason might have been that lying would not have produced the most good possible. That is, you considered that not lying would have been productive of greater good overall than lying. Lastly, consider whether the reason why you decided not to lie was because you thought that lying was not an action that you could will as a universal law. You thought that, as a matter of logic, a world in which everyone, including you, consistently lied is not a possible world.

4. Assumptions to avoid

As we examine our moral beliefs some assumptions must be avoided. Many thoughts that will occur to us, intrude upon our reflections, or even pester us must temporarily be set aside. Since we are initially unsure which of our moral beliefs is true, or even which moral beliefs we really hold, we cannot make any assumptions about the ultimate results of our moral reflections. Consequently, we cannot assume that there is one supreme principle that implies, justifies, or explains all our other moral beliefs, or that there is no supreme principle at all. At this stage, we are unsure.

Besides avoiding assumptions that can misdirect our inquiry, we must also keep a watchful eye on our responses to our reflections. Biases, wishful thinking, hidden antipathies and affections, all must be acknowledged, and temporarily put aside as we proceed. Such self-watchfulness is especially important in moral inquiry, where our subjective preferences are most apt to be lazily reinforced or easily threatened. In particular, we must guard against responses to moral thoughts that might move us to abandon them without giving them their due.

Some other responses of which to be aware: at several points we are likely to doubt that we know a particular moral proposition that seems correct to us. Doubting whether we know a given proposition is almost always salutary in philosophical inquiry. But the important thing now is merely what seems correct to us. So doubts should be registered, then let go. As we sift through what we really think of moral propositions, we will likely want to justify the beliefs we currently hold. Justification of beliefs is a central task of philosophy. But once more, we are trying to determine what our moral thoughts really are. Also, any thoughts of whether our reflections fit or contravene today's social norms must be abandoned for now. Lastly, many people have a desire to reform society. This desire is not inherently bad, but it cannot influence our initial moral reflections.

5. Divisions in moral theory

We can now connect several previous points. I will state which of the moral propositions we have been examining are self-evidently true, and which are not, according to intuitionism.[4] This sorting of propositions provides an opportunity to explain the different kinds of issues investigated in moral theory, and clarifies the character, structure, and extent of intuitionism's claims of moral knowledge.

What we really think about morality can be divided along certain lines. Under each head I'll place the moral propositions which fall under it. According to intuitionism, what we really think about morality can mean: (A) What we know is moral, (B) What some at best rationally *believe* is moral, or (C) What some really think morality *is*.

We know that (A):

1 Depriving others of liberty is wrong.

2 Keeping promises is required.

3 Harming others is wrong.

Some at best rationally believe that (B):

4 Animals have no right to life.

5 Abortion is morally permissible.

Lastly, what some really think morality is (C):

6 Morality is subjective.

7 There are moral facts.

Intuitionism holds that our basic moral knowledge is of *fundamental moral principles*, such as depriving others of liberty is wrong. Moral propositions that apply the fundamental moral principles are *applied moral propositions*. Among them are the following pairs: animals have *no* right to life and animals *have* a right to life; abortion is morally *permissible* and abortion is morally *impermissible*. In the current state of ethics, these applied propositions are matters of opinion, and open for debate. Finally, what we think morality is, such as morality is subjective, consists of *metaethical propositions*.

"Harming others is wrong" is a fundamental moral truth. We know this, and we are secure in our knowledge of this. We are not apt to disagree about moral propositions of this sort. The reason why, according to intuitionism, is that such propositions are self-evidently true. And the reason we know them is that our minds can adequately understand these propositions, and know them on that basis. When intuitionism says *you know what's right*, this assertion is primarily about fundamental moral propositions. Discussions concerning these propositions are about the fundamental *content* of morality. The branch of ethics that inquires about moral content is called *normative ethics*.

The certainty we have about such truths is shaken when it comes to propositions like "Animals have no right to life." At most we rationally believe this, meaning we lack sufficient justification for knowing it. A clear indication that only belief is involved here is that reasons can be brought forth that can easily generate doubts. One reason we believe that animals have no right to life, if we do in fact believe that, is that we think that "Harming others is wrong" does not properly apply to nonhuman members of the animal kingdom. Others dispute this, claiming that this fundamental moral proposition does in fact apply to other animals. This disagreement of application facilitates the current animal rights debate.

Applied moral propositions are not self-evident. They differ from the fundamental moral propositions in that they include content that our intellects cannot know simply by understanding them. The concepts of "animal" and "fetus" are material concepts we cannot completely grasp by intellect alone. Therefore, we cannot determine a priori whether the corresponding propositions are true or false. This is the underlying reason for our disagreements about applied moral propositions. We ask, what is a fetus? What is an animal? Are beings in either class persons? This suggests we must learn more about animals and fetuses through empirical means to determine if they are beings which it would be wrong to harm.[5]

Our intellects alone cannot determine the truth of most metaethical propositions either. Propositions such as "There are moral facts" and "Morality is subjective" are not self-evident. Metethical propositions are about the *nature* of morality. Most metaethical claims are not self-evident, and that includes most of the metaethical claims of intuitionism. So two central intuitionist metaethical claims, "There are moral facts" and "Some moral propositions are self-evidently true," are not themselves self-evident. That means that they can only be established by means of argumentation, and so invite dispute.

Our most important objective is to establish the truth of the fundamental moral principles. If indeed they are self-evidently true, then intuitionism is the correct moral theory. I have only listed fundamental principles that we've been considering. As we proceed, I will introduce more. Since these fundamental propositions are believed to be true, or correct, by most normative theories, and since they form the foundation of intuitionism, from now on I will call them the "intuitive principles." Previously, I offered for consideration some alternative moral reasons for not lying: it's simply wrong, it would not produce the most good or we cannot think of a world in which lying is universal. Intuitionism holds that we recognize that lying is wrong, and that is our best reason not to lie. To paraphrase H. A. Prichard, the reason lies within the principle itself. The intuitive principles not only inform us of what is right, but also provide reason sufficient to do what is right.

6. Intuitionism

Having worked through several preliminary points, we can provide a fuller characterization of intuitionism. Robert Audi, a leader of the revival of intuitionism, defines it this way: "(1) It is an ethical *pluralism*, a position affirming an irreducible plurality of basic moral principles. (2) Each principle centers on a different kind of ground, in the sense of a factor implying a prima facie moral duty, such as making a promise or noticing a person who will bleed to death without someone's help. (3) Each principle is taken to be in some sense intuitively known" (1996: 102). I know that is quite a handful for an initial characterization of the theory. But if we keep in mind that intuitionism claims that we (1) *intuitively know* (2) *several* basic *moral principles*, (3) each of which has a *distinct ground*, then we will have a basic grasp of the theory.[6]

Intuitionism holds that we know several distinct moral principles. We know them to be true because they are self-evident propositions. So what is this property of being self-evident? In simple terms, a proposition is self-evident if it provides all the evidence necessary to justify believing it is true. Since self-evidence is central to intuitionism, we will have to discuss the matter at length. But some clarifications concerning self-evidence are in order here. Just because a proposition is self-evident does not mean that we know it from the beginning of our lives. We must be mature enough to see the truth of "Harming others is wrong" and other intuitive principles. Also, reflection is required to see the truth of all such principles.[7]

One confusion concerning judgments of self-evidence is imperative to eliminate up front. A judgment that "This proposition is self-evident to me," is much more complex and much less secure than one like, "This proposition is evident to me." A claim that a proposition *p* is *evident to* me implies that accepting *p* is epistemically preferable to withholding it. When I consider the proposition "Now I see words on my computer screen," it seems to me to be true beyond reasonable doubt. So it is evident to me.[8] On a given day, judgments that are evident to us run into the thousands.

Judging that a proposition *p* is *self-evident to* me involves much more. It includes (1) the just mentioned features of a judgment *p* being evident to me and (2) an additional judgment about the *basis* for believing that *p*: that the information in *p* provides all the evidence needed to know that *p* is true. This second condition is a theoretical claim that, I think, cannot be proved. Consequently, there is much more reason to doubt that a proposition is self-evident to you than to doubt that a proposition is evident to you. It is not even certain that $2 + 2 = 4$ is self-evident to us. So when a critic of intuitionism says, for example, "'Keeping promises is required' is not self-evident to me" it is a less effective objection than she hopes.

7. Morality in action

We have each experienced a moral quandary. Maybe as we were about to fulfill a work obligation we realized we had promised to do something else for a friend. Perhaps a parent or a boss has asked us to do something that seemed immoral. Such experiences provide one of the main reasons people reject the idea of objective morality completely. But do such moral conflicts imply that there is no objective morality? Well, think about it. If you have a work obligation and an obligation to keep a promise, it seems that you have two duties, not one and not none. Two duties can only conflict if each has some moral force.

The early analytic intuitionists, H. A. Prichard and W. D. Ross, take the existence of such moral conflicts to be one of the basic facts our moral consciousness reveals. In such cases, we are aware that we have one obligation to fulfill, and equally aware that there is another obligation that conflicts with the first. Reflection on such phenomena shapes the way we understand the self-evident principles of morality. And reflection reveals that any two moral principles can come into conflict in a moral situation.

In light of this, each intuitive principle is not absolutely binding, but rather what Ross calls a prima facie principle. Having a prima facie duty gives us a moral reason to act in one way that can conflict with another prima facie duty that gives a moral reason to act in another. Whichever prima facie duty has more moral weight is our *actual duty*. In the scenario just mentioned, you *appear to* have a work obligation and *appear to* have a duty to keep a promise to your friend.[9] When two principles genuinely conflict, that means we cannot serve both duties. Since we cannot fulfill both duties, that means that only one is our actual duty. So of two moral principles in conflict, one overrides the other. The duty that overrides the other is the actual duty. But just because a prima facie duty has been overriden does not imply it is without moral significance. So if a work obligation overrides keeping your promise to your friend, and you act on it, you have good reason to make it up to your friend somehow. Thus, prima facie duties are *"ineradicable but overridable"* (Audi, 1996: 104).

Ross defines a prima facie duty as a property "which an act has, in virtue of being of a certain kind (e.g. the keeping of a promise), of being an act which would be a duty proper if it were not at the same time of another kind which is [more] morally significant" (1930: 19) That is the metaphysical aspect of prima facie duties. Although principles inform us of the prima facie duties we may have, we must stress that prima facie duties are properties of acts we may perform. Intuitionism's commitment to prima facie principles means we must amend the intuitive principles. "Keeping promises is required" is more accurately stated as, "Keeping promises is *prima facie* required," and the same goes for all the other intuitive principles. For the remainder of the book, for brevity's sake, when an intuitive moral principle is stated it is to be understood as being a prima facie moral principle.

Intuitionism holds that we are certain of our duties in the abstract, but we are not certain of our actual duties. Situational moral knowledge is highly fallible. In many ordinary concrete moral situations we have at best *rational belief* or *strong justification* of what we ought to do.[10] In moral conflicts, although we may have rational belief about what is right, our justification is much weaker. Here is why our situational moral knowledge is so tenuous. As just discussed, often we have distinct prima facie duties that are pulling on us at the same time, making it difficult to know which is our actual duty, and requiring some moral discernment to get things right. Also, there are several metaphysical and epistemic reasons for the high fallibility of situational moral knowledge. We apprehend the truth of the intuitive principles. Our mind only apprehends abstract objects that it can immediately grasp such as concepts and propositions. Thus I can apprehend that "Keeping promises is required" because it is a proposition. An actual moral situation, in contrast, is a complex object that involves many physical objects in certain determinate relations, mixed with nonnatural entities. These nonnatural elements, which intuitionism insists exist, are very difficult to know. And moral situations are wholes that are not reducible to their parts. Our minds cannot apprehend such complex, mixed natural-nonnatural situations simply because our minds cannot penetrate them. Thus, we can be certain of the abstract moral proposition without being able to apprehend what it represents in the complex physical world.[11]

Since moral reasons for action are each independent of one another, and because it is concrete situations that determine what we ought to do, that means that there is no rule to determine which prima facie duty has more weight. Thus on one occasion "Stealing is wrong" will have more weight than "Helping those in need is required." But on another occasion, their weights can be reversed. For example, in ordinary circumstances it would be wrong to break into a warehouse full of food to feed people who are poor, even though it would help them. But in an unusually dire emergency situation it can be right. Thus there is no way to determine before a situation presents itself what is the right thing to do in every case.

How we determine what's right in actual situations is epistemic appraisal. We consider the morality of the alternatives, then contrast and weigh them. In some cases in which there is no apparent moral conflict, epistemic appraisal will give us strong justification for what is right, constituting instances of particular moral knowledge. But given the nature of such knowledge it is highly fallible. In obvious cases of moral conflict, epistemic appraisal will justify our judgment only weakly, and recommend a course of action more tentatively.

8. Commonsense morality?

Intuitionism is sometimes considered a commonsense moral theory. Proponents of intuitionism hold that the commonsense basis of intuitionism is a point in the theory's favor. They claim that all normative ethical positions must test their theories against the commonsense moral views most everyone holds. Opponents make this claim as a criticism. They think that because intuitionism stems from common sense, we have made no theoretical advance by adopting the theory.

Intuitionism is committed to moral reflection as much as any moral theory. It makes no prior commitment to any moral beliefs, not even the commonsense ones. However, the results of moral reflection on what we really think are often articles of common sense. But the explanation for this result is that people commonly believe "Keeping promises is required" and "Harming others is wrong" because these truths are self-evident, rather than intuitionists declaring that they are self-evident just because they are popularly believed. That means that one can reflect endlessly on what moral beliefs are true, and end up believing the intuitive principles.

Some assert that intuitionism is in the business of providing theoretical backing for our pretheoretical beliefs. But simply because we believed certain things before we reflected seriously on them is no conclusive reason to believe them now. Intuitive moral principles might have been pretheoretical beliefs for some. But the true moral principles are discoverable pre-theory, during-theory, and post-theory. So at any stage of reflection in a person's life, the self-evident truths of morality are there to be understood and thereby known. They are there just as much for the seasoned ethicist who has worked through a dozen moral systems as they are for the inquisitive layman.

9. Persistent data

That fundamental moral propositions are self-evidently true explains more than how we know what's right. Intuitionism explains the persistence of certain of our individual moral beliefs. It also explains why the data of moral inquiry remain more or less constant, available for use by ethicists of a variety of schools. But perhaps most significantly the self-evidence of our fundamental moral propositions helps to explain how humanity's moral beliefs are so persistent through the ages. The intuitive principles are the *moral constants* throughout human history.

It may be objected that though some moral beliefs have persisted over centuries, many have changed. Lying, killing, and stealing generally remain morally wrong. But it is now common to believe that, in certain circumstances, it is considered permissible to kill, acceptable to lie, and required to steal. We don't hold that whatever is wrong is wrong in all circumstances. So moral absolutes are dead.

Intuitionism can account for these changes. The intuitionist stance on moral quandaries is, once more, that what is wrong in many, even most, cases can be right in rare circumstances. The reason no one holds to moral absolutism is that it goes against what we really think about morality. Moral absolutism was a much more plausible theory in the distant past. Several events in the twentieth

century have forever shaken our faith in such views. Witnessing
two world wars, governments exterminating millions of their own
people, justified instances of intentional civilian bombing, have
reset our intuitions, making them in several ways more accurate.
All these factors together have convinced us that moral absolutism
is wrong.[12]

Ethicists try to show by various means that their theories
account for our genuine moral beliefs. Theories that try to but cannot explain our real moral beliefs are regarded as failures. Thus
it seems like our moral beliefs have an authority that no moral
theory has of yet. While ethical theories enter and exit the stage of
academic controversy, the intuitive moral beliefs remain. What is
puzzling is that rarely do ethicists ask, if such moral beliefs have an
authority that is such that they can confirm or overturn the viability of an ethical theory, why are we not paying more attention to
such beliefs? Intuitionism, in contrast, does focus on the moral
propositions with the most epistemic authority. Both the persistence of moral beliefs across eras and the persistence of the primary
data of ethics are best explained by the intuitive principles being
self-evidently true.

10. Prejudices and social support

Does the self-evidence of our moral beliefs really explain their persistence? Many are apt to think this exactly backwards. They will
say that society shapes the rules by which we must live, that it
conditions us to hold certain beliefs, and punishes those who do
not adhere to them. Such beliefs we call "moral." Furthermore,
civilizations over time have perpetuated many of these core beliefs
because they have learned that general obedience to them is condu-
cive to social survival, and is in the interest of the ruling class. And
because these prejudices have been forced on people for so long, we
find that we psychologically resist doubting them, let alone overturning them. All these facts explain why moral beliefs *seem* to us
to be self-evident.

This is a quaint old tune. Where it once was fresh and plausible,
it is now stale and obviously inaccurate. We don't live in a morally
repressive society, quite the contrary. To claim we do is to echo
a worldview based on a set of facts long past. One of the taboos

we face in our new world is the stricture against using the word "morality." It is considered immoral to say people are immoral! So if we have any prejudice today, it seems that it runs in the direction opposite of objective morality. That means that if people continue to believe certain moral principles to be objective, it is despite the common prejudices that have been widely inculcated in society's members, not because of them.

Nonetheless, we cannot wholly discount the role society plays in supporting our beliefs. It seems that whatever epistemic confidence we have in a given belief has two sources: our trust in our own reason and the support we get from our society. Most people will not dispute that $2 + 2 = 4$. Many who believe it will agree that reason gives them confidence in its truth. What they might not recognize is that part of their confidence is based on how society regards it. Their peers, teachers, and parents repeatedly reinforced belief that $2 + 2 = 4$ by their behavior. So it is a mistake to attribute widespread belief even in necessary truths to our confident use of reason alone. Social reinforcement has an important epistemically supportive role.

The best epistemic situation for fundamental truths is when society supports self-evidently true beliefs. Sixty years ago, if you asked someone if $2 + 2 = 4$ and if lying is wrong, they would have confidently claimed that both are true. Social epistemic support helps explain why we are so confident that certain mathematical propositions are necessarily true. And lack of social epistemic support explains why we are less inclined to believe that moral propositions are even true. Today's society does not reinforce our beliefs that keeping promises is required and lying is wrong as strongly as it did once. That means that our trust in reason, and diligent reflection, must make up for this absence of social epistemic support.

11. Chapter summary

This chapter's aim was to bring you into the intuitionist perspective as fully as a single chapter can. With this brief outline, I plan to build the central portions of the intuitionist edifice. The chief complaint against intuitionism is that it cannot explain morality. To put this notion to rest, I will summarize this chapter by reviewing many of the things about morality which intuitionism essays to explain. Intuitionism offers explanations for why we have the basic general commonsense moral beliefs we do, as well as for why we have the moral reasons we actually do have. Why in some rare cases it is right to do what is ordinarily wrong is explained by intuitionism. Intuitionism also explains the contrast between our certainty about morality in the abstract and our uncertainty about our actual duties, the practice of ethics, including how ethicists have a common constant subject matter, and why controversy continues in both applied ethics and in metaethics. Finally, intuitionism explains the historical persistence of fundamental moral beliefs and how average people can hold the intuitive principles despite countervailing cultural incentives.

Further reading

At the end of each chapter, I will suggest further reading. My aim in doing so is to give you the next step for advancing your understanding of a topic covered in the chapter. Two essential intuitionist readings are, in order of importance, chapter 2 "What makes right acts right?" of W. D. Ross's, *The Right and the Good* (1930), and H. A. Prichard's "Does moral philosophy rest on a mistake?" in *Mind* (1912). We will be reminded of their value throughout this book.

CHAPTER TWO

The story of contemporary intuitionism

Introduction

Setting the record straight and providing necessary historical background are two reasons to tell the story of contemporary intuitionism. But they are not the main one. Telling the contemporary intuitionism story is actually part of the case for intuitionism. And the moral of the story is this. In a large, active, and highly competitive ethics field in which the methods of analytic philosophy are predominantly in use moral thought naturally moves in the direction of intuitionism. In work on substantive moral issues, ethicists largely employ intuitionist methods. Additionally, intuitions about certain particular moral situations have had a decisive impact on debates in ethics. Consequently, rivals to intuitionism have been forced to retreat, and paths are cleared for intuitionism to advance.

Intuitionism had a very bad reputation in the middle of the twentieth century. It is no exaggeration to say it was treated with the utmost contempt. But intuitionism has recently been revived. The questions to be answered, then, are, why was intuitionism regarded with such contempt? Given its outcast status, how did it even get a hearing? And lastly, how did intuitionism make a comeback?

Intuitionism's recent history gives us a sense of the constructive possibilities of analytic philosophy. The return of intuitionism is based on two major factors—one general, one specific. General trends in ethics and in analytic philosophy have unwittingly contributed to vindicating intuitionism. Many old objections to intuitionism have lost their force because of the work of analytic philosophers and ethicists who are not intuitionists. In addition, many ethicists in subsequent years have taken positions and employed methodological practices that have ultimately contributed to intuitionism's return.

More specifically and directly, the work of contemporary intuitionists has brought intuitionism back to prominence. Recent intuitionists, such as Robert Audi, Russ Shafer-Landau, and Michael Huemer have wielded the tools of analytic philosophy to make a strong case for intuitionism. Also, a number of intuitionists and nonintuitionist moral realists set the stage for their work.[1] Both the general and the specific reasons for intuitionism's return are based on key methods and signal attainments of analytic philosophy.

Three characteristics of the analytic approach to philosophy help explain intuitionism's return. First, analytic philosophy generally gives more weight to "what we really think" about any subject under investigation, more commonly referred to as our "pretheoretical beliefs," than approaches that rely on theoretical propositions alone. Second, it makes distinctions with the utmost care and patience. As a result it has advanced our understanding of the differences between implication, logical truth, necessary truth, a priori knowledge, and a number of other important philosophical distinctions. Third, analytic philosophy takes great pains to determine what any claim does and does not imply and what any claim does and does not presuppose.[2]

In this chapter, I will briefly discuss the thought of early analytic intuitionists, such as H. A. Prichard and W. D. Ross. Then I will present some of the reasons why intuitionism was banished from polite philosophical society in the middle of the twentieth century. Along the way, I will discuss ways in which employment of the resources of analytic philosophy, by both intuitionists and nonintuitionists, has contributed to the return of intuitionism.

1. Prichard's point

Intuitionism goes back at least to the seventeenth century. Such figures as Cudworth, More, Clarke, and Price were leading intuitionists.[3] Some argue that Aquinas was an intuitionist.[4] And both Aristotle and Plato exhibited certain intuitionist traits.[5]

We pick up the intuitionist story in the middle, at the beginning of the twentieth century. H. A. Prichard is the first prominent twentieth-century intuitionist. His article, "Does Moral Philosophy Rest on a Mistake?" is considered a classic statement of intuitionism. Prichard does several things worth noting in that article. Although his successor, W. D. Ross is considered to this day the central figure in intuitionism, a close and careful reading of Prichard's article will show that many of Ross's ideas are found there in germ form.

Prichard establishes the basic intuitionist methodology and positions discussed in Chapter 1. He employs epistemic appraisal to bolster the intuitive principles while undermining the utility principle.[6] He recognizes that sometimes what would normally be our duty is overridden by a more urgent duty, thus setting the stage for Ross's notion of prima facie duties.[7] Prichard also identifies the ground of our moral duties, recognizing they are based on *moral relations*, a crucial but unexplored part of intuitionism.[8] Unfortunately, along with his several positive innovations, he also makes the first pitch for separating the "right" from the "good."[9]

So what's the big mistake moral theory rests on? It is "the mistake of supposing the possibility of proving what can only be apprehended directly by an act of moral thinking" (Prichard, 1912: 36). The mistake, then, is searching for *moral proofs*. Prichard's essential point is that we cannot *prove* propositions like "Keeping promises is required," and that, since we know they are true by directly apprehending them, no such proof is necessary. He also states that there is no proposition which will *justify* propositions like "Harming others is wrong" in some way stronger than it justifies itself. Since such propositions cannot be proved, and cannot find stronger justification from some other proposition, if Prichard is right then there can be no supreme principle of morality. Prichard is correct to ban moral proofs, and ethicists have since then generally agreed.[10] Not even ethicists who favor a supreme principle talk about proving anything in ethics anymore. Many ethicists, however, reject Prichard's strictures on seeking an external source of justification for our central moral beliefs.

Prichard was not content to identify the mistake of searching for moral proofs. He wished to find the origin of the mistake.

According to Prichard, the mistake arises from philosophers burdened with obligations who ask, "*Why* should I do these things?" His view is that we know that, for example, it is our obligation to keep our promise simply because we made it. No stronger reason can be offered. Prichard seems correct about the theoretical confusion which leads us to seek moral proofs. But his explanation of the motivation behind it has led Prichard to make his own mistake. Just because moral proofs are out of the question does not imply that *any* attempt to explain moral truths is misguided. A philosopher can inquire into why it is wrong to steal without once being tempted to steal. Critics rightly seized on Prichard's moratorium on all moral explanations as a defect in his theory.

There is one more Prichard claim to discuss. Our moral knowledge is immediate and evident according to Prichard. But what is such knowledge knowledge of? Prichard speaks as if not only are abstract moral principles known by apprehension, but actual duties are known this way too. He states, "We recognise, for instance, that this performance of a service to X, who has done us a service, just in virtue of its being the performance of a service to one who has rendered a service to the would-be agent, ought to be done by us. This apprehension is immediate, in precisely the sense in which a mathematical apprehension is immediate" (1912: 28). So on Prichard's account, it is not just that we know "Returning favors is required" because the proposition is self-evident. He is saying that our actual duties are self-evident as well.

If we take Prichard to have stated the official intuitionist line, once and forever, then critics are right that intuitionism claims that we know our actual duties, by "apprehending," "intuiting," even "detecting" them in moral situations. In Chapter 1, I stressed that we do not apprehend our actual duties. That was Ross's claim, and intuitionists since then have concurred. Perhaps critics have assumed that since Prichard and Ross have many points of agreement, that they agree on everything. But on this point Prichard does not speak for most intuitionists.

2. Ross's intuitionism

W. D. Ross is the central figure of intuitionism. Even today many ethicists are arguing for and defending parts of Ross's theory.

And his stature only continues to rise.[11] His main ideas are to be found in his *The Right and the Good*, and in particular its second chapter, "What makes right acts right?" This chapter deserves repeated readings, for its contents have been at the center of discussion about intuitionism since it was written. There are many treasures buried within: many that have not been fully explored, some that have been underestimated, and some that have gone virtually unnoticed.

Ross's methodology of consulting "what we really think" about morality is mainstream in ethics today. It is no exaggeration to say "we are all methodological intuitionists today," even though few ethicists would use that language. Early analytic philosophers like Russell and Moore made "what we really think" about the world central to their methodologies. They appraised our genuine thoughts about the world against the abstract theoretical claims of idealists and other opponents of realism.[12] They successfully showed that our real thoughts have greater epistemic strength than their opponents suspected. Quite puzzlingly, Moore did not consistently apply his own methods in ethics, which separates his theory from intuitionism as I have defined it.[13] By consulting "what we really think" about morality, and by using contrasting moral judgments to test rival theories, Ross brought moral theory in line with the methods of early analytic philosophy.

The idea of prima facie duty is the most important of Ross's theoretical contributions. A. C. Ewing described it as one of the most important twentieth-century contributions to moral theory.[14] It is certainly the idea which most often comes to mind when we think of Ross's theory. On the broadest interpretation of prima facie duty few in ethics disagree with this concept.[15] Where ethicists do disagree, it will be with the epistemology and metaphysics supporting Ross's notion of prima facie duty, not with the notion per se.

Ross also rejects supreme principles of morality. He argues that no fundamental moral reason can be reduced to any other. When we consider what we actually think in particular moral situations, we'll find that, most often, there is a direct and simple reason for us to act on our duty. So if avoiding embarrassment tempts you to lie, it is likely that you will think "I can't lie, because that would be wrong," not that it will not maximize the good. Since "Lying is wrong" gives us sufficient reason not to lie, and "Maximize the good" is not our reason for not lying, we have no justification for believing the former reason can be reduced to the latter, as utilitarians ardently wish.

3. The downfall of early analytic intuitionism

Intuitionism was a dead issue in the middle of the twentieth century. The most critical point to keep in mind about intuitionism's period of exile is this. The criticisms of intuitionism that convinced many of its falsity were not as strong as you would expect. Often they were not directed at intuitionists' stated claims. Many reasons that were given for rejecting intuitionism were based on the critics' assumptions about its presuppositions. Where legitimate reasons were given for resisting intuitionism, often the arguments were not explicitly laid out. Instead, unsupported statements were made and questions raised. And often the spurious reasons for rejecting intuitionism had the greatest persuasive impact.

Intuiting our duties in particular moral situations was not a cardinal plank in the intuitionist platform, as we have seen. Nor was there an intuitionist push for a special faculty of intuition. G. E. Moore held that certain propositions he called "intuitions," such as "pleasure is good," are true but incapable of proof (1903: x). He also claimed that goodness is a nonnatural property, that is, a property we cannot detect by the senses. But does Moore also claim that we have a special faculty of intuition for grasping good? On the contrary, he plainly states,

> I wish it observed that, when I call such propositions "Intuitions," I mean *merely* to assert that they are incapable of proof; I imply nothing whatever as to the manner or origin of our cognition of them. Still less do I imply (as most Intuitionists have done) that any proposition whatever is true, *because* we cognise it in a particular way or by the exercise of any particular faculty. (Moore, 1903: x)

This is an emphatic disavowal by Moore of any claim of any special moral psychological faculty. Prichard made no statement about the psychology of our self-evident judgments, except to say that they are akin to apprehensions in mathematics. The same is true of Ross.

But what reasons are given by Ross's contemporaries for rejecting intuitionism? In his *Language, Truth and Logic*, Ayer has this to say about a theory like intuitionism:

> It is "the view that statements of value are not controlled by observation, as ordinary empirical propositions are, but only by a mysterious 'intellectual intuition.'" (1952: 106)

Given the just quoted Moore passage, we might doubt that Ayer is talking about intuitionism at all. But the following passage makes it clear that he is. He states that the theory "makes statements of value unverifiable. For it is notorious that what seems intuitively certain to one person may seem doubtful, or even false, to another. So that unless it is possible to provide some criterion by which one may decide between conflicting intuitions, a mere appeal to intuition is worthless as a test of a proposition's validity. But in the case of moral judgments, no such criterion can be given" (Ayer, 1952: 106).

Let us evaluate Ayer's claims. The second passage presents a legitimate claim against intuitionism. It is the argument from disagreement, a main reason ethicists reject intuitionism. Later in this chapter I will examine it. The first passage shows Ayer disregarded what intuitionists actually stated, and cited no twentieth-century intuitionist to substantiate his claims. It seems he believed that, since old guard intuitionists claimed a special moral faculty of intuition, then, the analytic intuitionists *must* have the same view. The tactic of ignoring what intuitionists say and attributing views to them that can only be said to hold for their remote intellectual ancestors became common practice. The charge of being committed to a "mysterious faculty" is a main reason for the widespread contempt ethicists felt for intuitionism.

The early analytic intuitionists undoubtedly share some blame for their ouster. It seems that what the intuitionists *didn't* say got them into the most trouble. Intuitionists were silent about how we intuit self-evident truths. They told us we know them, and that we can grasp nonnatural simple properties, but did not explain how.

Opponents wondered how the mind could know certain propositions just by grasping them, or how the mind could grasp nonnatural properties without a special faculty. But if opponents thought
we require an extra faculty to know nonnatural properties, they
should have just said that. But then that would have been their
own view, not the intuitionists'. In any case, intuitionists did not
respond with convincing explanations. Inadequate responses com-
bined with the objects of thought they claimed to exist constituted
their most vulnerable point.

4. Strawson's case against intuitionism

P. F. Strawson attacked intuitionism in a 1949 article titled
"Ethical intuitionism." It was considered a decisive victory.[16] A
second look at Strawson's article will make us wonder why it
triumphed, and will induce us to look at the philosophical atmos-
phere of that time for answers. Strawson gave intuitionism one
empiricist challenge that many regard as still being unmet. But
Strawson and others only consider it a challenge because they
misunderstand the basics of intuitionism.

Strawson begins by having the intuitionist say: "rightness or
goodness—is unanalysable, and known by intuition alone. The
fundamental cognitive situation in morals is that in which we intuit
the rightness of a particular action or the goodness of a particular
state of affairs" (1949: 24). Strawson is obviously trying to cover
several ethicists considered intuitionists. But as was just mentioned,
only Prichard thinks that we apprehend the rightness of particular
actions. Ross explicitly says we do not. What exactly is involved in
knowing that particular things are good is not made entirely clear
by Moore, the intended target here. But he says enough about the
property of good to exclude this particular critique by Strawson.
For example, good, like the number 2, does not exist in time. We
cannot experience it in isolation from the objects that are good. And
we can determine what things are intrinsically good by "reflective
judgment," not by intuition of particular states of affairs.

Strawson tries to undermine intuitionism's account of moral
knowledge. He does this by considering what kind of experience
we must have to obtain it. To make his case for the indefinability
of "good," Moore argued that we already have knowledge of some

indefinable terms, color terms. We experience red and this allows us to know what "red" means. But we cannot define "red." Similarly, we have correctly judged things to be good, but we cannot define "good." Strawson picks up on Moore's analogy and turns it against intuitionism. Each of us knows what the word "red" means. But because of that, "it is self-contradictory to say: 'I know what the word "red" means, but I can't remember ever *seeing* red and I don't know what it would be *like* to see red'" (Strawson, 1949: 25).

According to Strawson, in the parallel case intuitionism comes up short. He states, "if the word 'right,' or the word 'good,' expresses an indefinable intuitive concept, then it is self-contradictory to say: 'I know what the word "right" or the word "good" means, but I can't remember ever *intuiting* rightness or goodness, and I don't know what it would be *like* to intuit rightness or goodness'" (Strawson, 1949: 25).

Call this the "Experience Test" for intuitionism. To pass it, intuitionism must explain what experiences are involved in grasping and coming to know good or right. Responding to Strawson's assumptions, he is likening intuition too much to perception and not enough to thought. An intuition is a kind of thought. Since Prichard and Ross compared self-evident moral judgments to self-evident mathematical judgments, Strawson would have done well at this point to continue the comparison. But he seized on an analogy that Moore only used to make the narrow point that some terms are indefinable, and thought he could undermine all intuitionist claims in one fell swoop. Because Strawson made Moore's analogy undertake tasks for which it was not intended, he did not succeed.[17] Most importantly, the Experience Test is not one that intuitionism needs to pass. Going back to square one, moral knowledge, for intuitionism, is based on what we really *think*, not on what we experience. Strawson was not the first, nor the last, critic who applied the Experience Test without recognizing that it is inapplicable to intuitionism.

5. General trends against intuitionism

Early analytic philosophy helped pave the way for intuitionism. Most notably by its insistence that what we really think be given more epistemic weight than skeptics and idealists allowed. But at the same time that intuitionism was enjoying a dominant position in the 1930s, particular currents of thought were stirring which would soon make an inhospitable environment for intuitionism. Several new ideas made intuitionism appear impossible. And many difficulties raised in the middle of the twentieth century continue to stalk intuitionism today.

Philosophers, logicians, and mathematicians raised doubts about self-evidence. Their attacks were so successful that for decades most philosophers stopped talking about it at all. For example, in their 1934 book, *An Introduction to Logic and Scientific Method*, Morris Cohen and Ernest Nagel assail the notion of self-evidence. They state,

> if by "self-evidence" is meant psychological obviousness, or an irresistible impulse to assert, or the psychological unconceivability of any contrary propositions, the history of human thought has shown how unreliable it is as a criterion of truth. Many propositions formerly regarded as self-evident, for example: *Nature abhors a vacuum; At the antipodes men walk with their heads beneath their feet; Every surface has two sides*, are now known to be false. (Cohen and Nagel, 1934: 131)

These points invite comment. First of all, the proposition that "many people have mistakenly thought that *p*, *q*, and *r* are self-evident" does not imply that "there are no self-evident propositions." Second, the entire passage begins with a big *if*. If all of these things were what is involved in a proposition being self-evident, then we would do well to reject the very idea. Later, I will show why none of the above attributes are involved in self-evidence. Lastly, look at those examples! Among the false propositions overturned the only one that appears intuitive is "Every surface has two sides." Looking at the others, especially the proposition concerning the antipodes, it becomes clear that the authors are using "self-evident" in the most wide-ranging and least plausible sense.

The intuitive principles are self-evident, synthetic a priori truths. A proposition is self-evident if all the evidence needed to show it is true is in the proposition itself. A proposition is synthetic if it provides substantive information. In contrast, an analytic proposition like "It is what it is" is empty of information, no matter what aura of depth it exudes. And an a priori truth requires no external or internal observation to justify believing it. The case against self-evident truths was made by observing the record of propositions that failed to be self-evident. Doing away with synthetic a priori truths took a more sustained campaign. In two successive waves of attack, the notion of synthetic a priori truth was severely damaged in philosophy.

Logical positivists launched the first attack. It came in the context of a general assault on metaphysics. Logical positivists hold that all our knowledge about the world comes through observation. Rationalists disagree by holding that we can know truths about the world through reason as well. Logical positivists question how this is possible, but do concede that we know some things a priori. Consider the proposition that "Every brother is male." This and other analytic propositions are true, according to the positivists, by virtue of the meanings of the words involved. It is true because the meaning of "brother" and the meaning of "male" make it so. Rational insight is not necessary to see such propositions are true, only an understanding of English. Consider now a supposed synthetic a priori truth: "Every event has a cause." Being synthetic, the meaning of "cause" and "event" are not such as to make it true. Since grasping meanings is not enough for us to know it is true, and since we cannot observe through the senses that every event has a cause, we must give up the idea of knowing any such propositions.

W. V. O. Quine attacked the synthetic a priori with even greater force.[18] He argued that the distinction between analytic and synthetic truths could not be maintained at all. His argument is complex. The most salient points are, first, that any attempt to explain analyticity relies on notions that cannot explain it, and require explanation themselves, including synonymy, definition, interchangeability *salva veritate*, extensional agreement, artificial semantic rules, and, finally, analyticity. Since the analytic/synthetic distinction cannot be explained, there is no basis for believing there is one. Second, Quine's disavows meanings. He asks, just what could these entities called meanings be? He thought it an error to claim that for every word I read or say or write or think that there is an entity called a "meaning" that somehow corresponds to it. By giving up meanings, Quine foils the logical positivist attempt to save analyticity from radical empiricism. And since there is no way to verify through thought the truth of analytic propositions, there is, again, no basis for making the distinction between analytic and synthetic propositions.

6. The power of intuition

We now have a sense of why intuitionism experienced such ill fortunes in the middle of the twentieth century. Intuitionism's turnaround came at the end of a long rehabilitation. Given its all around bad reputation, reviving intuitionism became possible only after some favorable background conditions for the theory were established. This required a shift in philosophical trends, which, not surprisingly, had nothing directly to do with ethicists arguing for intuitionism.

Even when "intuition" was a dirty word ethicists appealed to moral intuitions we hold in common to overturn theories. More than once a moral theory's viability was put into doubt by some powerful particular intuition, showing that the well-chosen intuition can deal a theory a heavier blow than a dozen arguments. This was done in each case by furnishing a counterexample scenario that a moral theory seemed to imply, and that appeared to many to be immoral. The result was a belief in many that the theory had been refuted.

We will discuss two cases that illustrate the power of particular moral intuitions. The first one was directed at utilitarianism. Utilitarianism claims that the right thing to do is to maximize the good. H. J. McCloskey, in his 1957 paper, "An Examination of Restricted Utilitarianism," considers a possible implication of the utility principle. In a single, seemingly incidental paragraph, McCloskey lays out "the sheriff" scenario. A sheriff in a small racist town is faced with a serious problem. A woman was raped, people believe a black man did it, and the sheriff has no leads. Given the town's history, the sheriff must either frame an innocent black man for the rape or allow antiblack riots to occur, "which would probably lead to some loss of life and increased hatred of each other by whites and Negroes" (McCloskey, 1957: 468). Since the framing would only harm one person, and riots would harm many, the utilitarianism recommendation seems clear: frame the innocent black man. Some take this as a decisive counterexample to utilitarianism.

Indicating that McCloskey is over the target, utilitarians to this day feel compelled to contest his verdict.[19] But a straightforward understanding of utilitarianism suggests that framing someone would be the right thing to do. So this raises the question, why have utilitarians been so eager to dispute this conclusion? It cannot be because utilitarians dislike holding unpopular moral opinions. They have done so in many cases. It seems that the best explanation of their response is that they recognize the force of the counterexample intuition against utilitarianism. An intuitionist interpretation of the general utilitarian response is that the utilitarians know, through rational intuition, that harming the innocent is wrong. It is only their belief in utilitarianism that prevents them from recognizing the real source of their drive to contest the conclusion of framing the innocent.

Kant's ethics was the victim of the second particular counterexample intuition. In this case, the force of the intuition was even stronger. Unlike in the utilitarian case, Kantians did not rush to the defense of Kant. The "would-be murderer" intuition of which I speak, more than any theoretical attack on Kantianism, kept Kantian ethics in dry dock for decades. Interestingly, it was Kant himself who provided the example here.[20] The would-be murderer case is this. You come out of a friend's place. A dangerous man, the would-be murderer, approaches you and asks whether your friend is home. Sensing that he has evil intentions, you are tempted to lie to save your friend's life. But Kant, being a moral absolutist, claims that the Categorical Imperative does not permit lying to the man, despite his criminal aims.

It is only recently that Kantian ethics has recovered from the would-be murderer. At one point few would claim to be a Kantian ethicist. Those whose original work bore distinct resemblances to Kant's simply called themselves deontologists. Only the work of the New Kantians has been able to bring Kantian ethics back to a position of respectability. How did they do this? Marcus Singer, in his seminal New Kantian paper in 1954, does this by denying Kantianism is absolutist, despite Kant's own statements to that effect. He states, "Kant's ethics has traditionally been thought of as issuing in 'categorical imperatives,' which take no account of individual situations, personal differences, or extenuating circumstances. Thus Kant has effectively been stereotyped as an 'ethical absolutist'" (Singer, 1954: 577). Aiming to overcome the stereotype that Kant himself originated and disseminated, New Kantians revised Kant's theory so that it is consistent with lying to the would-be murderer.[21]

7. Methods of ethics

The revival of normative ethics in 1971 was the first thing to facilitate intuitionism's return. But it was not merely the discussion of substantive moral issues that helped intuitionism along. It was the method employed in the discussion that mattered too. Prior to 1971 the main discussion in ethics was metaethical. The main concerns were about what "good" and "right" mean, and how to analyze moral reasoning. So what happened in 1971 that brought back normative ethics? What is special about this particular date? In 1971 John Rawls released *A Theory of Justice*. This book, along with some prior work in normative ethics, led to what has been called "The Great Expansion" in ethics.[22] But it was not Rawls's seminal work alone which spurred discussion of normative issues. Many moral and social challenges of the early 1970s spurred philosophers to use their skills in argumentation and analysis to grapple with them, motivating more philosophers to rely on their genuine moral thoughts.[23]

Rawls showed that substantive moral discussions could be philosophically fruitful. He did this by employing what he called the method of "reflective equilibrium." This method was soon widely adopted in ethics. So what is this method? Reflective equilibrium is a way of sorting out our moral beliefs, and moving toward a more coherent, intuitive set of them. Early in our lives, we hold many of our moral beliefs without having reflected on them. As we begin to determine what we really believe we consciously begin to question our moral beliefs. If we persist in doing so, we come to have moral beliefs that have withstood a process of reflection. Rawls calls these our "considered" moral beliefs.

In the process of considering where we stand morally, something else emerges besides our considered moral beliefs. In the attempt to justify our moral beliefs we think of more general considerations. By noticing that different moral issues have common features, we begin to think about moral principles. The moral beliefs might seem to stand on their own before we try to justify them.

But, Rawls thinks, for our considered beliefs to be justified moral principles are indispensable. All of this explains the "reflective" part of the method of reflective equilibrium. But what of the "equilibrium" part?

Rawls makes an important departure from prior ethicists on the issue of a supreme principle. He abandons the claim that we can deduce anything from a supreme principle of morality. Instead, he sees the relationship of substantive moral beliefs to principles as being a matter of mutual adjustment. If, through reflection, we come to hold a certain moral belief strongly, then we might wish to reconsider a principle which does not allow it. On the other hand, if we have found that a certain principle effectively justifies a number of moral beliefs, we might think about giving up a belief which is inconsistent with it. For Rawls, this whole process should move in a direction of improving and justifying our moral beliefs. He holds that our beliefs and principles should finally come to a state of equilibrium.

Let us assess the extent to which reflective equilibrium resembles intuitionism's general methodological approach. First, both approaches begin by abandoning commitment to a single unifying moral principle. Second, Rawls strongly encourages us to carefully consider what we really think about moral issues. So how do these two approaches differ? In two ways. First, reflective equilibrium assumes there must be moral principles that help justify, but are separate from, our moral beliefs. Intuitionism is open to there being a two-tier structure to our moral thoughts, but does not a priori assume it. On this first count, intuitionism takes the more epistemically cautious position. Second, intuitionism claims that the best way to explain both the convincingness and the persistence of certain moral beliefs, such as the promise principle, is to assert that they are self-evidently true. In contrast, reflective equilibrium would only make the psychological claim that these beliefs are ones we find compelling after extensive reflection. So on the second count, intuitionism makes a stronger second-order claim about our moral beliefs than does reflective equilibrium.

So the methods of reflective equilibrium and intuitionism are close relatives. One result of Rawls's popular success was that philosophers became unembarrassed in talking about their intuitions. "During the Great Expansion, moral intuitions . . . flowed abundantly" (Darwall et al., 1992: 123). Although many

philosophers resisted such talk, many came to the realization
that, even if intuitions are not the kind of indefeasible starting-
points early modern philosophers dreamed of establishing, they
are indispensable to checking, testing, and overturning philosophical theories. The result is that today, "the primary way that
contemporary philosophers defend their views is through the use
of rational intuition, and this method delivers non-inferential,
basic beliefs which are then systematized and brought into reflective equilibrium" (Hales, 2004: 271).

The general acceptance in philosophy of reflective equilibrium
and the use of intuitions opened the gate for intuitionism. And
reflective equilibrium can be employed in support of intuitionism.
But despite many years of intuition talk, the theory of intuitionism
remained discredited. Why? Mainly for the reasons we mentioned
previously: misinformation about intuitionist claims, suspicion
about self-evidence, doubts about synthetic a priori propositions,
and disbelief about the mind apprehending nonnatural properties.
But with philosophers of every stripe employing intuitions liber-
ally, it was inevitable that someone ask, "Why . . . do so many
ethical theorists strongly resist combining their appeal to intuitions
with some form of intuitionism?" (Audi, 1993: 295).

8. Audi's insight

Robert Audi led the intuitionist revival. His first major statement
of intuitionism was in his 1996 article, "Intuitionism, Pluralism,
and the Foundations of Ethics." In it he concentrates on epistemological matters. The most important thing he does is sort out what
the claims of intuitionism imply and do not imply, and what they
presuppose and do not presuppose. Most crucially, he concentrates
on the nature of self-evidence, revealing a number of prevalent misunderstandings surrounding it. In addition, he highlights where
Ross said things which did not help his case, and which he need not
have said. In this section I will review some of Audi's major claims
concerning the epistemology of intuitionism.

One of the main things that has hobbled intuitionism is its reliance on the concept of self-evidence. By making self-evidence a
defensible and plausible notion, Audi has forced ethicists to give
intuitionism a second look. Audi's most important insight is
that there has been a certain confusion concerning two different

mental acts. On the one hand, we can say that we have apprehended the *truth* of a proposition that is self-evident. An example would be where we apprehend that it is true that "Keeping promises is required," supposing it to be self-evidently true. On the other hand, we might think that we apprehend the *self-evidence* of such a proposition. So we might consider "Keeping promises is required" and believe we have apprehended not just its truth, but its self-evidence as well. Clearly, apprehending the truth of p and apprehending its self-evidence are two distinct mental states. Call this "Audi's insight."[24]

Unfortunately, these two mental states have not been well separated in ethics. Not even Ross clearly kept them apart.[25] Everyone can apprehend the truth of certain propositions. When we learn the basic concepts and notations of arithmetic, we can apprehend the truth of $2 + 2 = 4$. Intuitionism claims that everyone can apprehend the truth of "Harming others is wrong" in a similar way. When we do so for both cases we are making first-order epistemic judgments. First-order judgments are epistemic claims about the world, including perceptible things, like dogs and cats, and apprehensible things, like numbers and logical relations. But a claim of self-evidence is a claim of *the way* in which we come to know a given proposition. It is a second-order judgment, and concerns the epistemic basis of our first-order judgment. "'$2 + 2 = 4$' is true" is a first-order judgment. "I know that '$2 + 2 = 4$' is true because it is self-evident" is a second-order judgment.

We must keep first-order and second-order judgments apart. It is crucial to recognize our first-order knowledge judgments do not contain second-order judgments about our first-order judgments. When we apprehend that $2 + 2 = 4$ is true that does not imply that we know that the basis of our knowledge is its self-evidence. Concerning moral knowledge, Audi states, "As moral agents we need intuitive knowledge of our duties; we do not need intuitive (or even other) knowledge of the [epistemic] status of the principles of duty" (1996: 107).

Audi's insight helps us see that we might have been mistaken about self-evidence in several ways. For one, we need not apprehend the self-evidence of a self-evident proposition to know it is true. For another, employing similar thinking enables us to see that a number of other properties need not be apprehended for a proposition to be self-evident: its necessity, its certainty, or its capacity to compel us to believe it.

9. Moral disagreement

The argument from disagreement is a major reason ethicists reject intuitionism. But ethicists are not alone in this respect. It comes naturally to people to object to intuitionism by pointing out that people disagree on matters moral. Intuitionism makes the claim that we know what is right, at least where the intuitive principles are concerned, because they are self-evidently true. If that is so, the critic asks, then why is it that people have moral disagreements?

The argument from disagreement is not always put forth in the most perspicuous form, and more often can be described as a declaration from disagreement. Recall Ayer's claim quoted earlier: intuitionism "makes statements of value unverifiable. For it is notorious that what seems intuitively certain to one person may seem doubtful, or even false, to another. So that unless it is possible to provide some criterion by which one may decide between conflicting intuitions, a mere appeal to intuition is worthless as a test of a proposition's validity" (1952: 106). Here is Mackie's statement on the matter: "radical differences between first order moral judgements make it difficult to treat those judgements as apprehensions of objective truths" (1977: 36).[26] Apparently these authors think disagreement poses such a problem for intuitionism that laying out a clear, rigorous, well-structured argument for it is not felt to be necessary. And, sadly, most ethicists have agreed.

It would help to try to capture the argument common to these different statements of the problem. It would seem to have the following form. Call it the "disagreement argument":

(A) If we have intuitive moral knowledge, there ought to be no moral disagreement.

There is moral disagreement.

We don't have intuitive moral knowledge.

The argument appears valid. The fact of moral disagreement is inarguable. So if intuitionism is to survive, the first premise must somehow be shown to be false.

Recall once more intuitionism's bifurcation of moral knowledge. In thought we know, by means of apprehension, several self-evident moral propositions. Of these we have certain knowledge.

In particular moral situations, however, we often have at most rational belief about what is right. To test the effectiveness of argument (A) we must try out both of these claims by inserting them in arguments of the form of (A).

First, let us take "intuitive knowledge" in premise one to mean intuitive knowledge of self-evident propositions. Altering the first premise of (A) to tailor it to capture our evident knowledge of the intuitive principles, we have:

(E) If we have intuitive knowledge of self-evident moral propositions, there ought to be no moral disagreement.

There is moral disagreement.

We don't have intuitive moral knowledge.

Like (A), argument (E) seems valid. It appears to represent the disagreement argument so often thrust at intuitionists. To evaluate argument (E), consider that intuitionists have often compared intuitive moral knowledge to intuitive mathematical knowledge. Many will resist the comparison, asserting that there is certainty in math that is absent from ethics. But everyone will agree that if there is intuitive knowledge anywhere, it is in math. Given this consensus, if a mathematical variant of (E) fails, then (E) itself must likewise be acknowledged a failure. Let's consider the plausible parallel case of mathematical intuition:

(M) If we have intuitive knowledge of self-evident mathematical propositions, there ought to be no mathematical disagreement.

There is mathematical disagreement.

We don't have intuitive mathematical knowledge.

Again, if we have any intuitive knowledge at all, it is in mathematics. So the first premise seems true at first glance. But can we seriously entertain the thought that there is mathematical disagreement? Yes, we can. Let us consider a common case of such disagreement, a case for which there is much empirical data. Consider the following problem:

$$1/4 + 1/2 =$$

You might say the answer is obvious: 3/4. If anything is self-evident, if there is any proposition on which we can all agree 1/4 + 1/2 = 3/4 would be it. But others disagree. Even if you give them time to think it through, they will claim that the answer is 1/3. Ask any math teacher. Ask any university math teacher. There is a reason this is called a "common mistake" of adding fractions. So if mere disagreement is sufficient to demonstrate our ignorance concerning a certain subject matter, then we are ignorant that 1/4 + 1/2 = 3/4. Since we know this equation with certainty, and since our certainty about elementary mathematical propositions cannot exclude disagreement about them, that means that "If we have intuitive knowledge of self-evident mathematical propositions, there ought to be no mathematical disagreement" is false. To see this is so from a different angle, consider that the second premise of (M) is true and its conclusion is false. That means the only source of the conclusion's falsity must be the first premise. Since premise one of (M) is false, the first premise of (E), "If we have intuitive knowledge of self-evident moral propositions, there ought to be no moral disagreement" is false. That means that argument (A), as applied to our apprehension of self-evident moral propositions, in the form of argument (E), is unsound.[27]

The second epistemic doctrine of intuitionism concerns rational belief. When we are in a particular moral situation, that is often the most we can have about our actual duty. Let's alter the first premise of (A) to fit this intuitionist doctrine, resulting in:

(P) If we have rational moral belief, there ought to be no moral disagreement.

There is moral disagreement.

We don't have intuitive moral knowledge.

Two problems stand out in this argument. First, the first premise is false. Two people can disagree about an issue while each is rational in their belief. Second, this is a manifestly invalid argument. So neither argument (E) nor argument (P) is sound. Given that the first premises of these two arguments exhaust the epistemic claims of intuitionism, argument (A), the disagreement argument, is unsound.

Given the absence of a decent disagreement argument, how does belief in it come about? Every instance of the disagreement argument is based on one *lazy assumption*: there is *only one way* to explain moral disagreement.[28] However, different sole explanations can be given. Some claim the explanation is that we have no intuitive moral knowledge. Others explain disagreement by asserting that there is nothing objective about morality. Of course no one expressly presents this "only explanation possible" claim. It would seem reckless to do so. But, clearly, theorists lazily assume that every single other way of explaining moral disagreement is ruled out.

When two people disagree about a moral matter there are several possible explanations. Arguments about abortion, capital punishment, whether a given war is just, and animal rights tend to ignite passions, rather than silence them. But moral issues are not the only ones on which people strongly disagree. People disagree about who shot JFK, what religion, if any, is correct, what are the economic effects of government social programs, and whether there are paranormal phenomena.[29] But for all these cases no one would dispute that there is some objective truth of the matter. The same goes for philosophical disputes. As Shafer-Landau states, "If the argument from disagreement is sound, then this should lead us to an antirealism about all philosophical views. For the extent of disagreement within any branch of philosophy is surely as great as—perhaps greater than—that found among substantive ethical views" (2003: 220).

So what factors might explain disagreement in all these different areas? Since we are dealing with fallible human beings, we must allow for error. And error can be due to bias, miscalculation, confusion, misunderstanding, and lack of understanding, oversight, hasty judgments, false or incomplete information, unarticulated assumptions, fallacies, forgetfulness, the intrinsic difficulty of the issues, inarticulate evidence, and mental defects.[30] Because of the passions involved in moral matters, and because of the many causes of error, we should expect disagreement rather than agreement on points of morality. So even "if there were objective moral truths and we had available ways of knowing them, widespread, strong, and persistent disagreements could still be expected" (Huemer, 2005: 141).

What is conspicuously absent from all instances of moral disagreement used to undermine intuitionism is the intuitive principles. No one says, for instance, that people disagree about
whether, in general, harming others is wrong.[31] They will instead
have people disagreeing about whether harming someone in a particular instance is wrong. But we have covered all this already.
Intuitionism only claims that certain fundamental moral principles, like "Harming others is wrong," are self-evident, and
thereby certain to us. Any discussion of a particular moral situation involves *application* of such principles. And of most such
application we have at best rational belief. In the cases in which
we do know what's wrong in a particular situation, for example, where a man rapes a woman in a dark alley at knifepoint, it
does not pose a problem for intuitionism that someone disagrees.
They're just wrong.

Lastly, the argument from disagreement is self-refuting. As
Huemer states, "if the argument from disagreement is sound, then
it refutes itself, since many people do not agree with the argument
from disagreement" (2005: 146).

10. Chapter summary

For most of the twentieth century, intuitionism was popular
mainly as a target for attacks. Intuitionists bear some responsibility for that situation. On some points they were evasive or
silent about certain particulars of their theories. Also, they didn't
launch effective counterattacks at the criticisms. But their critics
were not as effective as is popularly believed. They attacked positions that intuitionists did not state; they did not present their
arguments in a perspicuous form; they often merely made statements against intuitionism and raised questions. The contemporary revival of intuitionism is partly due to several favorable prior
trends in ethics. Intuitions became indispensable tools for ethical
inquiry. The return of normative ethics, as well as the rise of
applied ethics, made them so. But a new wave of intuitionism was
introduced and defended by contemporary ethicists, led by Robert
Audi, and wielding the tools of analytic philosophy. The objection frequently thought to have the most bite against intuitionism,

the disagreement objection, was shown to be toothless by other ethicists, such as Russ Shafer-Landau and Michael Huemer.

Further reading

The key article of contemporary intuitionism is Robert Audi's seminal, "Intuitionism, pluralism, and the foundations of ethics" (1996). A quite useful collection of essays edited by Stratton-Lake, *Ethical Intuitionism: Re-evaluations* (2002), provides historically informed contemporary assessments of intuitionism. The editor's introduction is especially helpful.

CHAPTER THREE

Moral knowledge

Introduction

Moral knowledge is the most highly contested issue of ethics. I say "of ethics" deliberately because it is not always the most contested topic *in* the field of ethics. Ethicists recognize that no one has satisfactorily solved the *moral knowledge problem*: "How do we know what's right?" But much of ethical inquiry—especially in normative ethics—merely works around it, without indicating any urgency to solve it. Nevertheless, moral knowledge is the prime ethics issue. In the past, intuitionism has given the impression that moral knowledge is mysterious. This chapter takes the first step toward showing that intuitionism can explain how we know what's right.

Earlier I enlisted your moral consciousness to inquire into several possible items of moral knowledge. The result was to suggest that moral principles such as "Keeping promises is required" and "Harming others is wrong" are known by us. Many ethical theories will hesitatingly agree with intuitionism up to this point. They will not dispute the first-order claims of intuitionism. But when the question is raised of how we know these are our duties, disagreements immediately arise. Characterizations *about* the moral knowledge that intuitionism asserts we have are second-order claims. The positions that intuitionism takes on this level have invited the most frequent attacks against the theory. As I make the case for intuitionist moral knowledge, I will respond to many of them.

1. Empiricism and rationalism

A number of obstacles stand between intuitionism and its general acceptance. Most of them come in the form of specific objections that have been directed at intuitionism. But a longstanding suspicion of rationalism is perhaps the biggest underlying factor responsible for resistance to the theory, for intuitionism is a form of moral rationalism.[1]

Many reasons for dismissing intuitionism are based on the assumption that rationalism is not a viable epistemological stance. Obviously, if intuitionism is right, the world, and how we know about it, must differ in material ways from how empiricists envision it. Empiricism holds that all our knowledge has its source in our experience of the world. Rationalism disagrees, claiming that though a great deal of our knowledge is got through experience, we have significant a priori knowledge about the world. One point of contention upon which the empiricist-rationalist debate hinges is synthetic a priori knowledge. Empiricists reject it. Rationalists embrace it. Later I will present an argument for synthetic a priori truths that tilts the scales toward rationalism.

Most contemporary philosophers think rationalism is irreparable. But several prominent philosophers have recorded their dissent with major rationalist works.[2] However, nothing contemporary rationalists say will alone likely sway the empiricist throngs. But rationalists have an ally that seems capable of overwhelming any empiricist argument. A little red ball. Empiricism correctly claims that we know a ball is red through sense-experience. But how do we know that nothing can be red and green all over at the same time? A few moments of reflection will convince us that this proposition is true. But the observations that would be required to show it are unavailable. Thinking alone convinces us it is true. Empiricists will assert it is analytic, and attempt to provide definitions of "red" and "green" that will make it true. But they have been unsuccessful, despite years of trying.[3] Although I lack space to make a proper case for rationalism, recognizing that empiricism faces fundamental obstacles of its own will hopefully convince everyone to proceed with us open-mindedly.

2. Self-evidence explained

Intuitionism claims that the intuitive principles are self-evident. But what is self-evidence? In this section I will provide a characterization of *self-evident cognition*, or knowledge of self-evident propositions. Audi states that, "A self-evident proposition is (roughly) a truth such that understanding it will meet two conditions: that understanding is (a) sufficient for one's being justified in believing it . . . and (b) sufficient for knowing the proposition provided one believes it on the *basis* of understanding it" (1996: 114). Audi gives a *two condition* account of self-evident cognition, consisting of what we may call the "understanding condition" and the "acceptance condition." The traditional view of self-evident cognition often seemed to be a kind of one condition account: a proposition is self-evident if understanding it is sufficient for one to know it. I believe that, in light of our current understanding of what knowledge is, a two condition account more faithfully captures what self-evidence cognition is, and avoids giving rise to numerous misunderstandings.

To understand self-evident cognition we must have some understanding of knowledge. Knowledge has three necessary conditions. For a person A to know that *p* it is necessary that: (1) A believe that *p*, (2) *p* is true, and (3) A is justified in believing that *p*. To say that these conditions are necessary for someone to know something means that *all three* conditions must be in place, and that one or two of them can be in place for someone without their having knowledge.[4] Suppose Jones spontaneously believes her mother, who lives in a different town, is now gardening, and she just happens to be gardening now. Although Jones has true belief concerning her mother's gardening, she does not have knowledge of it, because her belief is not justified. Consider another situation. Smith receives his paper by 9 a.m. every morning. So the proposition that Smith receives his paper every day by 9 a.m. is true. On each day Smith picks up the paper when he notices the sun rising. So Smith has justification for believing that he receives his paper before 9 a.m. every day. But since he never thinks about the general pattern of the paper's arrival, he does not believe that he receives his paper every day by 9 a.m. Therefore, Smith doesn't know it. So to have knowledge that *p*, we must have justified true belief that *p*.

On Audi's account of self-evident cognition, if someone adequately understands s then they are justified in believing that s. And it seems that if anyone adequately understands a self-evident proposition s, it *seems* to them to be true. That is, they have an intuition that s. But as we have seen in the case of Smith, we can be justified in believing that p without believing it. So a person can understand a self-evident proposition s, have an intuition that s, but yet not believe s on the basis of their understanding. And that would mean that they do not know s.

We must handle self-evident knowledge with some care. For many people doubt that they know any self-evident propositions at all. And what makes matters worse for the case for self-evidence, self-evidence has often been thought to imply infallible belief. Traditionally, philosophers, mathematicians, and scientists have believed certain propositions are self-evident. As we discussed previously, many propositions that were thought to be self-evident turned out not to be. At this point it would benefit us to recall Audi's insight that it is one thing to apprehend the *truth* of a self-evident proposition; it is another to apprehend its *self-evidence*.

I doubt that any mortal ever apprehends the self-evidence of a proposition. I believe that such a judgment is always based on an inference to the best explanation. It works like this. Take the self-evident proposition "All triangles have three sides." By fully understanding this proposition we can see its truth. That's a first-order judgment called an *apprehension*. It is when we try to explain our apprehension that judgments of self-evidence come into play. By understanding that our intuition is based on the proposition alone, without any experience-based information being necessary, we conclude that something about understanding the proposition made it evident to us. So we *infer* that the proposition is self-evident. And I believe it is this inference we intuit when we think we are apprehending the self-evidence of a proposition.

To consider the alternative, what would it be like to apprehend the self-evidence of a self-evident proposition? Take the proposition (A) "All triangles have three sides." Apprehending (A)'s truth would require apprehending it. Apprehending (A)'s self-evidence would be another matter. It would seem we would have to apprehend the truth of the proposition (B) "'All triangles have three sides' is self-evident." "Having three sides" has a natural relation to "being a triangle" which "being self-evident" does not have to

"All triangles have three sides." And that accounts for why we can apprehend the truth of (A) in a way we cannot (B).

What about the claim that self-evident propositions are necessary? Every proposition that is self-evidently true would also be necessarily true, that is, true in every possible world. But just because a proposition is necessary does not imply that its necessity is ever apprehended as its truth is. Claims of necessity of self-evident propositions are inferences we make based on two features of our intuitions of them: (1) we apprehend the truth of such propositions and (2) we are unable to see how they can be otherwise. For a proposition to be self-evident, our inability to see it being other than true must be based on features of the proposition, and not be due to a psychological limitation. Directly apprehending the necessity of self-evident propositions is not at issue. "Necessity" is clearly not part of the content of the proposition "All triangles have three sides." But its necessity is a property of the whole content of the proposition.

Having an intuition of a self-evident proposition does not imply infallibly having it. Intuitions are fallible. For example, clever arguments, involving thought experiments about our dreaming or being deceived by an all-powerful evil genius, can make us momentarily doubt even the most sturdy specimens of self-evident truths, such as $1 + 1 = 2$. Relatedly, previous critics and proponents of intuitionism were right that convictions concerning self-evidence can be mistaken.[5] Just because we are convinced that p is self-evident, that is, just because the belief factor of knowledge is experienced as very strong, does not imply that p is self-evident, or even that we know it.

3. Moral proofs

The intuitive principles are standalone truths. Proofs of them, as early analytic intuitionists recognized, are not necessary. Being self-evident, they need no proof, though arguments of some sort can convince us of their truth. In addition, they cannot be proved. Audi has contested this latter doctrine, claiming that, "the concept of self-evidence does not rule out proof or evidencing by something else" (2004: 83).[6] There is good reason to hold the no-proof doctrine. What rules out proof is not the concept of self-evidence, but rather the kind of proposition that is self-evident. Each self-evident proposition contains one or more *generic concepts*. A generic concept captures an entity with maximal generality for entities of its kind—that is, it captures a generic universal.[7] Consider the self-evident proposition "Pleasure is good." In it both "pleasure" and "good" are generic. There are many species of pleasure and many kinds of good, but neither pleasure nor good is a species of a higher existing genus. On this account, there are simply no true, informative premises capable of implying "Pleasure is good." So proof of it is impossible. I doubt that proofs of the intuitive principles can be provided. But just a single intuitionist moral proof would decide the case for the pro-proof side. Other kinds of evidencing—that is another matter.[8]

Proof is a word philosophers used to throw around. Although philosophers are now more circumspect in its use, it is not clear the conditions of proof are widely understood. For propositions *p*, *q*, and *r* to prove that *s* two conditions are necessary and sufficient. First *p*, *q*, and *r* must imply *s*. Second, *p*, *q*, and *r* must be known to be true. The problem in ethics is that we do not know any supreme principle to be true. And although part of the case for any supreme principle is that it implies the intuitive principles, as things stand it is the intuitive principles that carry all the epistemic weight. That is the opposite of what we need for a proof of them.

Intuitionism is committed to self-evident moral principles. These principles are evident to us. Certain crucial implications of this latter fact have not generally been appreciated. Specifically, that the intuitive principles are evident to us implies that no other moral proposition is more convincing than they are. That means that attempts to prove them, to justify them, and to normatively explain them by other propositions will not be fruitful. The following set of propositions is incoherent:

1 *s* is self-evident and evident to us.

2 *p* implies *s*.

3 *p* is more convincing than *s*.

A moral proof of *s* by a supreme principle *p* would involve *p* implying *s* and *p* being more convincing than *s*. Of course, for *p* to genuinely prove *s*, *p* must be known to be true. We will temporarily relax that requirement, and only insist that p be more convincing than s. But if s is evident to us, at best p would have to be evident to us. But the very fact that people greatly disagree about supreme principles indicates that no extant supreme principle is evident, whereas people generally agree that harming others is wrong, lying is wrong, and so on.

Considering propositions 2 and 3 as necessary conditions of proof shows why intuitionists are skeptical of such a possibility.[9] As an alternative, propositions 2 and 3 could be considered necessary conditions of justification. But similarly, a proposition p that is supposed to justify s cannot convincingly do so if s is evident to us and p is not. The same goes for any normative explanation that uses p to illuminate s. Until ethicists provide a supreme principle which is evident, as the intuitive principles are, we have good reason to doubt that any can prove, justify, or explain them.

4. Justification structures

It is one thing to be confident that we know that assault is wrong. It is quite another to be able to say *how* we know it. Asking someone on what basis they know what's right concerning a particular issue is to ask for evidence for their belief. This might be put differently by asking what justifies their belief. Every justification of a belief has one of two possible structures. Examining them will help to remove one hindrance to accepting self-evident knowledge.

The first justification structure is a binary one. A *binary justification structure* has two components. The first part is the proposition that is known, or said to be known, *the knowledge content*. The second part is *the evidence* by which the knowledge content is known. The evidence is distinct from the knowledge content. The simplest case is one in which, say, s is what one knows, and some other proposition p provides evidence for s. More complex cases will involve numerous propositions that provide the evidence for s.

Knowledge exhibiting the binary justification structure is by far the most common. The vast majority of instances in which we think we have knowledge involve two or more propositions. Every strongly confirmed scientific theory has amassed a great deal of evidence to support it. Prosecutors in criminal trials marshal reams of detailed evidence in order to convict criminals. So one might wonder if any other structure of belief justification is possible. A *unary justification structure* is the only alternative. Knowledge situations of this sort are comprised of knowledge content and evidence for such content, just as for binary justification structure cases. The difference is that knowledge that has a unary justification structure involves the proposition that is known, or believed to be known, providing evidence for itself. So the knowledge content and the evidence for that knowledge are one and the same. Propositions of such sort are called "self-justifying" or "self-evident" propositions.

Instances of knowledge that have a unary justification structure are comparatively uncommon. They are uncommon enough that many philosophers deny their existence. We naturally assume that there is *always* a *separate* item of information needed to show a proposition to be true. For example, if someone asks you "How do you know that *s*?" it is clear that they are asking for something other than *s*. The very asking of the question shows that they do not regard *s* as self-evident. But the *separation assumption* leads to a notorious problem. If *p* is the separate evidence that justifies us in believing *s*, then if we believe knowledge content and evidence are always separate, we must ask how we really can be justified in believing that *p* if it is not on the basis of some *other* separate proposition *q*. Since the same question must be asked of *q*, an infinite regress emerges. Since proponents of a supreme principle accept the separation assumption, they must, to be consistent, either adequately justify their principle with a separate principle or acknowledge that it is not unreasonable for intuitionists not to rely on a supreme principle.

Self-evident propositions provide the evidence for themselves. To give some sense of what they are like, a few examples would help. $2 + 2 = 4$ is an obvious self-justifying proposition. We need no evidence outside of it in order to know that it is true. The same goes for these others: Nothing can be red and green all over. If A is greater than B, and B is greater than C, then A is greater then C. If A occurs later than B, and B occurs later than C, then A occurs later than C.

Such examples should boost the plausibility of self-evident propositions. If they do not, a look at the best argument for excluding unary justification structures will surely do so. The argument, as applied to an intuitive principle, seems to be this:

(A) 1. The vast majority of knowledge is not self-justifying.

     2. <u>"Keeping promises is required" is something we know</u>.

       "Keeping promises is required" is not self-justifying.

Many philosophers will happily accept the conclusion. But if we accept it on the basis of this argument, we must accept that humans do not think. Why do I say this? Because (A) is of the same form as:

(B) 1. The vast majority of animals do not think.

     2. <u>Humans are animals</u>.

       Humans do not think.

There is ample evidence that humans think. All that acceptance of argument (A) shows is that humans don't always think things all the way through. To further demonstrate this, consider the two possibilities concerning self-evidence. Either,

(E) Some propositions are self-evident.

or (F) No propositions are self-evident.

One reason given in favor of (F) is that,

(G) Every proposition we know is proved (or justified) by another proposition.

So the question for skeptics of self-evidence is, "What is the basis for believing that every proposition we know is proved or justified by another?" In order to know or be justified in believing (G) one must have knowledge of the propositions which imply it. Right? So what are they? I must confess, I would not know where to start.

    Now, if no such propositions implying (G) can be supplied, then either skeptics of self-evidence are holding it as an assumption without reasons or it is evident to them in such a way they simply cannot see how it could be false. In which case, the best explanation they can give for their position is that (G) seems to them evident in itself. But it would seem that the campaign to rid the world of belief in self-evidence would be better served if it were not based on the claim that "Every proposition known is proved by another" is self-evident.

As we will soon see, intuitionists have several reasons for believing that the moral principles are self-evident truths. But because they are self-evident, they cannot be proved. Thus intuitionists give up one of the apparent attractions of most other theories: the appearance of explanatory power. This is the bargain intuitionists have struck by maintaining the intuitive principles are self-evident. What this means is that intuitionists cannot offer the appearance of a deductive means to getting to the truth through other propositions. The most they can do is give other ways of establishing the true moral principles. Perhaps the best way of doing so is our next topic.

5. Epistemic appraisal

Some questions are likely to remain about self-evidence. For those still doubting the intuitive principles, how may we show that they are true? How can intuitionism overcome the apparent drawbacks of the unary justification structure it relies on? How to show that each intuitive principle is more convincing than any proposition proposed for proving, justifying, or explaining it?

To answer these questions, recall that I asked you to judge your moral alternatives in the natural habitat of moral knowledge: actual moral situations. First, I asked that you consider, concerning a situation in which you were tempted to lie whether it seemed to you that (1) You should not lie, (2) You should lie, (3) You may lie. Next, I addressed the possible moral reasons for your first response. Why make the choice you did? Assuming you judged that you should not lie, some possible reasons given were: (4) It is wrong to do so, (5) It does not maximize the good, and (6) A world in which everyone acts thus is logically impossible. Both comparative investigations employed the method of epistemic appraisal, which I will now explain.

If people reflect on what's right to do they will likely agree with the intuitive principles. Reflection on moral reasons is also likely to result in such agreement. But it is not as likely, because many people, ethicists especially, believe that reasons for acting morally must involve something other than what moral consciousness delivers. When we evaluate moral reasons, we are implicitly evaluating moral theories. There are a number of ways of comparing two moral theories. An often overlooked approach is a direct epistemic comparison of their principles in actual moral situations. Ross, following the lead of Prichard, Moore, and Russell, has us do exactly that.[10]

Suppose someone enraged you so much that you wanted to strike them. Realizing you shouldn't, you think "It's wrong to harm them," and regard that as sufficient reason not to. Ross compares this ordinary moral belief to the principle of utility in its generic form. When we consider attacking someone to be wrong, the thought that "It will not maximize good" plays no role in persuading us to stay our hand. So in such a situation, "Harming others is wrong" is what we really think rather than "It will not maximize good."[11]

This is a *direct epistemic appraisal* of two moral principles.[12] In an actual moral situation, the intuitionist belief for why we should do what's right is epistemically preferable to that of the utilitarian. Such comparative appraisal should be repeated for all of the intuitionist moral principles, "Keeping promises is required," "Lying is wrong," and so on, in the context of the relevant moral situations. The result will be that any intuitive principle will be found to be epistemically preferable to the principle of utility. Each intuitive principle is evident to us in its corresponding kind of moral situation, while the principle of utility is never thus evident to us, except in situations where maximizing good is our actual duty. The intuitionist explanation for why we believe it would be wrong to strike a person is that "Harming others is wrong" is self-evident. Any other proposed supreme principle must likewise be appraised against the intuitive principles.

The pioneers of analytic philosophy effectively used epistemic appraisal to rout realism's adversaries. Why did it work? Epistemic appraisal helps us determine what we really think about any subject. In the process, it often brings into focus what we really know. Recent empirical work shows that we handle information we are considering for knowledge in the comparative fashion of epistemic appraisal.[13] Often our best reason for believing something is simply that it is epistemically preferable to the alternatives. For any two beliefs about a given subject we will have different degrees of epistemic confidence. That we have more confidence that p than that q, after considering them, is itself a reason to believe p over q. It gives us strong prima facie justification for believing that p.[14] So contrasting our options concerning lying in the proper context will justify our judgment. Likewise, by contrasting "It is wrong to harm others" with "It will not maximize good," when harming someone is a real temptation, the intuitionist moral principle provides strong prima facie justification for why we should not harm them. The principle of utility does not.

Not everyone will accept this way of examining theories. Some will question the claim that just because we are more confident in one proposition p over another q, it constitutes evidence for the former over the latter. Merely being inclined to believe p over q, they will say, contributes absolutely no evidence for p. Rather, it only informs us of our psychological bent at some time. Psychological confidence is not epistemic confidence, and epistemic appraisal seems based on confusing the two.

In response, I must stress that epistemic appraisal does not provide conclusive evidence for a proposition. Instead, it provides strong prima facie justification that can be overturned in a number of ways. Subsequent evidence can provide reason enough to reverse our initial epistemic preference. Or our initial appraisal can be overturned by discovery that it is inconsistent with a proposition we have greater reason to believe. Also, intuitionists recognize that a person's epistemic justification for a belief can be challenged, or even defeated, by identifying likely nonepistemic psychological causes of it, including evolutionary factors, bias, and personal issues.[15] Nonetheless, the intuitionist way of establishing the intuitive principles begins with the initial contact of our moral consciousness with actual moral situations. Whether they hold up depends on whether defeaters emerge as inquiry proceeds.

The context for much epistemological inquiry is the immediate epistemic situation. And for epistemic appraisal to have any value it must prove itself in that context. But epistemic appraisal shows its worth over the long term. Our ordinary perceptual experiences inform us over and over again of its general reliability. More

often than not, when we judge an object to have a certain shape
or color, rather than another shape or color, subsequent evidence
confirms our initial appraisal. So with regard to sense-experience
the maxim to follow is: "the senses should be regarded as innocent
until there is some positive reason, on some particular occasion,
for thinking that they are guilty on that particular occasion"
(Chisholm, 1973: 24).

Intuitionists take a similar approach with regard to moral
knowledge. In actual moral situations, we should trust our intelligence and accept that it is informing us that we ought not to lie,
break promises, and so on. The general principle to follow over
all domains, then, is "phenomenal conservatism": "Other things
being equal, it is reasonable to assume that things are the way they
appear" (Huemer, 2005: 99). Any attempt to overturn this principle must be based on considerations that *appear* to overturn it, and
would thereby be self-refuting. Given the general reliability of epistemic appraisal in other domains, the opponents of intuitionism
must offer compelling reasons for why epistemic appraisal should
break down in just one area: morality.

6. Intuitions

"Intuition" is a word with a number of meanings. In its most popular use it means a hunch. In some social circles, intuition is considered a mystical cognitive power. Intuition in its main philosophical
sense carries no such connotations. To separate our subject of study
from all others we might call it "intellectual intuition." But since
my explanation of it will make clear that intellectual intuition is
our only interest, the term "intuition" will do.

Intuitions are essential tools in contemporary philosophy. And
they have a critical role in the sciences. A few examples will be
helpful in understanding what they are. These examples are meant
to indicate that intuitions need not always be correct. When we
consider a philosophical theory for the first time, and it seems to
us that it has an absurd implication, that *seeming* is an intuition.
As we begin to learn a scientific theory, one strongly supported
by available evidence, we will often find that some element of it is
counterintuitive. But what seems so to us is also an intuition. When
someone offers a single principle for consideration such as "Every

exchange implies equality of value," and it seems right to us, that is an intuition, even though this particular one is mistaken.

The most important intuitions within intuitionism are of self-evident propositions of two kinds: those about what is morally right and those concerning what is intrinsically good. Such intuitions of self-evident propositions are intuitionism's starting-points, the *primary* intuitions of the theory. However, to bolster our confidence in the intuitive principles we consider *secondary* intuitions, which we compare to rival moral principles, through epistemic appraisal. These secondary intuitions that support the primary intuitions of the self-evident moral principles should be kept in mind, for they are often overlooked in criticisms of intuitionism. Also, intuitions inform us that in moral situations where duties conflict, one principle overrides another. Since intuitionism uses intuitions in several areas of investigation, we need a general theory of intuitions.

Having an intuition involves three things. The first is the object of an intuition: a proposition. The second thing is the intuition itself. It is a kind of mental entity, which I will define shortly. The third thing involved is our attitude concerning the intuition, commonly called a "propositional attitude." We can believe, disbelieve, or take an epistemically neutral attitude to an intuition we have. It is important to keep these three things separate as we proceed, for two reasons. They are difficult to separate in our mental experience. And each one of them has been considered an intuition by one philosopher or another.[16] Michael Huemer provides the most workable characterization of an intuition. It is an "*intellectual* appearance" (Huemer, 2005: 102). An "intuition that *p* is a state of its seeming to one that *p* that is not dependent on inference from other beliefs and that results from thinking about *p*, as opposed to perceiving, remembering, or introspecting" (Huemer, 2005: 102).

Intuitionism's primary intuitions have been highly criticized. By separating intuitions from their objects and the attitudes we might have about them, much of this criticism is neutralized. Let us first discuss the objects of the primary intuitions: the self-evident moral principles. These principles are necessary truths. That they are such has led to confusions among both adherents and opponents of intuitionism. It has been believed that if one apprehends a self-evident proposition then one is compelled to believe it. Part of the confusion here seems to be based on an ambiguity in the word "necessary." Many have mistakenly inferred from "p is necessary," that is, that p is a necessary truth, that "p is psychologically necessary." And that does not follow. Awareness that the object of an intuition is separate from the intuition itself removes the need to think that an object of intuition, in this case a self-evident proposition, can compel only one way of its seeming. Any proposition that appears true to Jones can appear false to Smith.

Intuitions and beliefs about them can be at odds. On one hand, a person can believe p consistently while their intuitions about p undergo changes. Beliefs we have are influenced by our other beliefs. Such influence is often independent of whether we have reflected on such beliefs. Take Jones, a young woman raised as a moral nihilist by her parents. She believes that there is nothing wrong with harming others, and her intuitions accord with that belief. But then Jones witnesses someone being severely beaten. She thinks about it, continues to believe there is nothing wrong with what happened, but when she considers "It is wrong to harm others" it seems to her to be true. At some point, if she is alert to changes in how things seem to her, she may begin to question her beliefs.

On the other hand, a person can change their beliefs concerning p while their intuition about p remains the same. Smith's parents brought him up to believe that keeping promises is required. As a result Smith had the intuition that he ought to keep his promises. But when Smith took a class taught by Jones, a notorious nihilist, he was persuaded to believe that there is nothing sacred about promises. He then gave up belief in obligation to keep promises, but his intuition about keeping promises remained. Intuitionists argue that "Keeping promises is required" is self-evidently true. Separating intuitions both from their objects and from the attitudes we can have about them helps explain why people can disagree with these truths.

7. Skepticism about intuitions

The simplest way to reject intuitionism is to reject intuitions. In past years, this was much easier for philosophers to do. Intuitions used to be objects of suspicion and scorn among analytic philosophers. But now intuitions have widespread methodological use in philosophy. Now if philosophers wish to reject intuitionism, they must explain why it is a mistake to employ intuitions in ethics, but acceptable to use them in metaphysics or epistemology. Furthermore, one who abandons all disciplines that rely on intuitions must perforce abandon all observational judgments and any hope of valid inference. So she must abandon science.

But why doubt that we have intuitions? Up until recently, it must be acknowledged that philosophers asserted that they had intuitions, or that a certain proposition simply seemed true to them, without having a good account of intuitions. This lack made it easy to confuse intuitions and the psychological mechanisms that generate them. So if someone asserted that they had a particular moral intuition, other philosophers wondered by what mechanism the intuition came about. But the confusion of intuitions and their mechanisms was accompanied by a major unfounded assumption: intuitions require a special psychological faculty.[17]

Intuitions are one thing. The mechanisms by which they are produced are another. That means that the first question is whether there are intuitions at all. And only on the condition that there are intuitions does it make sense to inquire into what causes them. The intuitionist need only establish that there are intuitions to carry on. With an intuition being defined as an intellectual appearance, skeptics are put in a difficult position. They must claim that propositions that we consider do not appear to us to be true, false or indeterminate. They must claim that propositions do not have *any* *way* they seem to us. And that is absurd.

Intuitions are necessary for any intellectual inquiry. To bolster this point, let's discuss how intuitions are necessary to science. Science rests on logical reasoning.[18] Even probable reasoning implicitly relies on the standards involved in deductive reasoning. The one indispensable mental act in reasoning is drawing an inference. How do we do that correctly? And how do we know when we have? Consider these two propositions:

1 All skeptics are rigorous inquirers.

2 Jones is a skeptic.

The question is, what can we validly deduce from these two propositions? One obvious answer is the proposition that "Jones is a

rigorous inquirer." Now, how do we do this? We look at propositions 1 and 2, then we judge that "Jones is a rigorous inquirer"
seems to follow from them. But how do we know that we have
drawn this inference correctly? We check the premises and the
conclusion we have drawn and judge that the premises *seem* to
imply the conclusion.[19] There is no other way for deductive reasoning to take place. Intuitions enable us to correctly draw and check
inferences. Without them we could not discern the implications of
propositions, and there would be no logic. So we must accept that
there are intuitions, and that without them science would not be
possible. As to the mechanisms behind intuitions, we will leave
that to psychologists to explain.

8. Self-evidence, mathematics, and morality

Mathematics is often enlisted on the side of intuitionism. Many
intuitionists have argued that, if one accepts that there are self-
evident necessary truths in math, then she should be inclined to
accept there are such truths in ethics. Also, it is claimed that, if
intuitions are all we need to know mathematical truths, then intuitions are sufficient for knowing certain moral truths. The effect
of such claims is not always favorable to intuitionism. In fact, it
often invites skepticism.[20] Some philosophers will agree that math
involves self-evident truths that we know through intuition, but
that moral truths are nothing like that. Math, they will say, provides a paradigm case of certainty and consensus on the truth.
Ethics, in contrast, can boast of neither of these attributes. In brief,
some take the position that rationalism about mathematics is well
justified, while rationalism about moral truth is absurd.

Obviously, math and ethics have had different levels of success. In terms of the extent of agreement, and degree of certainty,
the two fields seem at opposite ends. And the subject matters of
math and ethics are completely different. But, as I shall argue, the
main reason for their appearing so incredibly different to critics
of intuitionism is not that the basic sources of truth and means by
which we know them are completely different. Both math and ethics rest on self-evident necessary truths, and we know these truths

by apprehending them. The main explanation for their appearing vastly different to us is that they rest on very *different kinds* of self-evident truths. The simplicity or complexity of self-evident propositions, the number and variety of their components, or the preciseness or vagueness of their concepts, make for different self-evident propositions.

Since more than one kind of proposition is self-evident, we should not expect the ease or difficulty of apprehending one self-evident proposition to hold for all others. Not even all truths of arithmetic are equally easy to apprehend. 2 + 2 = 4 is often used as an example of a self-evident truth. But a true arithmetical equation expressed by 17 numerals will be just as self-evident as 2 + 2 = 4. That is, it will provide all the evidence necessary to see it is true. It just would not be *evident to us* because of its magnitude, although it might be evident to a mental calculator. The world's longest tautology is as self-evidently true as any instance of the law of non-contradiction. But they are vastly different in terms of their being evident to us. To mark this difference, I call self-evident propositions like 2 + 2 = 4 *immediately evident* because they are obvious to us. An instance of a nonobvious tautology, on the other hand, is *mediately evident* because the medium of reflection is required for us to see its truth.[21]

Similar considerations explain why the moral principles are not evident to us in the same way 2 + 2 = 4 is. "Harming others is wrong" is difficult to adequately grasp because the vagueness of "harming" can often make proper application a challenge. "Keeping promises is required," on the other hand, can tax our attempts to grasp it because of the complex nature of the concept "promise." But each of these moral principles is as self-evident as 2 + 2 = 4. Adequate understanding is sufficient for grasping their truth. But since the intuitive principles contain vague or complex concepts they are not as easily evident to us.

9. Mere truisms?

Self-evidence gets more respect today than previously. But objections remain. For one, propositions considered self-evident often seem trivial. In many cases we accept them because they are mere truisms, or analytic truths, the kind of thing that everyone in our culture believes. If we accept the intuitive principles merely because we belong to a culture that pushes us to accept them, then that would be a serious blow to intuitionism. So here I will face the charge that self-evident propositions are mere truisms, and are therefore not substantive truths.

One moral truth considered to be a mere truism is (*m*) "Murder is wrong." Judge Posner, a critic of the enterprise of moral theory, claims that, "there are no *interesting* moral universals" (1999: 6). So, according to Posner, there is not really anything for intuitionists to investigate. But he does not deny that there are moral universals. He only denies that there are interesting ones. There are, however, "tautological ones, such as 'murder is wrong,' where 'murder' means wrongful killing, or 'bribery is wrong,' where 'bribery' means wrongful paying" (Posner, 1999: 6).

"Murder is wrong" expresses an analytic proposition on this view. The "linguistic" account of analytic propositions asserts that a proposition is analytic if it is true *by virtue of its meaning*. So if (*m*) really is analytic, it seems that our discussing it will not advance ethics in any way. As Väyrynen states, "We cannot reasonably infer substantive ethical claims just from such non-substantive claims as 'Murder is wrong'" (2008: 506). But this raises the question of why it is analytic. The brief answer is that it is a linguistic convention in our society that whenever the word "murder" is uttered, it carries with it the meaning of "wrong." As a result, "Murder is wrong" is true by virtue of its meaning, which can be traced back to the conventions of our predecessors.

Such an explanation of (*m*) has neatness to recommend it. But it overlooks a couple of things. First, it never asks why society considers murder to be wrong. And, second, it only is convincing if we ignore ambiguity in language. Conventionalists claim that people ordinarily believe such things as that murder is wrong or caring for your children is right because of social convention. There are no timeless truths involved, and variations of social practices seem to support this claim. But intuitionism has another explanation for the same phenomena. It is a social convention that murder is wrong. But the reason why societies believe (*m*) is because people understand that murder is, by its very nature, wrong. So the social convention is based on common moral knowledge.[22]

It is true that convention dictates that (*m*) is trivially true. The meanings of the terms assure it. But just because "murder is wrong" is analytic by social convention does not imply that it is not also a substantive truth. "Murder is wrong" is ambiguous. It expresses two propositions. It expresses (c) "Murder is [conventionally] wrong" and (n) "Murder is [naturally] wrong." It is the latter proposition that is synthetic and known a priori. It is substantive. And the reason why it is such a strong convention in every society that murder is wrong is because the majority of people know that substantive truth. Convention in turn establishes it in language that "murder" simply implies "wrong." And that is how a substantive truth (n), over time, produces a trivial counterpart (c). But it would be a serious mistake to conclude that, just because (*m*) expresses a conventional truth, it *only* expresses such a truth. Besides, there are reasons to doubt that terms such as "murder" can be defined as "wrongful killing." Since manslaughter is also wrongful killing, this would commit us to holding that "manslaughter is murder."[23]

10. Synthetic a priori truths

If our self-evident propositions have any substance, they must be synthetic a priori propositions. Propositions of this sort have long been controversial in philosophy because of the age-old battle between empiricism and rationalism. What is a synthetic a priori truth? A proposition is synthetic if grasping the meanings of its terms is not enough to determine if it is true. This implies that for any synthetic proposition there must be something beyond the meanings of the terms of which we must inquire. The term "a priori" and its opposite "a posteriori" concern ways in which propositions can be confirmed or disconfirmed. A priori propositions can be known without testing them against experience, such as "All brothers are male." Propositions that require that we consult experience to determine their truth, such as "All brothers are loyal," are a posteriori propositions.

The principal question for synthetic propositions is what could possibly be that "something beyond" by which we could determine if they are true? Many twentieth-century philosophers thought that their truth can only be determined by empirically testing them against the world. That is, they held that all synthetic propositions are necessarily a posteriori propositions. On this basis, they regarded synthetic a priori propositions as a fabled species.

But synthetic a priori propositions have refused to die. Such clearly true propositions as "Nothing can be red and blue all over" and "No material object can be in two places at the same time" have not been effectively analyzed out of existence by opponents of synthetic a priori truths. And rationalists believe that the "something beyond" the meanings of synthetic propositions that is required to determine their truth is not in all cases the world of sense-experience.

We have more reason to believe in synthetic a priori truths than to doubt them. Oliver Johnson showed why with an argument that is widely and shockingly overlooked.[24] Let's concentrate on the doubters' claim, the proposition that "There are no synthetic a priori truths." Now, what kind of proposition is this? Is it synthetic or analytic? Given our definitions, it seems to be synthetic. We cannot say, based on the meanings of the words alone that it is true. Next, we must ask, is it known a priori or a posteriori? Although I anticipate that, after reading this, thousands of empiricists around the world are now putting on their jackets and boots in the hopes of observing enough propositions for a confirmation of their theory, it really does not seem that we can confirm or disconfirm this proposition through empirical research. So the only alternative is that we know it to be true a priori. So we are forced to accept that the proposition "There are no synthetic a priori truths" seems to be a synthetic a priori truth. This, of course, does not prove that there are such propositions. It only shows that it is more rational to believe in them than to doubt them.

11. You know what's right

I can now establish a central intuitionist claim: you know what's right. How, you ask, can I assuredly assert that? Many readers will be stunned to be told that they know what's right, especially those who believe there is nothing to morality at all. The challenge, then, is to show that moral doubters know things that they say they do not even believe. Is this possible? I think so.

To start, we must look more closely at Audi's account of self-evident cognition. A proposition p is self-evident if (1) having adequate understanding of p is sufficient for one to be justified in accepting it and (2) if one accepts the proposition p on the *basis* of that understanding, then one knows it. There is no need to change anything about the account. But I must clarify one point about the acceptance condition. I wish to forestall a narrow understanding of what it means to come to accept a proposition, for there are roughly two ways. Asking how someone might come to accept that 2 + 2 = 4 will help clarify them.

Children learn the symbols of arithmetic at the same time they learn arithmetic. They learn what "2" means and what "4" means partly by appealing to examples. So the teacher places two wooden blocks on the table and says, "That is two blocks." Adding two more blocks, she says, "And now we have added two more blocks. The result is that we have four blocks, total." In teaching both the meanings of the numerals and the equations involving them, it is important to understand one thing. The two blocks exemplify 2; they *are not the reference* for it. Likewise, when the second pair of blocks is added we have an instance in the world that exemplifies 2 + 2 = 4. But it certainly *does not confirm* it.

All school children know that 2 + 2 = 4. They understand the proposition that 2 + 2 = 4. And they accept it on the basis of their understanding. But there is one thing that they clearly do not, and need not, understand. They need not understand exactly *how* they understand 2 + 2 = 4. Allow me to explain. Most people will not grasp that they know 2 + 2 = 4 by being aware that their knowledge is formed on the basis of their understanding a proposition. They might not even have ever heard of the term "proposition" or thought about what a proposition is. They will often say, quite falsely, that they learned the symbols making up "2 + 2 = 4" in class, and that the four blocks *proved* it was true. So they believe that they believe 2 + 2 = 4 *because* they experienced the blocks on the table, and not because they consciously considered a proposition.

Nonetheless they still understand 2 + 2 = 4 and believe it on the basis of their understanding. That is how they know it. Such a person, an average grammar school student, *innocently accepts* the proposition that 2 + 2 = 4. That is, they accept it in all metaphysical and epistemic innocence. So while they understand the content of the proposition, they don't understand exactly what kind of entity is the object of their understanding. A more abstract thinker, say a budding mathematician, who is familiar with the concept of a proposition, might understand directly that it is a proposition that

2 + 2 = 4 that is true. Such a person would *cognizantly accept* the proposition: they grasp the content and the entity containing it. But both the budding mathematician and the average student understand and accept the same proposition.

Audi's account of self-evidence is compatible with both ways of accepting propositions. But it lends itself to being read as allowing only cognizant acceptance, and that would create a problem for it. The reason why is that everyone knows that 2 + 2 = 4, but few know that they do so on the basis of understanding a proposition. In other words, they are unaware or confused about how they know that 2 + 2 = 4.

If two requirements of knowledge are that one must know the metaphysical status of the object of her knowledge and know *how* she knows it—the cognitive means by which it is known—then most people do not know 2 + 2 = 4. Understanding the content of a self-evident proposition is sufficient to be justified in believing it. People are not aware of such categories of entity as propositions and abstract objects. They can accept a proposition *p* on the basis of understanding it without clearly knowing the object of their understanding. And people can know that 2 + 2 = 4, even though they believe there are no mathematical truths, but only arbitrary conventional arrangements of mathematical symbols.

Likewise, every normal adult knows that keeping promises is required. They know this by understanding the proposition and accepting it on the basis of their understanding. This is so, even though many people don't believe they know it. But how is this possible? For one to know that *p* there is no necessary condition that she believes that she knows that *p*. She must only believe that *p* as a condition of knowing it. An illustration should make this clear. Philosophy students dabbling with skepticism can be convinced that they do not know that they are experiencing a door, a car, or other humans. But that does not stop them from exiting and locking their apartment door and going for a drive. Nor does it stop them from braking for a pedestrian at an intersection. All that matters for such a student to be said to know there is a door in front of her is to accept that there is one when she's exiting it. Likewise, all that is needed for a person to be said to know that lying is wrong, assuming the other conditions are in place, is to believe it in an actual situation in which lying is at issue. And that is what most adults do: believe the intuitive principles in the moral situations that they are personally involved in. That moral belief constitutes moral knowledge for people when it most counts—whatever wild metaethical beliefs they hold the rest of the time.

12. Chapter summary

Intuitionism must grapple with a number of deeply held assumptions that block its acceptance. A dogmatic stance against rationalism will prevent a fair hearing for intuitionism. So will an insistence that every proposition must be proved, justified, or explained by another proposition. Audi's two component account of self-evident cognition makes the notion of self-evidence more plausible and more defensible. Epistemic appraisal of intuitive principles in actual moral situations gives them prima facie justification. Appraising them against any supposed supreme principle gives them further justification and demonstrates that they have much greater epistemic strength than the supreme principles. Contrary to previous beliefs, intuitions are best thought of as intellectual appearances. Keeping them distinct from beliefs and propositions helps to avoid many old criticisms of intuitionism. The thesis that "There are no synthetic a priori truths" is an interesting hypothesis, especially interesting because it seems to be an instance of the kind of truth it denies exists. Lastly, it is easy to deny that lying is wrong in non-moral contexts, while believing it in moral contexts, if you innocently accept the proposition "Lying is wrong."

Further reading

Chapter 5, "Moral knowledge" of Michael Huemer's *Ethical Intuitionism* (2005) explains intuitionist epistemology, and defends it against several misunderstandings and objections. Laurence BonJour's *In Defense of Pure Reason* (1998) provides a contemporary defense of moderate rationalism.

CHAPTER FOUR

New challenges to intuitionism

Introduction

The previous chapter argued for core tenets of intuitionism: we know what's right, and self-evident moral principles are what we know. Maybe you were convinced. Your reservations about intuitionism having been removed, you now believe that we have a priori moral knowledge. You feel you have adequate justification for believing the intuitive principles. Even so, there are good reasons to believe that the case for intuitionism isn't closed.

So what is missing? In order to see, consider how I described knowledge. Knowledge requires justified true belief. If either justification, truth, or belief of that truth is missing, then knowledge is absent. Recent converts to intuitionism would think themselves well justified in their beliefs. But such justification only takes us so far. For even the most justified of believers falls short of knowledge if their beliefs are not *true*. And getting to the truth about morality is extraordinarily difficult.

We think of the truth as being outside us, as being something that has the last word, no matter how diligently we have inquired. The challenge we face here is, even if we believe we are justified in holding the intuitive principles, how is it even *possible* that any particular moral judgment is true? It would be possible if there are genuine moral facts external to our minds. The key question, then, is this: Does the world as we know it through science have room for moral facts? Those who say "yes" are called "moral realists." Moral realism comes in two kinds. Nonnatural moral realism, or preferably "nonnaturalism," is the metaphysical component of intuitionism. Natural moral realism, or simply "naturalism," differs from nonnaturalism in holding that moral facts are natural through and through. But both kinds of moral realism agree that there are moral facts.

Moral skeptics say "no"; there are no moral facts. Based on everything that we know from science, they say, the world cannot contain moral properties, implying that there are no moral facts. Intuitionists disagree about the existence of moral facts, but agree with the skeptics that moral properties are not natural properties. Moral properties, they assert, are "nonnatural" properties, properties that are sui generis. Intuitionist assertions of nonnatural properties have raised eyebrows in the past. Here I make a fresh case for nonnatural moral properties being inhabitants of our world.

The bulk of this chapter confronts the charges leveled by moral skeptics. I will also raise some other recent challenges to intuitionism. By now it is clear that many old criticisms of intuitionism lack force. These new challenges—the challenge of nihilism, the problem of supervenience, and the problem of expert disagreement—require new responses by intuitionists. This chapter provides some.

1. Where in the world is morality?

On one point philosophers agree with everyone else today. The natural sciences are our best bet for knowledge of the external world. The extent of our scientific knowledge is great and ever-growing. We know many things about our planet, its inhabitants, and our physical being. And we have a very good idea of how science works. All of this scientific information and information about science raises a critical question for ethics: *Where in the world is morality?* Among atoms, microbes, energy fields, zebras, weather patterns, humans, where are moral properties located? It is perhaps the most difficult question in ethics.

Nonnaturalism takes the stance that moral properties exist, but that they are not natural properties. Because moral properties are different from natural properties, it is a mistake to consider them along naturalistic lines. Our confidence in moral facts is not, and cannot be, found in empirical evidence for them gathered by scientific researchers. Rather, it is found in our confidence in our moral thought and beliefs, in the way we actually respond to moral issues, in our ordinary use of moral language, and in our theories. But because intuitionism starts from our intuitive moral perspective, it has been at a pronounced disadvantage in providing metaphysical explanations of moral facts, giving the impression that it can't.

Moral nihilists think there is no need to explain moral facts, for there are none. The scientific picture of the natural world convinces moral nihilists that there is no room for moral properties at all. This view holds that *all* moral propositions are false. To illustrate it, nihilists hold that *both* the pro-choice and pro-life positions on abortion are utterly false. Compared with all of the natural properties in the world, moral properties do seem remarkably strange. Moral values are supposed to somehow simply be in existence. And when we come across them, they supposedly somehow instruct us on how to act. They *command* us to do good. They do so because they somehow have moral *authority* over us.[1] In short, moral nihilists claim that such entities are simply too strange, simply too queer, to exist. Mackie's well known *queerness objection*, embraced by nihilists, is this: "If there were objective values, then they would be entities or qualities or relations of a very strange sort, utterly different from anything else in the universe. Correspondingly, if we were aware of them it would have to be by some special faculty of moral perception or intuition, utterly different from our ordinary ways of knowing everything else" (1977: 38).

Moral nihilists and nonnaturalists disagree about the existence of moral properties. But there is one thing on which they, and almost everyone else, agree. *Morality is different from everything else.* Nonnaturalists hold that moral facts require certain nonnatural properties. They hold that morality's being different from everything else is explained by moral properties being different from all other properties. Intuitionists do, however, recognize that it is hard to understand how moral facts can fit seamlessly into the natural world. Their opponents have been understandably puzzled by the claims of nonnaturalism. Moral nihilists think that moral properties are different enough from everything else that they must not exist. Historically, intuitionists have emphasized our moral knowledge without devising metaphysical explanations of moral facts. But to fully establish intuitionism both the epistemic and metaphysical parts of the theory must now be developed.

"I do not understand how moral facts could fit into the natural world" is a thought had by most everyone who seriously inquires about morality. It is perhaps the central source of moral perplexity today. But how to respond to it? Consider the situation of a person having this thought. He believes the intuitive moral principles, but cannot quite understand how there are moral facts in the external natural world. It seems there is a chasm between our ordinary moral beliefs and a world that contains the properties that would make them true. How should a philosopher approach this?

Philosophy is the venture of trying to understand everything. So it seems the natural philosophical inquiry would be to seek to find out how something as common as strongly believing it's wrong to harm others could be squared with a world that apparently contains only natural properties. Another response to the moral perplexity is to take the thought "I don't understand how moral facts could fit into the natural world" as a premise, and conclude, "Therefore, there are no moral facts." Obviously, that doesn't follow. Lack of understanding cannot be rectified by giving up the attempt to understand. Intuitionists embrace the philosophical task of increasing our understanding of the world and persevere in the quest to make the existence of moral facts understandable.

2. Moral skepticism and moral nihilism

Moral nihilism gets its appearance of strength from science. Nihilists see the contest between nihilism and realism as a clash between two kinds of epistemic authority: the authority of science and the authority of our intuitive moral beliefs. In discussion among ordinary people, there is no question of which authority commands greater respect. Science wins out almost every time.[2] Intuitionists see matters otherwise. The authority of science deserves great respect. But we should not hold that just because science has indisputable epistemic reign over *all physical* domains of inquiry that it has dominion over *all* domains of inquiry. For intuitionism, moral knowledge is beyond the reach of the sciences.[3]

There are many forms of moral skepticism.[4] What all of them are skeptical about is objective morality. They all enlist the authority of the sciences for their skeptical aims. Moral nihilism is the brand of moral skepticism that poses the greatest threat to nonnaturalism. The reason is that it concedes several strong points of intuitionism. Each of us has moral convictions that we take seriously. We believe we are justified in holding our moral beliefs. And no matter what we say, in moral situations in which we are personally involved, we certainly behave and respond as if morality were an objective affair.

Nihilism and nonnaturalism agree that our moral beliefs make objective claims. Subjectivism, expressivism, and cultural relativism, three other varieties of moral skepticism, are less plausible, in part, because they cannot account for what we actually think about morality.[5] People can say that morality is subjective, but they can't help but make moral claims as if they are objective. We can tell people that morality is just an expression of our feelings, but when it comes to some moral issue about which we take a strong position, we are not prepared to be told that we're just venting our feelings, and nothing more. And while cultural relativists can tell everyone that culture completely determines what is moral, it is rare to find a cultural relativist who completely accepts the mores of his own culture.

So the inherent objectivity of the moral judgments we make is something nihilism and nonnaturalism agree on. Where they differ is on the matter of whether there are any moral properties answering to such judgments. Nonnaturalism says "yes," nihilism says "no." So nihilism poses a great threat to nonnaturalism because it concedes to it the sense of authority that is attached to our ordinary intuitive moral beliefs. It just says that such beliefs are gravely in error, and that there is nothing external to our minds that can give morality its supposed authority. Nihilism implies that even after intuitionism marshals forth all of its clear intuitive evidence for objective morality, even after intuitionism succeeds in having us agree that "what we actually think" about morality reveals the truth of some moral principles, all of our moral beliefs will be false.

3. Responding to moral nihilism

What we really think about morality excludes moral nihilism. It does not require extensive reflection to see it is true that "Murder is wrong." The nihilist position that it is false that "Murder is wrong" is something that, if we are reflecting directly on the matter, we are unable to see. Nihilists will counter that our resistance to their claim is psychological, not substantive. Some people, I recognize, will think the nihilists have a point. But to my mind this is only a reflection of the fact that our contemporary culture has nihilist strands running through it, distorting our judgments. A small sample of popular movies and TV shows will reveal this. We are used to seeing simulated murders—many of them.[6] However, I think that if the proposition in question were "Rape is wrong" more intuitions would land on the intuitionist side of the fence. Extensive reflection on both propositions favors intuitionism's position, and should bring the nihilist around.

Moral nihilism's posture is not as secure as it appears. Science has truly earned its place of high epistemic authority. But does science itself endorse moral nihilism? No, it does not. Even if some scientists signed on to moral nihilism, their position would not be based on any scientific evidence. The authority of the sciences is transferred to moral nihilism without the nihilists providing any scientific research as evidence for their view. Nihilists cite no studies from the fields of physics or biology to make their case. So it is rather the *presuppositions* of the natural sciences that are employed against moral realism. And the presuppositions being employed are those not of scientists, but of the nihilists themselves. So the scientific authority that nihilism relies on is there only on the say-so of the moral nihilists themselves.

Deeper problems for nihilism are found in its point of departure. It rightly recognizes that morality is different from everything else. It wonders only very briefly how morality might be assimilated to the worldview of the natural sciences. It decides that it can't. Nihilists assert that any subject worthy of epistemic respect *ought* to be neatly incorporated into the natural sciences. Nihilists offer no argument for this *ought*. And given their worldview, how could they? Do they expect us to believe that in a hard, material world of natural facts there somewhere lurk these queer facts that somehow inform us that all knowledge ought to be scientifically testable? Nihilism says, in effect, we should doubt the *oughts* of morality based on the fact that morality doesn't fit into the framework from which all genuine knowledge claims *ought* to emanate. It seems then that the challenge for the nihilist is to convincingly argue for why we should believe their unsubstantiated *ought* but reject the *oughts* our moral intuitions justify us in believing. Nihilism has other problems, which I will discuss later.

4. Naturalism and nonnaturalism

Uncovering the weaknesses of moral nihilism puts intuitionism in a relatively better light. But intuitionism is not yet in the clear. Just because we have undercut nihilism's *basis* for claiming that moral facts cannot fit into the natural world does not imply that moral facts do so fit. We are still far short of showing just *how* moral facts can fit in. In order to do so I must first explain what nonnaturalism is. And the best way to do that is to provide some idea of naturalism.

General naturalism is the metaphysical stance that all the properties in the world are physical properties. Think of the physical objects that surround you. There are tables, chairs, walls, cats, TVs, and so on. All of the properties that make up such objects are natural properties; they can be studied by the natural sciences.[7] General naturalism applied to morality holds that there is nothing to morality that is not natural. Taking this standpoint, however, does not commit one to any particular metaethical view. There are several naturalistic metaethical positions. Nihilism, which we've just discussed, asserts that naturalism excludes moral properties altogether. Starting from general naturalism, we can arrive at subjectivism, expressivism, cultural relativism—all nonobjectivist metaethical theories.

Natural moral realism, or just "naturalism," on the other hand, holds to objective morality just as tightly as intuitionism. However, naturalists assert that all moral properties are natural properties, just like everything else in the world. That makes naturalists the exception to the general rule of agreement that morality is greatly different from everything else. Naturalists reject intuitionism because it asserts there are nonnatural moral properties. However, since moral properties are not now, and are not likely to be, a subject of study of the natural sciences, naturalists are inadvertently targets of their own objection to intuitionism.[8]

Nonnaturalism asserts that moral properties are unlike the properties of all the natural objects. But this commitment does not deny that the world is brimming with natural properties. It merely asserts that in addition to the natural properties, there are some properties that cannot be detected, discovered, or investigated by the natural sciences. Why assert that there are nonnatural moral properties? The intuitionist looks toward them, at first, because morality is different from everything else. Second, the evidence indicates that there is something substantial to our moral thoughts. We can't but think that some acts are wrong, others are right, even if we are convinced of a metaethical theory that rules right and wrong out. Nonnaturalism is the theory of moral properties that makes the most sense, given what we really think about morality. No variety of moral skepticism does full justice to our genuine moral thought. And, as we'll now see, neither does naturalism.

What can explain the meaning of moral predicates like "wrong"? Three options are available.[9] Either moral predicates have meaning or they do not. The option that moral predicates are meaningless is out of the question, given our previous investigations into what we think. If moral predicates have meaning, there are two remaining options. Their meaning is found in natural properties or in nonnatural properties. Natural properties require no defense. They surround us. The problem for the ethical naturalist is to identify these properties in the external world and show these properties are *moral properties* in a way we can recognize.

G. E. Moore famously argued for nonnatural properties. In particular, he aimed to show that good is such a property. Moore attempts to establish nonnaturalism by showing that naturalism is an inherently faulty view, setting his sights on any naturalist view that would claim that (1) moral properties are identical to natural properties and (2) moral predicates are synonymous with natural predicates. Such views might be called *analytic naturalism*—"analytic" because of the second requirement, "naturalism" due to the first. Philosophers propounding such a view would claim "The very meaning of 'good' is 'pleasure'," or something similar by substituting an alternative for the predicate "pleasure."

Moore employs his famous "open question argument" against such views. It works as follows. Suppose we identify good with pleasure, and say that "good" and "pleasure" have the very same meaning. We already know that "good" and "good" are synonyms, and that their corresponding properties, if they exist, are one and the same. When we ask, "Is good necessarily good?" we unhesitatingly answer "yes." So that question is a closed question, with no room in our minds for doubt about it. But if we ask "Is pleasure necessarily good?" we are not sure. We think it might be or might not be. Since the last question is open, that shows that "good" and "pleasure" are clearly not synonyms, as "good" and "good" are.

Moore successfully shows that numerous attempts to analytically define "good" fail. But many doubt that he shows that good cannot be identical to any other property through this method. Here is why. Water is identical to H_2O, despite "water" and "H_2O" being nonsynonymous. Contemporary naturalists have convincingly argued that it is possible that a property such as moral rightness is identical to some natural property N1, but without their corresponding predicates being synonymous. Such views may be called *synthetic naturalism*. But imagine, please, that one day the world's smartest naturalist comes to believe that he discovered the natural properties that are identical to moral properties, and that the identity between these two kinds of properties is expressible in a chemical equation: moral rightness = $CH_4 + NH_3 + 1.5\ O_2 \rightarrow HCN + 3\ H_2O$. The urgent questions are: How did the naturalist discover this property identity? What was the process of investigation? What was the investigation's first step? And it is at the first step that naturalism is halted.

To see why, consider a more easily identifiable natural property, pleasure, which many naturalists have asserted to be the natural property identical to moral rightness. To see if morality is identical to pleasure, the first step would be . . .. It is hard to say. We can observe the occurrence of pleasure in the natural world, but morality is not something we can see, touch, feel, taste, or hear. It is only through our thinking that we are acquainted with morality at all. So, unlike the case of water and H_2O, we have no discernible observational route to determine whether morality and pleasure are identical—at the outset of our inquiry, when we are testing the hypothesis or at the inquiry's completion. That our sole epistemic access to morality is through thought, and that naturalism has no idea how observation can lead us to knowledge of moral-natural identities are two reasons to consider a nonnaturalist route to moral explanation.

So what are nonnatural moral properties like? Moore claims that good is a nonnatural property. To make his position more easily understood we might say that good is a generic universal.[10] Being generic, good is ultimate. Consequently, the predicate "good" is truly applicable to numerous and various kinds of good, and is used define them, but cannot itself be defined. Although "good" can be predicated of many things, little that is informative can be said about good as it is in itself. Its generic nature makes it also unanalyzable. In that respect we can liken it to the property of being extended, which every object in our environment possesses, but of which, when considered in isolation, we can say very little.

Moore considers good to be a simple object of thought. Because of its simplicity, if you have no knowledge of it, it cannot be explained by any other concept. But he thinks we do know it and that it is something we are constantly aware of. Moore considers good to be a unique object, something for which we can find no substitute in thought. We can recognize it before our minds, and so we are capable of seeing that it differs from other things like desire. So what relation does good have to the objects that are good? Well, it is not part of the things that are good, like a leg is a part of a chair. Thus, it cannot be separated from natural objects, like the leg of a chair can. According to Moore, we cannot imagine good existing by itself: it is always attached to another object in our minds. Our judgments of what things are good are determined by "reflective judgment," not by perception. Metaphysically, he likens good to a number like 2 in that it *is* and is timeless, and so lacks spatiotemporal existence.

After reviewing the many properties Moore ascribes to good, we might ask, can we know all this? The concept of a nonnatural property has one thing in common with the concept of self-evidence: it seems highly capable of explaining how we have strong ethical knowledge, but is at first blush difficult to know or explain. I think that if we look at the steps of Moore's inquiry, we learn how he might have arrived at his position. Also, reflecting on the general process of inquiry among philosophers concerning the good will also move us in that direction. The process of reflecting on good in the philosophical community indicates that good is in some sense prior to any supposed equivalent natural property that can be offered. That good can be, in quite a natural way, ascribed to each of them is an important clue. Some say it is pleasure, some say it is what is desired to be desired, and so forth. Thus it seems that the term "good" is something many different inquirers understand as they offer and criticize definitions of it.

Imagine a dozen Greeks arguing over whether Theaetetus resembles Socrates. One says that Socrates is taller than Theaetetus. Another disagrees, but claims that Socrates is more snub-nosed than Theaetetus. But, actually, none of them has ever seen Theaetetus! The history of philosophers arguing endlessly about the nature of good, while believing they have grounds for criticizing the accounts of others, is much like that spectacle, if "good" has no unique meaning. We make judgments of what is good all the time. Many attempts have been made to capture what good is identical to. But good has escaped all of them, seeming to rest securely outside of all our reductionist plans. Thus, it makes sense to consider that good is a generic universal. Our all knowing good would explain our ease in talking about it, as well as explain how we can consider various proposals for defining it, without losing sight of it. It would also explain our difficulty in analyzing it. Any proposal to identify good with some natural property N1 will run up against the question, "But is N1 always good?" Since the answer is "no," it seems naturalism can never succeed.

5. Supervenience problems

The poor prospects for the alternatives help make the case for nonnatural moral properties. But intuitionism must do more than establish such properties exist. It must show that moral properties *rigidly depend* on natural properties in certain specific and predictable ways. It must meet the challenge of explaining moral supervenience.

"Where in the world is morality?" is the question with which this chapter began. Solving the problem of moral supervenience would answer it. There is but one *problem of moral supervenience* for nonnaturalism: how to explain *the connection* of nonnatural moral properties to natural properties. More specifically, how can we explain the supervenience of moral properties on natural properties? Anything else considered a supervenience problem is merely this general problem applied to a specific setting. I will first explain the general idea of supervenience, then move to its moral variety. Many Caribbean island bays have blue waters. But being blue is not an essential property of water, for if it were, your drinking water would be blue. The property of being blue (S) in this context supervenes on the properties of water (U), as well as on other external conditions. S is the *supervening* property. U properties are *subvening* properties.

An instance of a supervenience relation implies several things. First, the S property and the U properties exist in some determinate form. Second, the S property could not exist in its current form without the U properties being as they are. But the U properties could exist without the S property existing. So in this case S is *ontologically dependent* on U, but not conversely. Third, if two things have the same exact subvening properties, they have the same exact supervening properties. So if two bodies of water are the same in all their subvening properties, and one is blue, the other must be blue as well. If one body of water is blue, and the other is not, their subvening properties must differ in some way. This means that if two things have different supervening properties, they must have different subvening properties. So supervening properties not only depend on subvening properties, they *covary* with them. Call this the *covariance thesis*.

The moral supervenience thesis is held by most ethicists. It is that every moral property supervenes on some set of natural properties. Many assert that this claim is "conceptually necessary," that someone who denies the supervenience thesis "would thereby give evidence that he is not a fully competent user of normative terms" (Ridge, 2007: 331).[11] Once we gain a better understanding of the thesis, we'll see why it so severely tests the theoretical adequacy of nonnaturalism.

Moral supervenience tells us that moral properties are grounded in the natural world. Nonnaturalism would be an implausible theory if the moral were completely disconnected from the natural. But how are nonnatural properties supposed to be interwoven into the natural properties of the world? How is it that moral properties bear necessary relations of ontological dependence with properties that are completely unlike them? Nonnatural moral supervenience implies that moral properties are not identical to natural ones. This keeps moral properties and natural properties distinct. But nonnaturalism's insistence on property differentiation burdens it with fresh difficulties.

Two issues in particular make nonnatural supervenience appear metaphysically problematic. The first concerns global supervenience. "Global supervenience theses claim that no two possible worlds can differ in the supervening respect without also differing in the subvening respect" (Ridge, 2007: 332). Here is one global supervenience thesis:

> (G) Necessarily, two entire possible worlds cannot differ in their moral properties without also differing in their natural properties.[12]

An illustration will show how fundamental (G) is to our moral thought. In our world the wrongness of Hitler's actions supervened on all their natural properties. Denying (G) would allow that the world could have been exactly like the actual world in all of its natural properties, yet Hitler's actions were not wrong. The *global supervenience problem* is: nonnaturalism, it seems, would allow for such an absurd state of affairs. To see why, consider the Hitler situation in the actual world. Hitler's actions, X, supervene on the natural properties N1, N2, and N3, and such actions are *wrong.* Nonnaturalism asserts that nonnatural moral properties and natural properties are properties of distinctly different kinds. But if that is so, then why is it impossible for moral properties to drastically differ between two worlds, while the corresponding natural properties are the same? That is, why is the following situation impossible?

	Actual World Hitler Actions	Remote Possible World Hitler Actions
Supervening property:	Actions X are *wrong*	Actions X are *permissible*
Subvening properties:	N1, N2, N3	N1, N2, N3

The subvening properties are identical across the two worlds. But the supervening properties differ greatly. Given that moral properties are not identical to natural properties, but only supervene on them, apparently nothing excludes a possible world in which Hitler's actions are permissible. Surely, such a world would be very different from ours, and thus far removed from it. But it is the nonidentity relation of supervenience that seems to ensure such a possibility. Since the supervenience thesis tells us any two such morally varying worlds is impossible, and since nonnaturalism seemingly allows such worlds, it must be wrong.

The *particular supervenience problem* has to do with particular moral situations. Suppose that a given act A is wrong, and wrong because of a set of natural properties, N1, N2, and N3. Recall that the covariance thesis implies that moral properties will be present with natural properties in predictable ways. So if an act B, which is just like A, supervenes on natural properties N1 through N3, then B, just like A, will be wrong. That corresponds to the part of the covariance thesis that runs, "if two things have exactly the same natural properties, then they also have exactly the same moral properties"(Miller, 2003: 31). The other part of the covariance thesis is that "If you find two things that have different moral properties, you must also find that they differ in some way in respect of their natural properties"(Miller, 2003: 31). This implies that if a third act, C, is, unlike A and B, morally permissible, that implies that is impossible that C supervenes on N1, N2, and N3. Either one of these subvening properties must be missing in this situation or an additional property, N4, is present, and is such that it alters the supervening moral property.

The particular supervenience problem is to explain why "moral properties supervene on the particular ones that they do" (Shafer-Landau, 2003: 90). The covariance thesis asserts that there are strict regularities between supervening and subvening properties. It explains such regularity by supervenience. But has nonnaturalism genuinely explained how this works? Two things put nonnaturalism at an explanatory disadvantage here. First, it is the party responsible for claiming there is something quite different about morality. By itself, asserting that there are irreducible nonnatural moral properties is not necessarily mistaken. Also, stating that such properties supervene on natural properties is by itself unproblematic. But, second, trying to explain why a particular moral property holds of a particular action by appealing to properties that are *entirely unlike* moral properties sure looks like a problem.

6. Supervenience solutions

Water is H_2O. Science informs us this is necessarily true. Stated differently, it is true in every possible world. This proposition has this status because "Water" and "H_2O" are rigid designators. That means they identify the same object in every possible world. When two rigid designators flank an "=" sign in a sentence, then the proposition it expresses, if true, is logically necessarily true. So an identity that is true of the objects or properties designated by rigid designators is a necessary relation.

Supervenience is a weaker relation than identity, because it "can hold with varying degrees of modal force" (McLaughlin and Bennett, 2005). If a property F supervenes on a property G in this world, then F cannot exist without G *in this world*. But that does not imply that F cannot exist without G in any other possible world. Even if the predicates for these properties, "F" and "G," are rigid designators, it is not clear that "F supervenes on G" is a logically necessary truth. For ". . . supervenes on___" is clearly not as strong a connective as ". . . is identical to___." It is possible that moral supervenience is a logically necessary relation. But whether it is at this point is not clear.

Russ Shafer-Landau offers a most promising account of moral supervenience. If it holds up, it appears to be able to withstand both the global and particular supervenience problems. Suppose act A is wrong. So it has the property W. The property W supervenes on a particular set of natural facts, N1–N3. The particular supervenience problem asks, why does W supervene on *this* particular set of natural facts? Shafer-Landau's explanation is simple. The moral fact that A is W is *constituted by* natural facts N1–N3. And such natural facts exhaustively constitute the moral fact that A is W—meaning, no supernatural or nonnatural properties take part in constituting it.[13]

Shafer-Landau's constitution account of moral supervenience is backed up by a "companions in guilt" defense. It consists in showing that supervenience explanations are widely used, both in science and in philosophy. Mental facts are explained as supervening on physical facts; color facts are claimed to supervene on primary qualities; chemical facts supervene on atomic facts. Although the first two of these explanations are disputed, none are disputed simply on the grounds that they make use of supervenience explanations. That dishonor is reserved for moral supervenience, thus signaling another application of double standards against objective morality. So the opponents of moral realism have a dilemma: either allow that supervenience might work in the case of moral explanation or hold that it can work in none.[14]

The constitution relation that Shafer-Landau invokes explains several things. First, it explains why the moral fact that A is W and the natural facts N1–N3 are in the same location. By N1–N3 constituting A is W, the two facts are coextensive. Similarly, the statue of Achilles and the bronze that constitutes the statue are located in the same place. The coextensiveness of the moral and the natural is important because "If moral and descriptive [natural] properties are necessarily coextensive, then there are metaphysically necessary and sufficient conditions allied with moral properties that can determine the conditions under which moral properties are instantiated" (Shafer-Landau, 2003: 93). And that makes it possible for nonnaturalists to specify conditions under which moral properties are present.

Questions have arisen about the compatibility of intuitionism's pluralism with its supervenience claims. The constitution relation helps explain how intuitionism's variety of wrong-makers is consistent with moral supervenience. Consider two quite different moral acts, both of which are wrong. The natural facts N1–N3 explain why A is wrong because N1–N3 constitute A being wrong. Other natural facts N4–N6 constituting B's being wrong explain why B is wrong. Likewise, the property of resembling Achilles can belong to a statue, whether it is made of bronze or marble. In such a case bronze would constitute one statue resembling Achilles, marble would constitute another. Since constitution is not an identity relation, Shafer-Landau's account respects the nonnaturalist insistence that moral properties and natural properties are not identical. Finally, it opens a promising avenue of inquiry for more fully explicating the nature of moral supervenience.

Shafer-Landau has cleared a path for a fuller positive nonnaturalist account of morality. As it stands, however, it seems vulnerable to tactics to separate moral supervenience from the companions in guilt he identified.[15] Perhaps its greatest point of vulnerability is that it leaves unclear *exactly what* is being discussed. We are told that the moral facts supervene on the natural facts because the natural facts constitute the moral facts. But what natural facts constitute which moral facts? What we need now are positive details of a constitution account. This is not to single out Shafer-Landau. Everyone discussing moral supervenience avoids stating exactly what is involved in any particular case of moral supervenience. No one offers examples to illustrate what they are talking about.

Because no connection is made between the content of supervenience theory and the content of our ordinary moral consciousness,
the entire discussion is riddled with obscurities. As a result, we
have no way of knowing whether everyone discussing moral supervenience is close to talking about the same things.

The remedy for this is a positive constitution account of supervenience. In the following two chapters, I will offer one. My aim is to
show that the inner structure of self-evident moral truths, the moral
facts, and our knowledge of such facts, can be explained in such a
way that their connections become evident. As I do this, I will bring
the supervenience discussion down to earth, providing examples
of moral supervenience so the discussion gains greater clarity. My
account answers the particular and global supervenience problems,
and it blocks attempts to separate moral supervenience from successful or plausible supervenience accounts in other areas.

7. Expert disagreement

The disagreement objection has plagued intuitionism. And it just
won't go away. Although I gave several reasons previously for
dismissing old disagreement objections, new versions of it have
emerged recently. Thomas Carson attempts to strengthen the objection so that the previous responses to it fail to overcome it. Call it
the "expert disagreement" objection to intuitionism. Carson considers the role of experts in ethics and in mathematics, and concludes that, "There is no comparable consensus about the truth
of moral principles among those who might qualify as 'experts'
or authorities about moral questions. Ross, Moore, and Sidgwick
arguably count as 'experts' about morality. However, they do not
agree about the truth of such principles as 'Lying is *prima facie*
wrong'" (2005: 149).

It cannot be claimed that ethics experts do not adequately
understand the intuitive principles, that they do not reflect on them
sufficiently, or that they are not mentally mature.[16] Previous intuitionist responses to the disagreement objection, while adequate to
most versions of it, appear to have a new challenge in expert disagreement. Can we truthfully say that ethicists, researchers who are
trying to find out the truth about morality, are employing a double standard against intuitionist moral knowledge? Also, expert

disagreement apparently bypasses the problem of the lazy assumption that undermined previous disagreement objections. Thus, it appears that the expert disagreement objection is more of a threat to intuitionism than the plain old disagreement objection.

I am afraid that appearances in this case are deceiving. True, experts have second-order disagreements about the intuitive principles. Why, even *intuitionists* disagree about which principles are self-evidently true. What can explain the mistakes of the expert anti-intuitionists? In order to determine whether the intuitive principles are self-evident, one must consider them each directly and alone. The story of modern ethics is of a quest for a single supreme principle of morality, a quest inspired ultimately by Descartes's philosophical methodology: find reasons for doubting the way things seem to us in the search for one certain principle that can explain everything. Ethicists previously committed to believing a supreme principle of morality do not directly attend to the intuitive principles to see if they are independently true. They would consider such principles, but only to derive them from their supreme principle. Moreover, the incentive structure of ethics research is such that *greater disagreement* should occur among ethicists than among lay people. Why? Ethicists are highly rewarded for devising novel explanations or supreme principles with explanatory promise. If such theories can license unconventional behavior all the better.

Take an extreme case of expert disagreement, disagreement with the moral nihilist. Nihilism offers a tidy explanation of moral phenomena. And its central thesis, that all moral judgments are false, is thrillingly unconventional. Sinnott-Armstrong argues that no moral theory adequately justifies moral beliefs unless it can rule out moral nihilism. He thinks that the strategy the intuitionist might take to overcome nihilism is to consider a moral belief that seems obvious to most people, and see if the nihilist can object to it. The proposition that Sinnott-Armstrong says seems to be obviously true: (T) It is morally wrong to torture innocent children just for fun. He then says,

> Almost all normal people would happily take this belief for granted. But suppose that a moral nihilist appears on the scene and denies (T). What could the moral intuitionist say against such a moral nihilist? Not much. Moral intuitionists can point out that (T) seems obvious to them even after they reflect on

it carefully. However, to appeal to such a moral belief in an argument against moral nihilism clearly begs the question. (Sinnott-Armstrong, 2006: 191)

I think the intuitionist has much more to say than that. Intuitionism accepts the challenge that nihilism poses, that it must explain how moral facts are related to natural facts. What has previously gone unacknowledged is that with regard to another source of knowledge, intuitionists and nihilists are not on equal terms. Intuitionism draws from one source of knowledge that nihilism neglects: what we really think about morality. Even nihilists have some intuitions about fundamental moral principles. And hopefully the nihilist accepts the creed, "do not bar the way of inquiry." Since the intuitionist is drawing from one source of inquiry that the nihilist neglects, it would seem that the nihilist owes us an account of his own intuitions about basic moral principles. Once he has taken the time to reflect on how his own moral beliefs appear to him, then theorists from the two schools can begin to have a more fruitful discussion about morality.

Granted, the nihilist may have reflected on his genuine moral thoughts, and not seen what the rest of us do. But I have my doubts. The nihilist recognizes that our moral language is objective, as it would be if we had the kind of objective moral knowledge intuitionist argue for. But when it comes to explaining that feature of our moral language, the nihilist must resort to the once-plausible, old-fashioned claim that society strongly conditions us that way. The way to bring the nihilist to see that we are no longer in such a morally uniform and repressive society is to press him on his commitment to empiricism and present him with the current facts. By looking at how people actually behave we can determine whether strong moral conditioning is really in effect.

Take the issue of cheating. Intuitionism claims that cheating is wrong. So what are the facts about cheating today? Consider marriage and academic integrity. Research shows that among college students "cheating is prevalent and that some forms of cheating have increased dramatically in the last 30 years" (McCabe et al., 2001: 219). Self-admitted serious test cheating has gone from 39 percent in 1963 to 64 percent in 1993. Marital infidelity has experienced a similar rise, based on the most reliable data, the General Social Survey. Cheating rates "among older women

[60 and older] tripled from 5% in 1991 to 15% in 2006; rates among men rose from 20% to 28%. About 20% of younger men and 15% of younger women [those 35 and younger] say they cheated, up from about 15% and 12%, respectively" (*USA TODAY*, November 17, 2008).

We learn several things from these statistics. First, that different forms of cheating are so prevalent shows that any thesis of strong moral social conditioning is false. A large percentage of people overcame whatever conditioning there is in society against these behaviors. That more people are not overly concerned about how they would look if they would get caught also indicates that society has become much less punitive about cheating. Next, since people often do not wish to share unflattering details about themselves with others, the percentages for all these cases is probably higher than the surveys and interviews report. Lastly, since reflection reveals to us that it is wrong to cheat, and since society is not giving us the message that it's wrong, our strong belief that it's wrong must be coming from our reflecting on the matter. In short, that cheating is wrong is evident to us, despite society's not promoting or enforcing that position.

The moral nihilist has the same rational faculties as everyone else. Since the nihilist excludes a priori our moral intuitions as a possible source of knowledge, the intuitionist has one source of information the nihilist neglects. The problem for nihilism is that this is the most important source of inquiry concerning moral matters. The nihilist, once more, owes us an account of his moral intuitions or at least owes an account of why he excludes them. The nihilist ought to conduct a sustained inquiry into his own moral thoughts, and do the necessary work to find out what he really thinks about morality. Without this, it seems the nihilist has no plausible way to account for our sense that moral language is indeed objective.

8. Intuitionism and disagreement

As newer forms of the disagreement objection arise, it might seem that intuitionism cannot escape it. But it can. It is time for intuitionism to retire the disagreement problem. But how? I have shown that the disagreement argument is unsound. Here I will show that intuitionism explains moral disagreement better than any other theory by drawing upon only its basic tenets. The result is that intuitionism obviously is not hurt by disagreement, but rather makes the most sense of it.[17]

A moral theory that could not explain moral disagreement would be unsatisfactory. There is currently no account of disagreement that is based on the foundations of intuitionism, although intuitionists have adequately explained why people might err in their moral judgments and how disagreement objections are based on faulty assumptions. Two rival theories offer plausible accounts of disagreement. Expressivism claims that people morally disagree because they feel differently about moral issues. And Mackie argues that disagreement "about moral codes seems to reflect people's adherence to and participation in different ways of life" (1977: 36).

What are the facts of moral disagreement? First, there is moral disagreement. Second, there are different kinds of such disagreement. Sometimes people disagree about the morality of a particular case. Other times people dispute a general moral proposition, such as whether animals have rights. Third, the positions in the disagreement are logically incompatible. That is to say, that people morally disagreeing are contradicting one another. Fourth, each person in a disagreement situation has strong feelings about the matter. Fifth, each person believes that their position is correct. If just one of the disputants had serious doubts about their position, they would not sincerely disagree with the other person. A sixth feature of moral disagreement is often overlooked, but its inclusion is essential to understanding moral disagreement: There is something to each side of the case. Each person in a moral disagreement has *some* justification for their position. That helps explain why each of them believes their position is correct, and why each has strong feelings about the matter.

Intuitionism best explains these features of moral disagreement. Let us examine an instance of a particular moral disagreement given by one of intuitionism's critics, Richard Brandt:

> Let us suppose Mrs. A, who is very unhappy with her husband and is planning a suit for divorce, is discussing the matter with her sister, who is familiar with the problem, so that there is no disagreement between them about the facts of the case. But the sister thinks the contemplated suit for divorce would be wrong,

that Mrs. A is obligated to stay with her husband—for the reason of principle that promises are sacred, that the marriage vow was a solemn vow "until death do us part." It seems that there are different "intuitions" about the obligations of a person who has taken a marriage vow, and whose reasons for breaking it are those Mrs. A has. How will the sister show that Mrs. A's "intuitions" are only pseudo intuitions? (1959: 195)

Let's suppose that Mrs. A does not simply want to strike out on her own because she is bored, or because she's fallen in love with her auto mechanic. In such cases, Ms. B, her sister, would be right, and no explanation of moral disagreement would be needed. In the case we are considering, Mrs. A was aware of the content of the marriage vow, and understood its intended duration. So it seems breaking the promise to stay with Mr. A would be wrong. Suppose now also that Mr. A has for a long time prevented Mrs. A from developing her moral character. In such a case, Mrs. A and Ms. B have a genuine moral disagreement.

Intuitionism claims that in Mrs. A's situation there are two prima facie duties present. Mrs. A is concerned with the prima facie duty of developing her character. Ms. B is concerned with the prima facie duty Mrs. A has to keep her promise. Since Mrs. A is subject to two prima facie duties in this situation she faces a conflict of duties. The sisters have all of the facts at their disposal. Intuitionism holds that one of the sisters is right. So why is the other sister wrong? Neither sister is certain about the actual duty involved. Each has at best rational belief of what is right. The right sister correctly believes that the prima facie duty she is defending is the *stronger duty* in this case. The wrong sister incorrectly believes the opposite.

We can now explain the several features of moral disagreement. The disagreement that Mrs. A and her sister are having involves a contradiction. One is really right, the other really wrong. The right one correctly believes what she is arguing for is an actual duty. So the contradiction is based on their being a truth about the matter. Most importantly, Mrs. A and Ms. B each has some justification for their position about this would-be divorce. To each of them their position seems to be correct. And each is right about how things seem to her. The sisters are confident in their beliefs because each believes a particular self-evident proposition that is evident to her.

That explains why they sincerely believe they are in the right, and why each quite reasonably has strong feelings about the matter.

The reason why there is moral disagreement, ultimately, is because it is one thing to know that a prima facie duty is present. That is relatively easy, and we're all capable of doing that. It is another to know what the actual duty is. And that is often very difficult. In many cases what makes moral disagreement so strong is that the people disagreeing don't understand the difference between prima facie duties, on which both disputants can be right, and an actual duty, on which only one can be right. So part of what makes Mrs. A and Ms. B's disagreement especially sharp is that each has only a part of the picture, not the whole. The two self-evident propositions they are well aware of drive them on. But they don't recognize that actual duty is distinct from what each is apprehending. Knowledge of intuitionism would allow them to better understand the position of the other person, and be open to a practical solution to their disagreement.

Intuitionism has the resources to explain moral disagreement. My account also shows the shortcomings of rival theories. Expressivism argues that moral disagreement is explained by people feeling differently about moral issues. Intuitionism explains why people feel differently—each has some justification for their position—in a way that better matches our moral experience. Mackie explains disagreement based on different "ways of life." But this only explains cultural disagreement, not individual disagreement. So unlike my account, it doesn't explain different kinds of disagreement. Also, Mrs. A is married, so she *is* living the way of life of her culture. Her disagreement with Ms. B involves the two sisters accepting the same moral code. This reveals a further limitation in Mackie's view.

My theory puts us in a position to explain each kind of moral disagreement. The first kind is disagreement in a particular situation. Mrs. A and her sister's spat illustrates disagreement of that kind. Other disputes arise not because of such a particular situation, but because of a general moral matter, such as abortion. As I discussed in Chapter 1, this general disagreement is largely due to neither "Abortion is morally permissible" nor "Abortion is morally wrong" being self-evident. The third kind of disagreement arises because of the nature of certain moral concepts. Some moral concepts are difficult to apply because they are vague and open. Their openness is due to such concepts containing few conditions of application. "Harm" is an example of an open moral concept. There are many kinds of harm that we are aware of.[18] And the openness of "harm" suggests that we will find more in the future. Finally, there is metaethical moral disagreement. Some argue that morality is subjective. Others disagree, claiming that morality is an objective matter. As I argued in Chapter 1, such disagreements are to be expected, given that few metaethical theses are self-evidently true. Thus, if we have a thorough understanding of intuitionism, the disagreement between the nihilist and the intuitionist—due to the intuitive principles being substantive—along with all other kinds of moral disagreement is to be expected, and should not surprise us.

9. Chapter summary

"Where in the world is morality?" is the toughest question for moral realism. What makes it especially tough is that, as most agree, morality is quite different from everything else. Moral nihilists take this difference as a strong indication that morality does not exist, that all moral propositions, however objective seeming, are false. But nihilists only do so based on the queer fact that somehow the world is telling them that all knowledge *ought* to fit neatly into the scheme of the physical sciences. Naturalists agree with intuitionism in holding there are objective moral properties. Naturalists, however, don't explain how scientists can possibly investigate through observation and experiment these supposed natural moral properties.

In order to explain where in the world morality is intuitionists must tackle the basic problem of supervenience: How are nonnatural moral properties connected with the world's natural properties? Shafer-Landau's claim is that physical properties constitute moral facts, an account I will expand upon in the following two chapters. Lastly, an adequate intuitionist account of moral disagreement, which explains disagreement based on the fact that each side in a moral disagreement has some justification for their position, makes it much harder to object to intuitionism on moral disagreement.

Further reading

Shafer-Landau's *Moral Realism: A Defence* (2003) critically examines naturalism and nonnaturalism, and provides a constitution account of moral supervenience in chapter 3 "Ethical non-naturalism" and chapter 4 "Supervenience and causation." Sinnott-Armstrong's *Moral Skepticisms* (2006) studies a variety of positions skeptical of objective morality.

CHAPTER FIVE

The grounds of morality

Introduction

We intuitively know several basic moral principles, each of which has a distinct ground. That's the definition of intuitionism with which we started. So far I have given the matter of intuitive knowledge the most attention. Throughout intuitionism's history both adherents and adversaries have done likewise. The issue of the plurality of the intuitive principles has also been widely treated. But, in stark contrast, the grounds of intuitionism are generally regarded as being of little consequence.[1] The early analytic intuitionists, I believe, identified the grounds of our several moral duties, but that is all they did. Explicating these grounds was not a high priority, and no one since has given the matter the treatment it deserves.[2]

Prichard and Ross identified *moral relations* as the grounds of our several duties.[3] We enter into moral relations with other agents, whether intentionally or not. The existence of any moral property of any action is always based on some moral relation. Moral actions, in the broadest sense of the term, are of different kinds, such as harming, helping, or cheating another person. Such *moral kinds* are abstract intelligible entities, which we can grasp with our minds and consider alone and apart from their particular instances in the world.[4] A fuller description is that moral kinds are complex, relational, mind-independent, generic, nonnatural abstract wholes. They are universals. Grasping a moral kind allows us to grasp a number of self-evident truths about it, most of which, surprisingly, are not moral principles. Examining moral kinds shall equip us to explain how we can have adequate understanding of self-evident propositions and how we can correctly judge what's right in particular situations.

The moral explanations I will examine give new prominence to moral kinds. It has long been recognized that moral acts come in different kinds. In this chapter we will see why they are explanatorily important. I will examine the nature and structure of promises, which shall serve as a model for all other moral kinds.[5] Our a priori understanding of the kind "promise" explains how we know so much about promises. Generally, understanding moral kinds is the basis of all our moral knowledge. Throughout this chapter I will counter this view's main objection, that moral kinds can just as well be explained by conventions.

The moral realism I am developing might be described as *stout nonnaturalism*. Moral kinds and moral relations are platonic entities. Contemporary nonnaturalists claim that right is a non-natural property. And they suggest that it—along with wrong, good and bad—is the only kind of nonnatural moral entity. But if only right is nonnatural, then natural facts alone can explain why something is right. That would make the difference between nonnatural moral realism and ethical naturalism appear negligible, while preserving, not removing, mystery. My view is that the grounds of right are nonnatural too. By extending the range of the nonnatural this way I engage in metaphysical speculation. Generally, intuitionists have not gained credibility by being silent about morality's grounds. So I proceed. And actually, a close look at Ross's moral theory suggests that it presupposes the theory of moral kinds.[6] So it will serve intuitionism well to open the issue for investigation.

1. Moral explanation

Why is a given act *a* wrong? The fundamental task of moral explanation is to answer this and like questions. The central charge against intuitionism, once again, is that it cannot explain morality. Sometimes intuitionism's disavowal of supreme principles is why it is considered bereft of explanatory resources. Other times its irreducible nonnatural realism is taken to signify that moral explanation is out of intuitionism's reach. But some ethicists carry the explanatory impotence complaint further, claiming that intuition-ism is a wholesale form of resistance to moral explanation.[7]

All these views are mistaken. Intuitionists have often given the impression that they are averse to giving moral explanations. And intuitionism itself might seem incapable of moral explanation. But it's not. Intuitionism is only incapable of explanations favored by naturalists and empiricists. Consider intuitionism's doctrine that the intuitive principles are self-evidently true. It is sensible to wonder what could explain truths not having and not needing some further basis. But, as has already been pointed out, a crucial implication of intuitionism's commitment to the intuitive princi-ples being evident is that no moral explanation *can possibly be* more convincing than they are. Many seeking explanations crave to discover explanations more convincing than what they wish to explain. But that outcome is inconsistent with intuitionism.

The plurality of the intuitive principles is as central to intuition-ism as is their self-evidence. This fact alone fosters the image of intuitionism as an explanatory dead end. An implicit assumption in most moral theorizing is that there is a single explanation for every kind of moral act. Witness the long search for a supreme principle of morality. But a theory's capacity for moral explanation does not imply that it has one explanation for every kind of moral act. So it most certainly does not imply that there is a single prin-ciple that provides all moral explanations. There is no reason why there cannot be substantive intuitionist moral explanations. But such explanations will be nonnaturalist, not naturalist, and plural rather than singular.

2. Moral relations

Our daily lives are lived at the center of a web of moral relations. A typical day in Jane's life illustrates this. After leaving her house, her first stop is to leave her children safe in the hands of people who will look out for their welfare, thus fulfilling an important parental duty. As Jane drives to work, she intentionally avoids endangering other drivers, in light of her duty to not harm them, even though she does not know them. As she parks her car, she takes care not to hit parked cars, so that her duty to not damage other people's property is upheld. Once in her office, Jane helps a customer dissatisfied with a product, out of her obligation to the person and to her company. Crossing paths with a distraught colleague, she recognizes that her duty is to be kind to him. Finally, realizing that she needs some pens at home, and briefly considering taking a few from work, she recognizes that she must not steal from her company.[8]

Moral relations are the foundations of our duties.[9] Any viable objectivist moral theory must include them. We have a duty to help *others* in need. Lying is wrong, and any instance of lying implies a person lying and another being lied to. Likewise, stealing requires in every case a thief and a rightful property owner. It appears impossible that there is any moral act which doesn't involve a person other than the agent acting. No theory can adequately describe, let alone explain, "A's doing c is wrong" without including some agent B and A's relation to B. The challenge for the skeptic of moral relations is to find just one case in which we can say "A's action c is wrong" is true, without there being some other person B who is the patient, or recipient, of A's action. Absent such an example, we can safely assume every moral act by an agent implies a moral relation to another agent. So far from intuitionism being at a disadvantage in moral explanation, since, unlike every other theory, it acknowledges the necessity of including moral relations, it is strongly explanatorily situated.

The relations into which we enter found our obligations. I speak of "entering" relations in the broadest metaphysical sense, including cases where I find myself in a moral relation involuntarily. Such relations provide moral reasons for performing certain acts, and they contribute to explaining why such acts are morally right or wrong. As Prichard states, "The rightness of an action consists in its being the origination of something of a certain kind A in a situation of a certain kind, a situation consisting in a certain relation B of the agent to others or to his own nature" (1912: 27). The "relation B" of which Prichard speaks is what I am calling a "moral relation." Such relations are real and exist between agents in actual situations. The "kind A" Prichard speaks of is what I mean by moral kinds.

Since there are several independent intuitive moral principles, there are necessarily a number of kinds of moral relations. In a famous passage, after claiming that utilitarianism reduces our many moral relations to a single one (which I'll soon discuss), Ross states that other agents "may also stand to me in the relation of promisee to promiser, of creditor to debtor, of wife to husband, of child to parent, of friend to friend, of fellow countryman to fellow countryman, and the like; and each of these relations is the foundation of a *prima facie* duty, which is more or less incumbent on me according to the circumstances of the case" (1930: 19).

Establishing the existence of moral relations requires we take up the starting point of all intuitionist inquiries: what we really think of morality. In our moral experience, we find that we have definite moral relations to some people which we do not have to others. I have a duty to feed and clothe my children, but not yours. I have a duty to teach a number of classes for my university, but none for yours. Also, we find that as our relations to others change, so do our moral obligations. When you leave one job for another, your obligation to realize the aims of the organization employing you shifts from one organization to another. When you end a conversation with me and strike one up with Jones, your duty not to lie is now to Jones, and not momentarily to me. The favor you have done for me is the foundation of my obligation to return a favor to you. Jones, having done no favor for me, I owe no favor to. These initial reflections indicate the existence of moral relations.[10]

Many moral theorists look for the properties of beings that give them moral status, and that make acts toward them right or wrong. A more adequate view is that it is not properties of persons alone that make it wrong to harm them. Instead, it is their properties *in relation* to other agents and the kinds of acts they might perform that make it wrong for those agents to harm them. So directly it is moral relations, and the kinds of acts we perform in view of them, that make some acts right, others wrong. Indirectly, certain properties such as rationality or sentience qualify certain select entities to enter into moral relations. These relations exist independently of what we think or what our attitudes are, but, importantly, their instantiated existence does depend on our existing.

No objectivist moral theory can do without moral relations. Despite Kant's attempts to eschew real moral entities, in practice his theory requires them. We see this with regard to the humanity formula of the Categorical Imperative: "Act in such a way that you never treat humanity merely as a means but always at the same time as an end." On Kant's view it is immoral to treat persons as means only. But what is it to treat persons as means? A means is a necessarily relational entity. Nothing is a means in isolation from an agent who can employ it. The same is true of ends. Our having ends is, in Kant's view, what gives things value. Kant argues that persons, in contrast, are "ends in themselves." But barring duties to self persons can only be ends in relation to other agents. So all entities, whether humans or things, are ends and means only in relation to agents.

Utilitarianism also requires real moral relations to work as a theory. Ross claimed there is but one utilitarian relation others can have to agents, that "of being possible beneficiaries by my action" (1930: 19). Although utilitarianism asserts that there is only one kind of moral relation, it is committed to there being incredibly numerous instances of it in existence. In fact, on utilitarianism, each one of us has real moral relations to every sentient being on earth, regardless of their location. The reality and pull of these relations is such that we have a strong obligation to help all our poor fellow humans, even those on other continents.[11] Utilitarian moral relations are real and obtain between each of us and others merely by their having a single property: the capacity to experience pleasure and pain, or well-being and ill-being. Bear this in mind when intuitionism is criticized for its real moral relations. The capacity to have pleasure and pain, or well-being and ill-being, seems a poor basis to explain all moral relations between agents. Intuitionism more plausibly asserts that moral relations are of several distinct kinds, and exist based on the existence and proximity of rational agents.

3. Properties of moral relations

Our thought and experience tell us there are moral relations. But what can explain their existence? Surely, an impoverished metaphysics will prevent any attempt to account for them. So too reckless an employment of Ockham's razor will mutilate any moral explanation in the womb. Moral relations will be considered by opponents to be queer entities. The queerness charge has previously been met by intuitionists pointing out that many other kinds of entities are queer, which is true. But a stronger response is to illuminate the many ways in which moral entities appear queer, but only from a limited naturalist framework. Only a theory that is deeply aware of just how different morality is from all else can begin to make sense of it. If our metaphysical vision of the world is broad enough, and it includes a system of nonnatural moral relations, then morality should seem less strange.

Moral relations seem to be queer entities. They will not and cannot appear on any naturalist metaphysical map. But that's a problem for naturalism, not intuitionism. Promise relations provide an instructive example of what I mean. They have the following features:

1 By a simple speech act a promise brings new moral relations into existence: an obligation for the promiser, a claim for the promisee.

2 The promise relations exist over time, are carried by their bearers through any and all movements through space, and in no way depend on the cultures, experiences, thoughts or feelings of the promise relations' bearers for their existence.

3 Promise relations have a necessary circuit. A promise forms them. Keeping the promise necessarily dissolves them.[12]

When we make a promise to someone our relation to them changes. We recognize that we are *bound* to do for them what we promised. This burden stays with us until the promise is discharged. Promises have the curious property that they bind us over time, with no need to reaffirm or reestablish the obligation. If we promise someone we will have a report for them in six months, both the promiser and the promisee understand the obligation remains in existence for the whole duration of the intervening period. No physical science can locate these promise relations. Yet they exist.

4. Transactions

In each situation we enter with another person we enter several moral relations. But nothing is ever right or wrong without action. The rightness or wrongness of an action depends on the moral kinds it instantiates in view of the situation's existing moral relations. Any action involving two agents I will term a "transaction." The following are transactions in the wide-ranging sense I give the term: a greeting, a kidnapping, a consoling, a commanding, an insulting, a complimenting, and a murdering. Transactions always involve two agents, whether their involvement is voluntary or involuntary. Though there are many kinds of transactions, only some, such as lying, promise-keeping, and helping others, are inherently moral, in the broad sense. Moral kinds, then, are a subset of transaction kinds.

Intuitionism would do well to shift attention to transactions. Conducting plural *transaction analyses*—one for each moral kind—will put it on firmer ground. Moore focused on the importance of the concept of good, which he thought was simple, unanalyzable, indefinable, and nonnatural. Ross thought that both right and good have such properties. These are undoubtedly central concepts of ethics. But that does not imply that they ought to be analyzed first, or exclusively, or that they should have all our attention. Unfortunately, intuitionists, along with everyone else, have concentrated on these *thin* moral properties as if their importance did imply such research strategies. As a result, intuitionism has been vulnerable on several fronts.

Intuitionist transaction analysis directs attention away from abstract, thin normative terms, such as "good" and "right" and toward more concrete, but nonetheless abstract, *thick* terms such as "promise," "harm," and "benefit." All moral terms in the first instance refer to transactions. Thinner terms such as "wrong" and "bad" refer to thinner properties of transactions. Thicker terms such as "promise-breaking" and "lying" cover everything in transactions of those kinds required for determining the prima facie wrongness of their instances.

All naturalists, and even some intuitionists, will say that lyings, promises, and so on, are conventional entities. But that view matches poorly with the claim that we can have a priori knowledge of "Lying is wrong" or "Keeping promises is required." My account argues instead that our understanding of these transactions is based on understanding different moral kinds. Fundamental kinds of transaction have a set of invariant conditions for a given act to qualify as an instance of that kind. We have a priori knowledge of such conditions because our minds grasp these abstract kinds. Analyzing transactions as being abstract intelligible entities allows us to see how good and right are embedded in wholes of discernible kinds, and equips us to explain how we can recognize the presence of right or good in actual situations.

5. Moral kinds

Picture, if you will, this scene. You're on your break in the lunch room at work. As you sit down to eat your lunch, you are aware of a conversation between Peter and Paul. They both appear serious. Peter then asks, "Are you sure you can be there at five o'clock tonight?" Paul responds, "Don't worry. I *will* be there at five." "Good, I'm counting on you," replies Peter. Paul nods once while maintaining an assuring look.

What do you think just happened? I have not given much detail, just a brief description of a brief exchange between two men. You might be curious about what they are planning, but I would guess that you are quite confident that Paul just made a promise to Peter. It seems remarkable that from so little information we can know what is going on with people who we cannot see, and who don't even exist. On any day we can recognize a promise being made merely by chancing upon strangers in a conversation just like Peter and Paul's, even without the word "promise" being uttered.

We have thorough implicit knowledge of what promising is. The explanation of this is that we understand the moral kind "promise" that we grasp a priori. Particular acts of promising, lying, and harming are produced by individual humans. So it is a contingent matter whether anyone lies or promises. Each such transaction has a certain determinate structure, which requires that a set of necessary conditions is satisfied. When all of the necessary conditions of a kind of transaction are present, that is sufficient for a transaction of that kind to be instantiated. If even one necessary condition of a promise is absent from a transaction, then a promise-instance is momentarily impossible. Actual promises are made by individual agents, billions of them. But there is only one formal structure of a promise, which we cannot alter. The necessary conditions of a moral kind are not a mere list of unconnected requirements, like the list of requirements to qualify for a specific tax exemption. Each moral kind is a whole, having unity, and being constituted by a network of necessarily related components. In actual situations, like the one involving Peter and Paul, we recognize the whole immediately and fully.

Adolf Reinach offered the first substantial modern account of real transaction kinds. Although his approach and account are models for my transaction analysis, I do not follow him in details.[13] Most of our experience of transaction kinds is in the context of their being actually instantiated in concrete situations. But these intelligible entities can also be considered abstractly. We can contemplate and examine them, and we can determine what their structural components are. Analyzing the components of transaction kinds may seem like an activity that is secondary to experiencing them in action as instantiated wholes. But this is not so. For in everyday situations, by considering the abstract kind itself, we can be quite acute about whether all the components of a promise are present.

Suppose now your lunchtime scene were a little different. Just like in the other case, Peter says, "Are you sure you can be there at five o'clock tonight?" but he is holding back a laugh. Paul, hardly containing himself, responds, "Don't worry. I *will* be there at five." They both burst into laughter. In that case we would recognize that Paul was not making a promise at all.

Philosophers argue about what promising, harming, and lying is. Enlisting the theory of moral kinds on behalf of moral realism is new in analytic philosophy. But philosophical attempts to arrive at the correct account of the just mentioned moral kinds has proceeded as if there are such real kinds. According to the theory of moral kinds, philosophers are trying to determine what the genuine essences are which corresponded to our words for them. In discussions of promising, philosophers can come to agree that one theory provides a better account of promising than another. Shortcomings of a particular account of, say, lying can be pointed out by an effective counterexample. Defending such an account will often require making adjustments in order to deflect such counterexamples. All appearances suggest what is going on in such discussions is that people are talking *about* a real thing with essential properties. The theory of moral kinds best fits the behavior of philosophical discussion about what is a lie, a promise, or a case of harming.

Every moral kind provides the basis for several self-evident propositions. To see how, consider the act of lying. Self-evident propositions concerning lying relate parts of lying to the whole.

When a lie has been told it implies that every single part of the kind exists. Without the corresponding parts, the whole would not exist. But the parts, in contrast, can exist without the whole being instantiated. Suppose that A lies to B. Consequently, every part of the whole "lie" is instantiated. Suppose also that (*a*) is a proposition that highlights and corresponds to a part of A's lie to B and connects it to the whole: (*a*) "If A lies to B by saying that *p*, then A believes that *p* is false." (*a*) is self-evidently true. Suppose now that things are different, and that A believes that *p* is false, but A does not say *p* to B. Then, even though (*a'*) "A believes that *p* is false" is true, it is not self-evident. So each self-evident proposition that corresponds to a moral kind relates a single part of the kind to the whole kind. And such truths capture a part of any action of that kind and relate that part to the whole of it.

6. Promises

"What, exactly, a promise is, is not so easy to determine," says Ross (1930: 35). That is true, but we should take steps toward a satisfactory promise analysis. My starting-point is that we already know a priori what a promise is. My task is to take this implicit understanding and make it explicit.[14] The theory of moral kinds lays out a set of necessary conditions for something to be a promise. When all of the condition components of the whole kind are present, that is sufficient for a transaction to be a promise. While the set of conditions offered here may not be complete, it seems a good start. And actually, any missing condition that is later found to be necessary for a transaction to be a promise only serves to support the theory I am offering: we already understand the intelligible kind "promise."

Examining the structure of the promise as a whole will enable us to explain why the promise principle, "Keeping promises is required," is self-evidently true. In addition, the result of this examination will allow us to determine several other self-evident propositions for promises. An example of such a proposition is: "If A made a promise to do x, then A performed a speech act *p* to do x." Since there are many self-evident propositions concerning promises, and not just moral ones, this poses a problem for opponents of the self-evident promise principle. The critics of intuitionism actually have a cluster of self-evident promise propositions to contend with. That means they will have to provide circumstances in which propositions like "If A made a promise p to B, then A understands p," are false. When this fails, and they must concede that there are several self-evident promise propositions, then they will have to explain why the promise principle's self-evidence should be singled out for doubt.

Here is the structure of a promise:

1 Two distinct agents, A and B, encounter one another.

2 A performs a speech act p: "I will do x."

3 A understands p.

4 B understands p.

5 A believes that B understands p.

6 A believes that B will believe p to express his intention to x.

7 B believes that A's speech act p can most naturally be interpreted to expresses his intention to x.

8 B accepts, either expressly or tacitly, A's intention to x.

...

n A has a prima facie obligation to x.

m B has a prima facie claim against A concerning x.

Conditions 1 through 8 of a promise refer to familiar inhabitants of the world. People encounter one another. Some perform speech acts, which they and others understand. And so on. So where do (n) and (m) fit in? They involve obligations and claims—entities that are no less familiar, but entities of an altogether different metaphysical sort. Many ethicists say that obligations and claims are not a part of the world's fabric. So the question is, how exactly do (n) and (m) relate to promises?

Obligations are not conditions of a promise. They are relations, consequent on whole promises, for the agents who have made a promise. Only a whole promise can obligate one to perform a certain action. So having a prima facie obligation to keep a promise (n), is a necessary *implication* of having made a promise, and therefore (n) cannot be a condition of a promise, like conditions 1 through 8. If Jones attempts to make a promise to Smith to do x, and Smith rejects Jones's attempt, then a necessary part of a promise (condition 8) is absent. In such a case Jones has no obligation to do x.

The *whole action principle* states that the rightness, the wrongness, or the obligation-generating character of an action is determined by the whole action and nothing less than the whole action. About a right action Ross states, "its rightness depends on its whole nature and not any element in it" (1930: 33). Ross asserts this in the context of discussing cases of moral conflict, where two prima facie obligations are at odds. But the whole action principle holds even for situations in which one's duty seems obvious and appears unopposed by any conflicting prima facie duty. That is because for an action to be of a moral or immoral kind all of its component conditions must be present. Suppose Wilson tells a falsehood to Cooper. If one condition of lying, her belief that she's uttering a falsehood, is absent, then she's not lying, so it's not wrong. If Wilson kills Cooper, but unintentionally, then she might be guilty of manslaughter, but not murder. Thus the properties of rightness, wrongness, and being obligated to do something are not components of certain acts, but rather properties of whole actual acts based on what kinds of acts they are.

7. Variations of conditions for promises

All promises have the same essence. That essence is understood by each of us. To see that the components I have offered are necessary conditions for a transaction to be a promise, we must consider transactions with and without each of the individual conditions. I do not have space enough to carefully consider each component condition of a promise, but by exploring variations on some of them, we will better understand the theory of moral kinds and be in a position to see if the account is correct.

Promises require two agents to be in communication with each other. That is the first promise condition. But why can't we make a promise to ourselves? The main reason is that if Jones makes a promise to Smith, only Smith can release Jones from her obligation. Jones cannot unilaterally decide her obligation is null and void. But if Jones could make a promise to Jones, Jones could unilaterally decide she is released from her obligation. Therefore, there are no promises to oneself, perhaps only resolutions we make.[15]

Without someone performing a speech act of some sort, making a promise is impossible. So condition 2 is necessary. Suppose Jones is walking down the street and passes Smith, someone she's never met. Jones nods to Smith and Smith responds with a nod. Nothing else takes place between them. Would it not be insanity for Smith to claim that Jones owes him $500 "because she promised it"? Absolutely.

The first five conditions seem to take us a long way toward accounting for what a promise is. But close examination reveals that they are not sufficient for a promise. The recipient of the promise must believe that the speech act of the promising agent can most naturally be interpreted as expressing her intention to carry it out. For example, suppose Jones and Smith are in a play together, a medieval fantasy. Jones says, "Forsooth, I promise to slay the green dragon." Because the utterance p takes place in a play, it cannot most naturally be interpreted as expressing Jones's intention to x (condition 7). So there is no promise.

Condition 8 may seem wrong. Why can't A make a promise to B that B doesn't accept? There are two kinds of cases to consider. First, cases where B does not accept an apparent promise because he cannot. If a young man pledges to his comatose father to avenge his injury, then conditions 1, 4–8 are lacking. Although we do use the word "promise" for such cases, the absence of so many conditions informs us that such *oaths* deserve an entirely different kind of account. The other kind of case to consider is unwelcome promises. In such a case, B might be present, and understand what A intends to do, but simply wish for A not to do what she intends. If A ignores such wishes, then A's action would be an intrusion. This implies that promises require mutual agreement.

It may be claimed that one essential part of a promise is obviously missing. That is, for there to be a promise A has to sincerely intend to do x.[16] But I include no component such as "A intends to x." Whether A intends to x or not, if A says p under appropriate conditions, a promise has been made. So promise is a genus that has false promises as well as sincere promises as species. If A's sincerity were a necessary condition, then A can legitimately claim, "I didn't make a promise. I was not sincere when I said p." But in actuality B would be in the right to reply, "I don't care what you intended. You made a promise."

A promise gives rise to an obligation for one agent, a claim against that agent by another. These are necessary moral implications of a promise, once more, not conditions of a promise. The instantiation of a promise means that all of the essential conditions of a promise have been met. Once a promise is made that is the ground of all subsequent moral properties being instantiated. If one keeps the promise, and doing so is not overridden by another prima facie duty, then it is necessarily right. If one fails to keep the promise, without another overriding prima facie duty justifying it, then necessarily it is wrong. Such necessary moral property instantiations are based on the necessary structure and nature of promises.

8. Understanding and a priori knowledge

Understanding plays a critically important role in intuitionism. For, as previously stated, adequate understanding of self-evident propositions is necessary for knowing them. The theory of moral kinds enables us to explain our understanding of the self-evident propositions that correspond to them. The primary things we understand are moral kinds. Everyone understands the nature of lying, and can recognize a lie when they see one. All of us recognize when someone made a promise to someone else because we understand what a promise is. We only understand the corresponding self-evident propositions derivatively. So if we did not understand what a lie is, we would not understand that it is wrong to lie. On this account, the moral principles are true, a priori and synthetic, because each captures a necessary relation of a part of a moral kind to the whole.

To have a priori knowledge of a moral kind is to have adequate understanding of it. The crucial question, "how do we get the concepts of 'good' and 'right'?" is to be answered by turning to moral kinds. We have a priori understanding, for example, of the moral kind, "helping someone in need." And we obtain the concepts "good" and "right" because they are necessarily true of such a

whole. By understanding other moral kinds such as "act of kind-
ness," "act of mercy" we further solidify our grasp of the concepts
"good" and "right." On the other side of the matter, adequately
grasping several moral kinds to which "bad" and "wrong" belong
is the means by which we come to possess these concepts. The
order of our coming to understand each moral kind is by first
encountering its instances in actual moral situations. That's the
theory in a nutshell.

Let us take stock of our mental capabilities concerning actions
like promising. Each of us is capable of understanding what a
promise is. We can also judge when a promise has been made, and
when one has not been made, often judging quite subtly of tough
cases. We can do this without having an explicit grasp of all of the
conditions of a promise. But after some reflection, we are capable
of judging whether an account of promising, like the one given
above, really fits what a promise is. So our knowledge of promising is extensive and subtle in practice, and equips us to rationally
evaluate different accounts of promising when theorizing.

Everyone makes promises. One condition necessary for their
actualization must be highlighted here, for it is critical. No promise is made without the agents involved understanding what a
promise is. If Wilson makes a promise to Cooper, that implies
two things: Wilson understands what a promise is, and Cooper
understands what a promise is. On my account, the knowledge
possessed by Cooper and Wilson of the essence of promising is a
priori.

Many think promises are merely conventions. Hume states,
"promises are human inventions, founded on the necessities and
interests of society" (1969: 571). But a brief comparison of promises with something that is clearly conventional, greetings, will
show they are quite different. Greetings are a kind of transaction
on which conventions disagree. Familiarity with a few different
greeting conventions allows one to make comparisons. For example, we can say China's greeting conventions are more like Japan's
than America's. But can we make similar claims about lying? Can
we say the rules concerning what is a lie in China are more like
what constitutes lying in Japan than they are like America's lying
rules? It seems not. It would be absurd to ask a cultural consultant,
"What is a lie in Bangladesh?" That this question is absurd tells
against the convention account of lying. However, what counts

as a *socially offensive* lie can differ from country to country, but is another matter altogether. When we think about transactions like lying and promising, they are universal, and not mere local social norms. For the theory of moral kinds I am developing, that is exactly what promises and lies are: *universals.*

The conventionalist will nonetheless claim that we learn about the nature of promising and lying as we do other conventions. We are taught them. This explanation encounters a problem. And employing the Experience Test will reveal what it is. Recall that the Experience Test was put forth by Strawson as an objection to intuitionism.[17] It relies on our supposed lack of experience of intuiting the properties rightness or goodness. He claimed that if we could not recall doing so, and if we could not say we know what it would be like to intuit such properties, then it makes sense to say that we have no grounds for saying we have direct knowledge of right or good.

Let's employ the Experience Test to the transaction of promising. If the word "promise" expresses a concept we grasp, and learned through social instruction, then it is self-contradictory to say: "I know what the word 'promise' means, and I know its many conditions of application, but I can't remember ever *being taught* the rules that constitute promising, and I do not know what it would be *like* to be taught the rules of promising." I certainly was never taught the essential rules of promising. And I cannot imagine in what kind of teaching environment I could be taught them. So I possess the concept of the promise a priori. Being exposed to some instances of promises was all I needed to understand the essential structure of promising. So the convention account of promising fails the Experience Test.

9. The metaphysical status of moral kinds

Transactions realism may not appear as strongly positioned as conventionalism is, but there are many things that favor a realistic account of transactions. Moral kinds exist in two modes. When we think about them directly, they are complex abstract objects, which include a network of conditions. "Lying" is a whole having different parts, parts that are connected in definite necessary ways, and not possibly in any other ways. Suspicions are bound to arise concerning abstract intelligible wholes, like moral kinds, first about the abstract element. Extreme nominalists will resist them tenaciously. But generally, such complaints would have met a more receptive hearing years ago, for now even moderate nominalists claim "abstract particulars" as building blocks of the world.

So perhaps the assertion that there are abstract *wholes* might spur greater opposition. The problem with this stance is that there are quite familiar abstract wholes that are regarded as denizens of our world by a variety of theorists: propositions. If one countenances propositions in one's ontology, then she accepts intelligible wholes that exist mind-independently. And actually, most people will be much more favorably disposed to accept that promises, lies, and harms have essential natures, than believe there are propositions, indicating that moral kinds are not contrived by theoreticians.

Actual concrete situations are the other mode in which moral kinds exist. Such situations never afford us direct knowledge of a moral kind. We directly see individual humans, their unique faces, their peculiar utterances, and idiosyncratic gestures, and so on. As Peter and Paul speak, the kind of interaction they are forming becomes intelligible to us, as it were, around all of the sensory information in the transaction. And that is how we discern a promise is being made. A concrete transaction, such as a particular instance of harming is an ontologically dependent entity. In the material world, a harming cannot exist without two or more agents. This makes real-world particular instances of moral kinds, such as harms, benefits, promises, lies, *multiply dependent* entities.

Monadic properties, like the property of *being green*, depend only on a single object, the surfaces they cover. A transaction *being a promise* is dependent on two agents, the various pertinent states of mind, such as their understandings and their beliefs, and the respective overt actions of the promiser to make a promise, and the promisee to accept it. By being multiply dependent on several objects, the existence of a promise-instance necessarily depends on the several objects existing and being related in certain determinate ways.

The nature of a lie is a *complex formal universal*. Although an instance of lying necessarily requires agents to exist, it itself is not a material thing like the agent's eyes, mouth, or the teeth through which she lies. Something is a lie when certain *formal requirements* are met. That lies, promises, and harms are universals explain why there are essential requirements for each of them. It also explains why the rules constituting a lie do not change from town to town, or nation to nation. The universal "lie" is what everyone predicates of a certain kind of act, and truly only of acts of that kind. Lastly, understanding these fundamental transactions as complex universals allows us to explain why they are recognized by people all around the world.

Someone might object that lies and promises are not universals. Take promises. They are greatly different. Some promises are to go for a walk in the park on Sunday. Others are to wire $500 immediately. Still others are to return that borrowed CD the next time you are in town. But think of what differentiates these promises. A difference in content is sufficient to differentiate two promises. But if the contents of two promise speech acts are the same, we say the promises are the same. If I promise to put my son through college, and my father made that promise to me, we say truthfully that I and my father made the same promise. If a woman in Ecuador promises to send her daughter to college, it too is the same promise. That all that is required to distinguish two promises is their content, and that having the same content is sufficient for two promises to be identical indicates that nearly everything about all promises is the same. So promises are universals. A similar argument works equally well with lies and their various contents.

Even those who disdain the idea of moral universals think and speak as if they existed. This becomes most obvious where identical instances of moral kinds are involved. We understandably feel duped when we discover a salesman hooked us in with the *same* lie they told to others. When we aim to be fair to our children we offer the *same* promise if they bring home a straight A's report card. We naturally consider it an injustice when two individuals receive greatly different punishments for the *same* crime. In order for two actions that are separate in time, and that differ from one another in numerous other details, to be considered the same, they must have something crucial in common. In the cases just mentioned they have a moral kind in common. A thoroughgoing naturalist will take issue with all of these natural thoughts we all have. Following their program will make nonsense out of the most basic claims of injustice. Where claims of justice are concerned, then, naturalism is the mysterious doctrine, not nonnaturalism. That provides yet another reason for favoring the theory of moral kinds.

10. The convention objection

I have made a case for a theory of real moral kinds. Every part of a lie is necessarily implied by a whole lie being made. People must understand all of the necessitation relations involved in a lie. And such understanding is a priori. But despite our counterattacks on conventionalist accounts of promising, the conventionalist will continue to insist that they are institutional facts. They will explain the necessary character of the relations that make up promises by appealing to a set of constitutive rules.

Constitutive rules are those that are necessary for a given kind of practice to exist. Walking is a behavior that humans engage in before there are *regulative rules*, rules that regulate and govern walking, such as laws against jaywalking. The practice of chess is quite different. It requires a set of rules for chess to even exist, and once such *constitutive rules* are in place and are understood, then humans can play chess. From the point at which the rules of chess were initially constituted till now, all people who have played chess have relied on the constitutive rules of the game. Conventionalists will argue that a similar set of constitutive rules were devised for the practice of promising, and that all those who promise make use of such rules.[18] With this outline in hand, the conventionalists appear poised to be able to explain what promises are, how they came to be, and how there are a number of necessarily true propositions that can be stated about any given promise, just as there are a number of necessary propositions about chess.

Two features of moral kinds confound conventionalism: the universality of their instances and their inner necessities. Take promising. Promising is ubiquitous, and is found in cultures continents away from each other. Also, internal to promising is the necessary relations that obtain between any part and the whole of a promise. Conventionalists will offer a sort of social evolutionary explanation. Prohibitions of lying, they will say, are necessary for the existence of civilization. Without such rules, society will dissolve. Conventionalists will grant that devising the convention of promising does require some intelligence, but it does not require an intelligence that "apprehends" the essential structure of promises. But the importance and efficacity of promising is not diminished by such an account.

Conventionalists have a plausible story. But several other considerations undermine it. First, even if the evolutionary account explains why promising is so widely practiced, it does nothing to explain why the necessary relations internal to a promise have taken the one and only form they in fact do universally have. Conventions are various, not uniform. Second, we are given a picture of people with social purposes devising conventions to assure the continued existence of their societies. How are humans *able* to do this? If society exists as they go about devising moral conventions essential for civilization, and if, as it seems to me, promises are the basis of society, then there is no need for them to invent the conventions. If society does not exist, then humans are not situated to devise and propagate rules that everyone will feel it important to follow.

Promises are not human inventions. Conventionalists who disagree greatly underestimate our inventiveness. For instance, popular celebratory gestures are clearly invented. At some point a "low five" was the way to acknowledge something worth celebrating. It was replaced by the "high five." Currently, the "fist bump" is becoming increasingly popular. If conventionalism were the correct account of promises, there would be nothing to prevent promises from taking any number of structures while still being promises. So promises, for conventionalism, could have any or all of the following features:

> The obligation is not discharged after the promise has been kept.
>
> The promise is not expressed in a speech act of any kind.
>
> A promise need not be understood by the promiser.
>
> A rejected attempt at a promise is still a promise.

The conventionalist must either accept that promises with such features are possible or explain why, if they are merely invented entities, their theory excludes them.

What has been most overlooked about a conventionalist account of promising is this. Two questions concerning promises must be separated: What *is* a promise? How did promising become a common practice? Conventions may help explain how promises became common. And conventions will surely explain why keeping promises is taken more seriously in some cultures than others. But conventions can have no part in explaining what a promise *essentially is*. Once a conventionalist essays to lay out the necessary timeless conditions of promising, she has drifted too far toward the theory of moral kinds to be a conventionalist.

11. Chapter summary

A complete intuitionism must include the grounds of morality. Moral relations are abstract entities that agents enter to form moral situations. From the standpoint of naturalism they are queer entities. But no objective moral theory can do without them. Moral kinds are abstract entities that we understand a priori. Self-evident propositions of moral kinds relate parts of a given kind to the whole. In actual moral situations we can recognize when an instance of some kind is present, say, when someone tells what we know to be a lie. A successful transaction analysis of a moral kind provides a number of self-evident moral propositions, including an intuitive moral principle. Opponents of self-evident moral principles must find a way to contest them all.

Conventionalist objections to moral kinds don't work. The structure of lying is universal, no matter how differently it is regarded in different cultures. Also, for two, or two million, people to tell the same lie, it is sufficient that the content of their lie is the same. Lastly, conventionalists underestimate our inventiveness, and along with the rest of us, are not willing to consider something a lie if it differs from its essential structure.

Further reading

The primary text to read on the nature of transactions is Reinach's work "The a priori foundations of the civil law" in a 1983 translation. An informative recent discussion of Reinach's theory is Barry Smith's "An essay on material necessity" (1992).

CHAPTER SIX

The right and the good reconsidered

Introduction

Our examination of intuitionism has proceeded from the intuitive knowledge we have of certain moral principles toward the features in the world that the principles capture. That is to say, we began with the basic moral knowledge possessed by us all, and are now firmly in the territory of moral metaphysics, attempting to explain just what makes the intuitive moral principles true. The theory of moral kinds, as outlined in the previous chapter, provides the structure of an account of what makes actions right: An action is right in virtue of the kind of action an agent performs in virtue of the moral relations that agent bears to others in the situation.

The entities that are distinctive of moral facts are nonnatural. People stand in various moral relations to one another. Such relations are necessary for any theory that includes moral actions. These moral relations are essential to explaining why we have duties, and why some acts are right, others wrong. Also, every human situation with two agents affords possible transactions between them. Certain transactions are, broadly speaking, moral: assaulting, helping, being kind, lying, and so on. We understand certain fundamental transaction kinds because they are intelligible objects about which we have a priori knowledge. The a priori understanding of these kinds enables us both to identify their instances in actual situations and to judge whether they are right or wrong.

Bringing together these separate elements of moral facts is this chapter's aim. However, before I can do this, there is one outstanding inconsistency in early analytic intuitionism that I must address. It concerns the matter of intrinsically morally good actions. Such actions are good simply by being done, and require no external good, such as an agent's good motive or good consequences, in order to be good. Prichard and Ross colossally blundered by excluding such actions from intuitionism. This has had a devastating effect on intuitionism and, more generally, deontological moral theories. By examining Prichard and Ross's theories, I will show that they actually give us more reason to believe than to reject intrinsically morally good actions. Including such actions helps us to better explain moral facts, to forge a more consistent and more powerful intuitionism, and, as we will see in the next chapter, to show intuitionism to be the stronger normative theory.

Particular moral facts are where resistance to moral realism seems strongest. What explains the existence and knowledge of particular moral facts? Intuitionism holds that there are both particular moral facts and general moral facts, the latter being represented in the self-evident moral principles. I'll explain how these two kinds of facts are connected. I will also explain how particular moral facts can coexist with natural properties. The kind-based constitutive explanation of moral facts I provide eliminates the supervenience problems discussed in Chapter 4.

1. What's wrong with deontology

A longstanding debate in ethics concerns a matter of explanatory priority. Is the right prior to the good? Or is the good prior to the right? Which of these two fundamental concepts is explanatorily prior? As the questions are currently understood, the answer is "neither." Deontologists typically hold that the right is prior to the good. Consequentialists have occupied the contrary position. As is often the case in philosophy, both sides are providing satisfactory answers to the wrong questions. In this chapter I try to set the whole misguided discussion of moral explanation right.

What is explanatorily prior is the *kind* of act in question. For a given act, being of a certain kind explains why it is, say, morally right and morally good. For another act, being of a different kind will explain why it is morally wrong and morally bad. Generally, the explanation of the moral rightness and moral goodness of an action is based on the kind of action it is. But each kind of act will explain goodness and rightness in its own distinctive way.

What's wrong with deontology today is it assumes the good is completely detached from moral conduct, and argues that the right is prior to the good. The early analytic intuitionists are responsible for the assumption and the rightness-priority stance. I believe that severing the good from morality is the colossal blunder of analytic intuitionism. Although many problems in deontology today can be traced to this source, I will focus on the problems it visits on intuitionism. For one thing, the "priority of the right" stance fosters the impression that intuitionism has no explanatory resources. For another, since any plausible moral theory will have some role for the good to play, it partly explains why intuitionism appears unplausible to some.

Since the days of Prichard and Ross some intuitionists have sought to bring the good and the right together.[1] But I think that fully repairing the moral good requires examining why these two intuitionists detached the good from morality in the first place. The reasons given for the detachment are not as convincing as they might have appeared. I'll argue for a distinct intuitionist moral good in two steps. First, I will show that Prichard himself conceded in several ways that our intuitions strongly indicate a moral good. Second, I'll show that Ross's own argument for objective intrinsic goods strongly supports moral action being among them. Later I will explain how good properly figures in moral explanations.

2. Intuitionists against intrinsically good action

Prichard and Ross's extracting the good from morality was unprecedented, and was recognized as such by their contemporaries.[2] Let us state precisely the kind of good they excluded from moral theory. Prichard and Ross claim that there are basically two categories of moral action. Some actions are morally right, others are morally good. Morally right actions are right by being a certain kind of action performed in a certain kind of situation. Morally good actions are just like morally right actions but have one other feature: they're done from a moral motive. So early analytic intuitionism holds that there are no *intrinsically morally good actions*, that is, no actions that are good independently of a moral motive. For brevity's sake, I will call such actions "intrinsically good actions."

On behalf of the right, Prichard filed for divorce from the good in his "Does Moral Philosophy Rest on a Mistake?" Recall that the mistake preoccupying Prichard was the search for moral proofs. To his mind, what motivated that search was ethicists being mistakenly dissatisfied with their plain knowledge of what's right. If an ethicist thought it would be wrong to lie to a neighbor, he sought an additional reason not to lie. Three ways of providing such an additional reason call on, one, what "will be for our good," two, the goodness "to which the act leads," or three, the goodness "of the act itself."[3] Exhausting the ways good can explain right, and rejecting them all, Prichard rules out egoism, consequentialism, and any possible good-based deontology.

Prichard does not give a distinct argument for declaring the right totally independent from the good. The good is simply an unfortunate casualty of his campaign against moral proofs. Asking "Why should we do so and so?" leads us to look for moral proofs. I agree with Prichard, as do most other ethicists today, that the quest for moral proofs is misguided. But because the good is employed as a means to the illegitimate end of moral proofs, Prichard rejects the good in the moral context. The mistaken assumption is that if some concept X is used for an illegitimate theoretical end Y, then the concept X is itself illegitimate. A parallel case would be where an atheist argues that because a theist uses the notion of possible worlds to argue for the existence of God, that there are no possible worlds. In each case the inference is erroneous.

Other reasons why Prichard and Ross separated the good from the right are not so clear. Especially unclear is what exactly convinced them that there are no morally good actions outside those done from a good motive. In this instance they strayed from their general methodology of cautiously considering what we actually think about different moral phenomena.

3. Prichard's case for intrinsically good action

There is a simple reason for an intuitionist to embrace intrinsically good actions. If we follow the intuitionist method, and look to what we really think about morality, we are bound to hold that morally right actions are intrinsically good. And that is exactly what Prichard himself saw.

In the process of setting up his case against intrinsic moral goodness, Prichard acknowledges in several ways the intuitive force propositions about intrinsic moral goodness have. When we carefully examine utilitarianism, he says, we see "its failure to correspond to our actual moral convictions" (Prichard, 1912: 25). Recognizing this, Prichard states, "we become driven to adopt the other form of the view, *viz.*, that the act is good in itself and that its intrinsic goodness is the reason why it ought to be done" (1912: 25). He proceeds: "It is this form which has always made the most serious appeal; for the goodness of the act itself seems more closely related to the obligation to do it than that of its mere consequences or results, and therefore, if obligation is to be based on the goodness of something, it would seem that this goodness should be that of the act itself" (Prichard, 1912: 25). He adds, "Moreover, the view gains plausibility from the fact that moral actions are most conspicuously those to which the term "intrinsically good" is applicable" (Prichard, 1912: 25).

After laying out all such intuitive points in favor of the intrinsic moral good, he cuts against it. He says,

> There is, of course, no doubt that we approve and even admire certain actions, and also that we should describe them as good, and as good in themselves. But it is, I think, equally unquestionable that our approval and our use of the term 'good' is always in respect of the motive and refers to actions which have been actually done and of which we think we know the motive. (Prichard, 1912: 26)

This is one intuition I fail to share with Prichard, partly because of the several intuitions he previously offered on behalf of intrinsic goodness. Let us gather all his intuitions, and see which side possesses greater weight. On the one side, our intrinsically-morally-good-action intuitions:

1 more closely correspond to our actual convictions than utilitarian claims;

2 have always made the most serious appeal to our intelligence in explaining right;

3 reveal the goodness of the act seems more closely related to obligation than its consequences;

4 suggest that if obligation is to be based on the goodness of something, it seems it would be the act itself;

5 suggest that moral actions are most conspicuously those to which "intrinsically good" is applicable;

6 inform us that we approve and admire certain actions and describe them as good, and as good in themselves.

On the other side, Prichard has the intuition that:

(1') "it is equally unquestionable that our approval and our use of 'good' is always in respect of the motive from which it is done."

Weighing the sides gives two results. First, it is hard to credit the claim in (1') that our consciousness informs us that our use of "good" with respect to actions is *unquestionably* always about the action's motive, partly because of the accumulated epistemic strength for the contrary stance found in (1) through (6). Second, as a result, the greater intuitive weight of Prichard's intuitions supports the conviction that there are intrinsically good actions.

4. Ross's case for intrinsically good action

Like Prichard, Ross offers no argument against intrinsically good actions. He only declares against them.[4] But a careful examination of Ross's ethical system reveals what Ross did not suspect: his own claims about intrinsically good objects quite strongly support the inclusion of morally right actions among them. Part of the case for intrinsically good actions employs Ross's own method of determining what is intrinsically good to show that right actions count as such. These considerations, coupled with Prichard's several reasons for believing in intrinsically good actions, make a strong case for their existence.

An aura of mystery surrounds intrinsically good actions. The early analytic intuitionists are responsible for this widespread impression. But there is nothing especially mysterious about them, as compared with other common metaphysical entities, such as the property of being blue. To see why, consider that everything that exists constitutes facts that are either intrinsically good, intrinsically neutral, or intrinsically bad. So morally right actions must be intrinsically something.

Now consider *Situation 1*, a pedestrian case of moral action. Brown refrains from lying to Johnson on a quite trivial matter. After being questioned, she admits to Johnson that she did not double-check the time of a movie that she and he are going to, and whose time she is certain of. She doesn't do this from a moral motive. Brown tells Johnson the truth because she fears he'll get angry if he finds out she lied. But her fear is misplaced because there is no way for Johnson to find out whether she had double-checked the movie time. When Brown tells the truth she feels about as good for doing so as Johnson feels annoyed that she didn't double-check the movie time.

In *Situation 2* Brown lies to Johnson. Since Johnson does not find this out, he is pleased because he thinks Brown double-checked, as pleased as Brown was in Situation 1. But Brown feels guilty in Situation 2, thus being as displeased as Johnson was in Situation 1. By comparing the consequences of the actions in the two situations, we can see that they are *counterbalancing consequences*.

Intuitionists say that Brown was right not to lie. But what is her action's value-status? Her telling the truth was surely an action. Since her action exists, it must have some value-status. It would be a mistake to declare Brown's action to be intrinsically bad, for nothing supports that judgment. Perhaps her telling the truth was intrinsically neutral, so there was nothing either intrinsically good or bad about it. But since there is no sense to saying her action was intrinsically bad, it can only be intrinsically neutral if it is not intrinsically good. And what reason do we have for believing that? Of course, some can say that intrinsic goodness is an unintelligible notion. But Ross can't. For he holds that there are intrinsic goods. He states, "Four things . . . seem to be intrinsically good—virtue, pleasure, the allocation of pleasure to the virtuous, and knowledge" (Ross, 1930: 140).

How did Ross determine his "four things" have intrinsic value? He employs a possible worlds thought-experiment to that end. Ross considers "two states of the universe" (1930: 134). In the two possible states all entities are the same, except for one. If the addition of the one thing makes the world in which it exists more valuable, then that thing possesses intrinsic value. If it does not make that world better, it doesn't. To illustrate this method, consider an actual use of it by Ross. Assume that World 1 and World 2 are the same in terms of pleasures, distribution of pleasure to the virtuous, and in amount of virtue. The difference between them is that in World 1 there is widespread knowledge, and in World 2 there is widespread ignorance. The question is, "Is the addition of knowledge in World 1 enough to make it of greater value than World 2?" The answer is "yes." That is Ross's justification for claiming that knowledge has intrinsic value.

Let's apply Ross's worlds test to morally right action.[5] Suppose that World 1 and World 2 are the same in the amount of pleasure, knowledge, virtue, and distribution of pleasure to the virtuous. The difference between World 1 and World 2 is that World 1 contains widespread ordinary moral actions, say twice as many acts of trivial truth-telling just like Brown's in Situation 1, with similar consequences. In World 2 the lies told are just like Brown's lie in Situation 2, with similar consequences. Is that addition sufficient to make World 1 more valuable than World 2? Yes. When people meet more of their obligations, that suffices to give a world greater value. Therefore, ordinary moral actions are intrinsically good.

Not everyone will accept intrinsically good actions on this basis. Utilitarians will characteristically look toward the consequences of the actions involved. The utilitarian will ask, "Might it not be the case that World 1 is more valuable, not because of the intrinsic goodness of all these extra acts of truth-telling, but rather because such acts produce consequences that make World 1 better than World 2?" In that case, better consequences, and not intrinsic goodness of certain actions, would explain our intuition that World 1 is more valuable than World 2.

But this objection does not work for Worlds 1 and 2. I said that *all* things are the same in the two worlds, except for the additional acts of truth-telling in World 1 and the immediate consequences of both actions. That means World 1 and World 2 have all the same consequences, except for the pairs of counterbalancing consequences. Recall that, in World 1, Brown's pleasure in telling the truth is counterbalanced by Johnson's annoyance. In World 2, where Brown lies, her lie is not detected, and her guilt about lying is counterbalanced by Johnson's feeling of assurance about the movie time. The situations use a right act and a wrong act, each of which does not make a major difference, thereby isolating for us the performance of the moral act itself. And isolating the act this way shows that what makes World 1 better is the multiple acts of truth-telling themselves.

5. Good and right

"Good," "right," and "ought"—these most fundamental ethics notions are also the trickiest to handle. On my account, actions that are morally right are also morally good, and vice versa. The main reasons for believing this are that's what we really think about morality, and no compelling reasons have been given for thinking otherwise. But just because "good" and "right" are present in our positive moral judgments does not alone imply that the former explains the latter. Attempts to explain one thin moral concept by another can guarantee only thin explanations, and do little to illuminate morality. Rather, moral kinds are the key to moral explanation. Moral kinds are sufficient for explaining what's right. But understanding how good is structured *within* moral kinds provides deeper, more satisfactory moral explanations.

What makes an action right?[6] The outline of my account, so far, is this. Persons enter moral relations. An action is right if it does not violate the moral relation that obtains between agents. The promise-relation is formed by one agent making a promise to another. Once a promise-relation obtains between Jones and Smith, Jones respects the promise-relation only by keeping the promise she made to Smith. When Jones violates the promise-relation by not keeping the promise Jones's action is wrong. Other relations form without our overt, intentional acts. When Taylor is walking down the street and encounters Robinson, then two no-harm-relations form between them, one binding Taylor, the other binding Robinson. So either Taylor or Robinson would be wrong by harming the other.

Moral relations are the foundations of our duties. Moral kinds indicate *the way* in which a moral relation is adhered to or violated. And importantly, these kinds inform us of what kind of moral relation is present in a situation, and inform us of whether the relation has been respected or violated. So moral kinds are our epistemic windows, so to speak, to moral relations. For there is no way that we can see through the senses or apprehend with the mind particular instances of moral relations directly. The only way is through intelligible moral kinds.

Likewise, we cannot see or grasp rightness in a moral situation. We can't see rightness because it has no visible properties. We cannot grasp rightness itself in moral situations because rightness, though a nonnatural property, is located within a situation all of whose visible parts are physical entities. Locating rightness in the world has been a notoriously difficult task. But based on the whole action principle, it is perfectly understandable why we can't locate it with our senses or directly through the mind. Rightness is a property of a whole action, not its mere parts, and since we only grasp a whole action based on its intelligible features, it is no wonder that we cannot directly epistemically access the rightness of an action. A concrete whole action is a multiply dependent entity, depending on several physical objects, actions, and events.

Since rightness depends on that whole, rightness is nonlocatable. In contrast, we can locate the material objects, actions, and events upon which the whole action depends for its existence. Instantiated rightness is not a independent entity, such as a corporeal agent, nor a natural first-level dependent entity, as actions are. Nor is it a nonnatural first-level dependent entity such as an instance of a moral ground. Instantiated rightness is a second-level dependent entity, depending as it does on a particular nonnatural ground, and on an action, which in turn is dependent on a host of objects and events that form the action as it is.

How kinds explain what is right is this. Recall that Brown confessed to Johnson that she didn't double-check the movie time. If we ask what explains the rightness of Brown's action, "It was not a lie" suffices. It suffices because the action was not the kind of action that is wrong. This may seem too obvious or trivial to serve as a moral explanation. But it only appears so because of our long familiarity with the moral kind "lie." Anything beyond that answer, if it does explain, only explains why more deeply.

The structure of a lie, consisting of several components, affords the next level of explanation. Brown's action was right, on this deeper explanatory level, because Brown did not intentionally tell Johnson something she believed to be false. Such structured explanations may be likened to mathematical explanations that derive properties from whole entities. For example, the fact that this figure is a triangle allows us to explain why it has three sides, is enclosed, and why it has interior angles equaling 180 degrees. The next level of moral explanation draws upon the value-statuses of the different components of the whole action in question.

6. Good and kind

Kinds are absolutely indispensable for moral explanation. Good also has an explanatory role. But if we lose sight of the structure of moral kinds in the quest to make good explain all, we will surely lose our basis for explanation. Previously ethicists who gave good the primary explanatory role only considered it independently of any intelligible structure. As the astounding volume of utilitarian literature has amply demonstrated, good without structure provides only the promise of moral explanation, or poor or erroneous moral explanations. But it is important to note that good itself has not led us astray. It is good unmoored from any intelligible structure and scattered everywhere that is to blame.

A complex, intelligibly structured moral explanation, which incorporates the good will succeed more fully in explaining right. Moral kinds provide the needed structure. By considering the value of each of the distinct parts of a kind of action, then determining the value of the whole, we can see more fully why it is right, wrong, or permissible. The method employed should be familiar by now. I will ask what we really think for each component of a kind of action. By proceeding step by step we'll arrive at a judgment of the complex whole.

What happened to Anderson yesterday will serve as the material for our moral explanation. Anderson died. He was a decent person, so he did not deserve to die. Death is bad thing. So we all understand that Anderson's death was bad. How he died is important to consider, for we think some deaths are worse than others. If Anderson died of natural causes while asleep we would think that is much better than if he were mauled to death by alligators. So the story behind Anderson's demise can alter our judgment of its badness. In this case, Miller killed Anderson. A little reflection will reveal that death by human killing is worse than death by natural causes. It is also worse than death by violent animals, even if dying that way seems more terrifying. Another human killing Anderson is worse for two reasons. For one, we assume that Miller is responsible for the death. For another, we think that Miller was capable of knowing the consequences of his actions and was free to have done otherwise. His choice led to Anderson's death.

How Miller killed Anderson is obviously important. Just the fact that Miller killed another human being is bad. Each of us would think we would be devastated if we killed someone, even if it were not on purpose. Sadly, Miller intentionally killed Anderson. So that is worse than if he had done so accidentally. As we proceed to determine the whole action Miller performed, we are seeing that its different components, taken together, are much worse than if any of the states of affairs that make up the whole had been different. If Anderson had not died, Miller had not done it, or Miller had not intentionally done it, if one or more components of his action were different, Miller's action would not have been as bad as it is. But it is worse than I have so far described. If circumstances had been greatly different, Miller might have killed Anderson because he found him in bed with his wife. But the fact is, Miller planned for six months to murder Anderson to take over his position at work.

Miller's premeditated murder of Anderson was very horribly wrong. It was wrong because of the kind of act it was. Good plays an important and integral role in this kind-structured explanation of moral wrongness. The wrong-maker in this situation is the act itself, as deontologists have long insisted. But a crucial part of the explanation is that the components of Miller's whole act have value because of what they individually are. When different combinations of action-components coexist then we have different kinds of acts, some of which are worse, some better. The reason premeditated murder is worse than manslaughter is simply because its component parts comprise a worse whole. This is what past ethicists meant when they spoke of an action's *nature* explaining why it is wrong.[7]

This kind of moral explanation shows that ordinary reflection is much better at judging the conditions of wrong-making than many theories previously devised. What has prevented us from recognizing this method of moral explanation is that we have concentrated on what concept ultimately explains rightness, and not on the structures of moral actions. Instead, effective moral explanations are to be found on the mundane level of moral experience, where the structures of moral actions are recognized.

The good and the right coexist as properties of moral actions. But each has a different focal point. Rightness belongs only to actions. Goodness is a property of actions and much else—states of affairs, states of character, states of mind, and so on. So they are distinct. In moral actions, goodness (or badness or value-neutrality) is located in each component of the action, as well as the whole action. Rightness, in contrast, belongs only to whole kinds of acts. When we speak of an action being good we are referring to *the action itself*, based on the whole arrangement of its components. When we speak of an action being right we are referring to *the decision* in taking that action. Take lying. Brown's lying, the whole action, itself is bad. And it was wrong of Brown to have chosen it.

7. Ought

"Ought" is a concept wholly different from right or good. How does it fit in? What we ought to do covers a wider range of action than what is morally right. For often we ought to do what is prudent. However, what one ought to do will often overlap with what is a morally good action, with what is right to do. What is most distinctive about "ought" is that, in its primary use, it is normative, and so directly guides action.[8] "Right" and "good" are primarily descriptive. They apply to existent entities, actual actions, and so are not directly action-guiding.

To determine the role "ought" plays in the moral life, let's consult what we really think about "ought," as it is reflected in language. The primary sense of "ought" is in assertions about actions, such as "I ought to do *a*." Call this the "action-ought." A secondary sense of "ought" is to be found when we say that "*b* ought to be." The difference between them is that when a genuine proposal is being considered, it is the action-ought we are thinking of. State-of-affairs-oughts often express mere wish, as in "There ought to be no more war." The principle that "ought" implies "can" only constrains action-oughts. For these reasons, from now on I will only use "ought" in the action-ought sense, the only sense that is important in ethics.

Many ethicists have thought that "right" is synonymous with "what ought to be done," including Ross.[9] But that's wrong. Take the sentence (A) "I ought to do what is right." If "right" means the same as "what ought to be done," then "I ought to do what is right," with some slight grammatical adjustments, means the same as (B) "I ought to do what I ought do." (A) and (B) are obviously different in two ways. First, (B) is a tautology, while (A) is substantive. Second, (A) states a reason for doing what one ought, (B) does not. So "right" and "ought" do not mean the same thing.

Furthermore, "right" and "good" are primarily descriptive, not prescriptive. That there is a clear divide between the good and the right, on the one hand, and ought, on the other, can easily be seen when we examine how sentences including these terms operate in various contexts. Running through several substitutions of terms makes this point. First, neither "right" nor "good" can sensibly function when they are substituted for "ought" in its primary sense. It makes sense to say "I ought to a." But it makes no sense to say "I good to a" or "I right to a." Clearly, "ought" is not interchangeable with these other terms where it most counts, in action.

The logic of "right" and "good" each involves an ineliminable "is." Any ought sentence including an "is" can eliminate it. For example, if we say "It is the case that I ought to a," we can say simply that "I ought to a," while retaining the meaning of the original. As an attempt to devise a substitute for "I ought to a" we can try these: "It is right to a" and "It is good to a." But in both cases these are descriptive expressions because of the "is." Can we eliminate these "is's" and thus form genuine normative sentences? By doing so we are left with "It right to a" and "It good to a," two absurd expressions. Other ways of trying to find substitutes for "I ought to a" are "It would be good if I were to a" and "Doing a would be right." But in both cases, good and right are predicated of actions that are counterfactually hypothesized to exist. They are equivalent to "If I were to do a it would be right." The action a hypothetically exists in such cases, thus giving more credence to the claim that "right" and "good" are descriptive predicates of actions, actually existing entities. Lastly, the descriptive "It is right to do a" and "It is good to a" find no substitutes with "oughts." It is absurd to say "It is ought to do a." From such reflections we can see that "ought" operates quite differently than the descriptive "good" and "right."

If right and good are properties belonging only to actual exist-ences, what in existence corresponds to "ought"? Nothing in the external world answers to "ought." "Ought" applies to agents, and implies changes in the world they have reason to effect. "Ought," however, does have some kind of existence. It exists only as part of thoughts in the mind, thoughts that point outward toward possible actions. "Right" and "good" function descriptively in propositions. That is because their corresponding properties can belong to acts. "Act *a* is wrong," "Act *b* is good" are factual assertions. "Ought" cannot function descriptively. There is no ought-property that can belong to acts. We cannot say "Act *a* is ought." We can only say "P ought to *a*," which is a normative claim, for a given person.

The relation between propositions containing "ought" and those containing "right" is not easily determined. If "Act *a* would be right" is true, then it seems to follow that "P ought to do *a*." If it is true that "Act *b* would be morally good" then it seems to follow that "P ought to do *b*." The gap that people are aware of in discussing the relation between is and ought is due to the fact that is-propositions have to do with facts of the world, while ought-thoughts are indexed to, and are only located in, the minds of distinct individuals. Our minds are such that based on certain information about the world, we form judgments that include "oughts" in them to direct our actions accordingly.

A consistent intuitionist categorization of moral action is now at hand. When we evaluate an action there are two things that can be said about it, depending on our focus. When we refer to *the thing done*, the action, we can say that it is good, bad, or neutral. But when we refer instead to *the doing* of the action, we can say that it is right, wrong, or permissible. And when an act is right to do, or most good, that seems to imply we ought to do it. I reject the notion that to say that an action is morally good implies an evaluation of the motive of the agent who performs it. To avoid confusion, how-ever, I will adopt a term that Ross employs for such actions, calling morally good acts from a good moral motive "conscientious."

8. Possible moral facts

Intuitionism must explain how there are particular moral facts and how we know them. Whether intuitionism can deliver on these counts has been much doubted. It is hard to tell whether it is self-evident truths or particular moral facts that has dissuaded more people from accepting intuitionism. But I suspect that even if someone were inclined to believe in self-evident truths, the matter of particular moral facts would likely discourage their doing so. And there are good reasons why. Given the natural world we know, how could there be moral facts?

Let us first explain how particular moral facts are possible. Intuitionism's nonnaturalism cannot merely be a claim about moral properties, such as being morally right. Nonnaturalism must figure in the grounds of moral facts somehow. Otherwise we have non-natural moral properties like rightness inexplicably emerging from nonmoral natural facts. With nonnatural grounds for intuitionism, we can make more sense of nonnatural moral properties existing. To see how, we must introduce the general notion of a *mixed fact*. A mixed fact is a particular fact that consists of both natural and nonnatural properties. Certain mixed facts are undoubtedly scientific facts, but not purely natural facts. Although many believe the natural sciences only study portions of the world that consist wholly of natural properties, this can easily be thrown into doubt. (F1) "Cows have udders" is obviously a natural fact. But are (F2) "There are four cows in the field" or (F3) "The cow gave birth to two calves" purely natural facts? Both are clearly scientific facts. They are *particular numerical facts*. But the fact that both propositions make use of abstract objects like 2 and 4 raises questions about whether F2 and F3 are purely natural facts.

What is the truth-maker for (F2) "There are four cows in the field"? The cows would certainly be involved. But would abstract objects called numbers necessarily be part of F2's truth-maker? If there were only three cows in the field, F2 would be false. So the additional presence of that other cow is crucial for F2 to be true. Her absence would make F2 false. But what accounts for the numerical truth-making component in the natural world? Neither the number three nor the number four would be in the field, standing alongside the cows. And it would seem that our symbolic numerical system is not necessary for the proposition "There are four cows in the field" to be true. For it would be true if there were four cows in the field, whether humans developed the number system, or whether humans ever existed. So the abstract 4 must *be* if it is to be true of the cows in the field.[10]

What has all this to do with moral facts? Particular moral facts are in important respects like particular numerical facts. They are both mixed facts.[11] Particular numerical facts, such as the fact that there are four cows in the field, and our knowing them, involve the following:

1 natural objects: the cows, the field;

2 nonnatural entities: the relations the cows bear to the field;

3 nonnatural entities: the abstract number which is true of the cows in the field;

4 this particular numerical fact cannot be known without numerical knowledge of 4.

Particular moral facts, such as the fact that Miller's harming Anderson is wrong, and our knowing them, involve the following:

1 natural objects: Miller, Anderson, and the physical event, Miller's attacking Anderson—the objects and actions that largely constitute the act of harming;

2 nonnatural entity: the no-harming moral relation between them, which binds Miller;

3 nonnatural entity: the act kind—the abstract harming whole;

4 nonnatural entity: the abstract property of being wrong that Miller's decision possesses;

5 nonnatural entity: the abstract property of being bad which Miller's act possesses;

6 this particular moral fact cannot be known without knowledge of the moral kind "harming."

To best understand particular moral facts let us contrast them with general moral facts. Numerical facts will once again serve as an example. General numerical facts, such as that 2 plus 2 equals 4, do not require agents to exist. Likewise, general moral facts, such as that keeping promises is required, do not require agents to exist. Particular numerical facts, such as the fact that there are four cows in the field, do not require human agents to exist. But here is where numerical facts and moral facts are quite different. Since every particular moral fact necessarily relies on their being a moral relation, and since every moral relation instantiation necessarily requires there being two agents, every particular moral fact necessarily requires that there are two agents. So the fact that Miller's harming Anderson is wrong requires Miller and Anderson.

Recognizing this difference helps to clear up misunderstandings about moral facts. General moral facts, such as those represented in the self-evident moral principles, are facts, with or without there being any humans in existence. But particular moral facts, on the other hand, do require that there are agents to exist. If a new species of rational agent emerges in a far-off solar system, it would be as true of them that its wrong for them to harm each other as it is for us. Only a correct understanding of the difference between particular and general moral facts can allow us to make sense of this.

9. Particular moral facts

Particular moral facts are possible. But what makes them actual? To explain, we must recognize that particular moral facts are complex metaphysical entities. They supervene on several physical objects. When we include everything involved in moral facts, we have a number of entities spanning the natural-nonnatural divide. But it is crucial to stress that just having the mere ingredients of moral acts is not sufficient for there to be one. All the formal conditions of a given moral kind must be concretely met. If they are then we have a moral act.

Agents enter moral relations. Some of these relations require our say-so for their existence, others do not. We are aware that we are in a moral relation by *recognizing* the moral kind that is pertinent to our action. When you encounter another agent, and interact with them, the do-not-lie relation comes into being between the two of you, as does the do-not-harm relation, as do others. Being civilized, you think of neither relation as your interaction begins. But suppose he asks you a question you are not comfortable answering. To satisfy his curiosity without revealing what you wish concealed, you consider lying to him. At that point you think that it would be wrong to lie because you recognize that the moral kind "lie" has application here. And that is the first point at which you recognize that the do-not-lie relation obtains between you and your companion. If the situation had been different, and your interlocutor were to say very nasty provoking things to you, if you considered striking him, you would recognize that it is wrong to harm him because you recognize that the moral kind "harming" applies in that situation. Note that in the case in which lying is contemplated, the recognition of the do-not-harm relation does not come to awareness; and in the case in which assault comes to mind, the do-not-lie relation is not recognized. But they nonetheless obtained from the start of your encounter.

Recognition is the crux of knowledge of particular moral facts. It is the bridge between understanding of abstract moral kinds and seeing what's right when Jones angers you. Recognition is needed to explain how we know that it's wrong when Brown lies to Johnson, that it is right when Taylor keeps his promise to Davis, that it is wrong when Adams detains Harrison. The theory of moral kinds explains how people can observe that a given act is wrong without observing the property of wrongness in isolation.

Our understanding grasps that harming is wrong. A human performs an action against another that constitutes a harming, based on its meeting the formal requirements of the universal "harming," which we all implicitly understand. We recognize that the case before us is an instance of harming, and we infer, based on our understanding of the moral kind "harming," that the act is wrong. Keep in mind that, although goodness and rightness are independent entities, universals, their instances are dependent on the physical acts of agents. *Being right* and *being good* depend on actual whole actions of certain kinds in order to exist. Just as we do not see through our senses that a promise has been made, just as we do not see through sight alone that one person is harming another, just as we do not see a merely physical act of lying, so we do not see an action's being right or an action's being wrong through the senses. Recognition allows us to identify acts of moral and immoral kinds. And it is through the medium of intelligible moral kinds that we can determine whether a particular action is right or wrong.

Observation of a morally wrong action is much like an observation of a triangle in the world. We never see triangles with our senses, because triangles are intelligible entities, and so are not delivered to our minds through the senses. But if we are hiking in the woods, and encounter some felled trees, it might happen that we recognize three trees that form an isosceles triangle on the ground. Without observing a triangle alone, we recognize in the arrangement of trees that it has taken on the form of the intelligible entity, an isosceles triangle.

So how do we decide what we morally ought to do? In many cases it works like this. We encounter other agents. Sometimes a particular course of action appeals to us, but we sense we ought not to take it. This happens because our understanding, which apprehends a number of intelligible a priori structures, helps us to recognize in the situation we are in that the course of action we are considering is of an immoral kind. That is, we think that a possible action would constitute an immoral kind. We then infer, if I were to do *a*, then that would be wrong. The counterfactual brings to mind the judgment "So I ought not to do *a*." In such a case, the wrong action does not exist, because we have not yet chosen *a*. Also, the "ought" does not exist externally. It exists only in our minds, and that can be enough for us to not do it.

10. Explaining supervenience

Moral properties are not natural properties, but in actual moral situations they supervene on them. This stance allows intuitionism to claim that morality is different from everything else, as it certainly seems to be, yet that moral properties fit into the natural world in a way we can predict. Intuitionism's supervenience thesis, however, has opened it to several criticisms. The main challenge is to explain the connection of nonnatural moral properties to natural properties. How can intuitionists assure that in other possible worlds in which all subvening properties are the same as ours all supervening moral properties are as they are in our world? Might there not be another possible world in which all actions Hitler performs are the same, but they are not immoral? Also, intuitionists must explain exactly how moral properties supervene on particular natural properties.

Shafer-Landau's constitution account of moral supervenience gives the framework needed for intuitionist moral explanation. In his theory, moral properties are constituted by particular natural properties. Recall one criticism of his view: just because superveni-ence works in other areas, such as in philosophy of mind, does not imply that it will work in the case of particular moral facts. The point is entirely correct. But it becomes moot once a supervenience account is shown to work in the moral domain. Since my constitu-tion theory provides greater detail, including a specific scenario to illustrate it, it is escapes this critical tactic.

The *moral kind constitution* account of moral supervenience explains how the property "being wrong" supervenes on one agent's particular action. This thesis holds that any physical action that constitutes a kind of action that is prima facie wrong is neces-sarily prima facie wrong. The two key elements in the account are *moral relations* and *moral kinds*. Including such nonnatural enti-ties in my constitution account separates it from Shafer-Landau's in one particular way. Recall that, on his account, the natural facts exhaustively constitute the moral facts.[12]

Recall also that a major hindrance to advancing our understand-ing of moral supervenience has been a dearth of helpful examples. To understand my account of moral facts, to understand exactly what supervenes on what, to allow for a firm grasp of the roles moral relations and moral kinds play in constituting moral facts, let us observe a case of one man lying to another. Davis and Harris encounter one another in the hallway. By virtue of this encounter, a moral relation, the do-not-lie relation, obtains between them in this scenario. Davis lies to Harris, and by doing so his action con-stitutes a lie. By instantiating the moral kind "lie," the moral prop-erty "wrong" is instantiated. Davis lies to Harris, right to his face. He says "I stayed at the Plaza Hotel in New York City," when in truth he stayed at the Holiday Inn. Davis lies, suppose, not because it is urgent that he do so for some moral end, but in an attempt to boost his standing with Harris.

As soon as Davis encountered Harris, he entered the do-not-lie relation to Harris. By Davis's speaking the words he did in this con-text, his words constituted a lie. Thus Davis's action violated the do-not-lie relation. We know what Davis did was wrong because we understand what a lie is. A lie has certain necessary conditions, and Davis's speech act happened to have met them all. Davis's action is also morally bad. The distinct components that make it a lie each has negative value. First, it is bad that Harris now believes a falsehood. It is also bad that another agent is responsible for getting him to believe that falsehood. And it is even worse that that agent intentionally brought that belief about. If any of these components had been different Davis's act would not have been as bad as it is.[13] Davis's particular physical act, including the pitch of his voice, the tempo of his utterance, the look on his face, his manner of standing, and his style of gesturing, constituted a lie.

What is significant in moral matters is the kind of act performed, not the particular physical facts that constitute the kind. Certain fundamental moral kinds of actions have necessary conditions that are invariant. But just because *the conditions* are invariant for an action *a* to constitute an action of a given moral kind does not imply that the *physical elements* that constitute the action must be of only one arrangement. On the contrary, the physical elements of a given kind of moral action can vary tremendously. Murder has a given invariant structured set of necessary conditions. But murder can be performed with a knife, poison, a gun, a speeding car, a falling safe, or a noose. Since murder is a universal, the term "murder" is a rigid designator.

The particular way in which Davis lied is likely unique. But the combinations of physical arrangements that would have constituted lying are inexhaustible. Even if he told the same lie, he could have done so in a higher pitched voice, or a lower one. Different mannerisms, postures and gestures could have been employed. Any other of numerous physical combinations of ways of delivering the lie could have been used. Davis could have phoned Harris from another state, or texted him, and told the same lie. All that matters is that the necessary and sufficient conditions for a lie were met. The conditions for lying, as well as other moral actions, are knowable a priori. The invariant structure of lying is not a physical object, but an abstract moral kind, with an ordered network of necessary relations constituting it.

One salient fact about moral supervenience is the covariance thesis: "if two things have exactly the same natural properties, then they also have exactly the same moral properties. If you find that two things have different moral properties, you must also find that they differ in some way in respect of their natural properties" (Miller, 2003: 31). Let us apply this to the Davis case. If Harris had beat Davis to the punch, and told him "I stayed at the Plaza Hotel in New York City," when he did not, in the same context, then it would have had the same moral property as Davis's action.

It would have been wrong. Also, if, contrary to what really happened, Davis's act was not morally wrong, then there must have been a physical difference, and, this is critical, a physical difference sufficient to *not constitute* an act of lying.

Any number of things could have made an act of Davis's morally permissible. For one, Harris might not have been around. If Davis spoke his sentence "I stayed at the Plaza Hotel in New York City" to an empty hall, it would not have constituted a lie, and would thus have been morally permissible. If Davis had merely mumbled the sentence to Harris, so Harris was unable to understand it, then Davis would not have done wrong. And if Davis had just slightly changed his utterance to Harris, saying instead that he stayed at the Holiday Inn, then his action would have been morally permissible. Through all these variations only one thing matters. Did Davis's action, no matter the physical elements, constitute a lie?

The moral kind constitution account fends off the global supervenience problem. It helps to explain how, although supervenience is a weaker relation than identity, if an action is wrong in our world, it is wrong in every possible world with the same natural facts. It does so by focusing on the fact that what makes certain actions wrong is that they are the kinds of actions that are wrong. It is understandable that a nonnaturalist supervenience account that does not recognize this fact would have a difficult time explaining why Hitler's actions in another possible world could not be morally permissible. But my account explains why Hitler's actions are wrong in every possible world.

Moral theory focuses on the physical acts that constitute kinds of moral wrongs. Hitler's actions were murderous. Having recognized the kind of actions he performed, and knowing that an act that meets the necessary and sufficient conditions for murder, we know his actions were wrong. The physical details of how Hitler conducted genocide are important historically. But if the physical means for murdering millions were different in some way, it still would have been genocide. So any possible world in which Hitler commits the identical physical acts as in our world, or even if he committed genocide by some alternative means, such actions would be wrong. Genocide is a universal wrong, and the term "genocide" is a rigid designator, picking out very bad actions in every possible world where it occurs.

Turning to the particular supervenience problem, why do moral properties supervene on the exact natural properties they are claimed to supervene on? Because those natural properties constitute a kind of action that is obligatory, permissible, or wrong. It is important to realize that, without our understanding of the necessary conditions of moral kinds of acts, no moral action would ever have been performed. The moral kind constitution thesis explains both how certain ordered sets of natural properties constitute a wrong action, and how numerous other ordered sets of different natural properties can constitute the same kind of wrong action. In any case, what is of paramount importance is what kind of act a given set of natural properties constitute.

11. Chapter summary

Explaining particular moral facts has been troublesome for intuitionism. With the theory of moral kinds, it can be shown to be achievable. However, to allow for the most effective moral explanations intuitionism must correct an inconsistency bred by the early analytic intuitionists. They favored excluding intrinsically morally good acts. But a careful look at Prichard's own intuitions and Ross's method for establishing intrinsic goods strongly supports their existence. Although the good has an important role in explaining an action's being right, moral kinds are the indispensable ingredient. Concerning a given act, identifying the moral kind in question is sufficient for informing us whether it is prima facie right or wrong. A deeper level of explanation is gained by considering the value-statuses of the several components making up a given moral kind, then determining the value of the whole act. Problems of moral supervenience are eliminated by moral kinds. Since moral kinds are universals, moral terms are rigid designators. That explains why Hitler's genocide cannot be permissible in any possible world. Numerous variations of physical elements can constitute a wrong action insofar as they constitute an action of a kind that is wrong, such as promise-breaking.

Further reading

In chapter 1 "Subjectivism" of his book, *The Definition of Good* (1947), Ewing shows many problems with a subjectivist view of the good, a topic I have not had space to treat. Audi explores the place the good should have in intuitionism in chapter 4 "Rightness and goodness" of his *The Good in the Right* (2004).

CHAPTER SEVEN

Intuitionism's rivals

Introduction

Intuitionism naturally spans the divide between metaethics and normative ethics. So fully treating it requires covering normative ethical ground. Determining the content of morality and explaining how agents can act on the intuitive principles are subjects of the next chapter. Here I examine intuitionism's rival normative theories, chiefly by examining their supreme principles. The principles of Kantianism, utilitarianism and one recent variety of virtue ethics shall be shown to be deeply flawed. Each of these supreme principles suffers from the same defects. They each break down at some point under the weight of clear counterexamples and their proper use cannot adequately be explained.[1]

Each normative rival to intuitionism appears to be true to the extent to which it relies on our common intuitive moral knowledge. That is, as rivals examine and attempt to argue for their supreme principle, they are relying on their knowledge of the intuitive principles to guide them. What we really think about morality is also what informs us that a particular counterexample has been effective against a proposed supreme principle. That intuitionism adheres only to those principles that constitute moral knowledge is indicated by the fact that intuitionism, unlike its rivals, has no counterexamples to it.

None of this is to say that there is no value to criteria of right action. Many obviously have use in actual moral situations. The point is just that no single one has exclusive value in the departments of epistemic justification and moral explanation, so that theories advocating these principles as the supreme basis of morality are mistaken. However, since some supposed supreme principles can plausibly be argued to be self-evident, the intuitionist is, on pain of inconsistency, bound to consider their potential as intuitionist principles. If such principles make the grade, they should be incorporated into intuitionism.

1. Moral knowledge and normative ethics

That we know what's right is crucial information for our moral lives. We do not need a theory to tell us what is right. But we must use our intelligence and reflect objectively on the kinds of actions we are contemplating performing. Also, we must keep in mind that the moral principles, "Keeping promises is required," "Lying is wrong," and "Harming others is wrong," and others are the moral constants of civilization.

Ethical theorizing is a practice that relies on our knowledge of these principles. Our moral intuitions, once more, are the data of ethics. All rivals to intuitionism use our ordinary intuitive moral beliefs to determine the correctness or incorrectness of their theories. But at the same time, all of intuitionism's rivals also distrust intuitionism's privileging these ordinary intuitive moral principles. Their trust is invested instead in their supreme principles of morality. Kantians have great trust in the categorical imperative, just as utilitarians trust the principle of utility.

The fact that there are normative rivals to intuitionism raises serious questions. If we really do know what's right, based on apprehending self-evident principles, and if normative ethicists believe morality is objective, then how is it that there are such rivals to intuitionism at all? In my view, adherents of other theories know what is right but assume that there are not several self-evident moral propositions. So they agree with intuitionism on the matter of first-order moral knowledge, knowing the content of the moral principles, but disagree about the second-order claim that such propositions are self-evidently true.

Doubters of intuitionism, not believing there are plural self-evident moral propositions, seek a proof or an explanation of the intuitive principles. Most often this search has been for a supreme principle of morality. The supreme principles Kantians and utilitarians rely on for proof or explanation have several attractive features. They capture important features of moral facts of the world, they have much intuitive plausibility, and they promise to provide moral proofs or moral explanations. So they have *explanatory promise*. If such principles had no such features, they would not be plausible, and few would accept them. And, I should note, a great many more contemporary ethicists have accepted such principles than hold to intuitionism. My job, then, is to show that accepting a supreme principle is an error.

2. Supreme principles of morality

Finding the supreme principle of morality used to be the highest task of moral theory. Modern ethicists began this practice as they sought to find a way to prove what is right. In the age of rationalism, with no previous failures to discourage them, it is no wonder ethicists were confident that moral proofs could be got. Kant certainly intended his categorical imperative as a proof-making instrument. He believed it could solve all moral problems we face. Bentham agreed with the general idea, but thought the principle of utility was better suited for the job.[2] Since then the role of supreme principles has shifted. Where proof of what is right is no longer sought, many ethicists confidently proceed as if their supreme principle can explain why certain moral rules, such as "do not lie," "do not harm," and so on, are correct.

Prichard rightly rejected moral proofs in ethics. He did so because we know, for example, that "Lying is wrong," and we know it because it is self-evident. Since the intuitive principles are self-evident, they need not and cannot be proved by any other principle. Today's consensus agrees with Prichard's conclusion, if not his premises. But although there is little talk of moral proofs today, there is much reason for examining the idea. For one, the conditions for adequate supreme principle explanation contain some critical conditions of proof. For another, the demand for moral proofs is still present in the general populace, and so must be addressed.

Supreme moral principles seem ideally suited for moral explanation. Most people are likely to believe that lying is wrong and harming others is wrong. But they are less likely to hold that "Always maximize good" or "Act only on that maxim that you can simultaneously will as a universal law" is true. Given that a condition of proof is that the proposition(s) providing proof must be known, since the proposed supreme principles are less epistemically preferable to any intuitive principle, it is unlikely that people would agree that the former could possibly prove the latter.

But what of explanation? Can't we say that a supreme principle is intended to *explain* such ordinary moral rules? Perhaps. Even as we consider a supreme principle for this role, we will continue to be convinced of our intuitive moral beliefs. But recognizing that we do not have an evident external reason for our moral beliefs, we might think that ethicists might just be able to fill the need for explanation. When we find that the utility principle seems to explain why "Lying is wrong," then find that it seems to explain why "Harming others is wrong" our confidence in the utility principle will increase. Although in itself the utility principle is epistemically weak, it seems to accumulate epistemic strength with each moral rule or moral case it seems to explain.

Two fundamental problems menace this strategy. First, a necessary condition for p to explain (or prove) q is that p is true. Consequently, ethicists hoping to explain what is right, either for individual actions or as a rule, are unrelieved of the burden of showing that their supreme principle is true. The second problem is even more serious. It comes into play when we ask whether the supreme principle's implying several true propositions indicates that it is itself true: that if, for example, the principle of utility implying many moral rules we believe true is an indicator that it itself is true. The answer is "no." Here is why. False propositions are just as capable of implying numerous true propositions as true ones. "Every number is even" implies "Two is even," "Four is even," and so on for the whole natural number system. That means that, once again, proponents of supreme principles must show that their principle is true before they can say it explains anything.

Supreme principle theories have two responses available. They can attempt to show that their principle is true by some form of argumentation. The other alternative is to hold one's supreme principle as self-evidently true, as Sidgwick did for the principle of utility. But once an ethicist commits to a moral truth being self-evidently true, we will respond by testing whether their principle seems more or less epistemically preferable to the intuitive principles, such as

"Lying is wrong." In the contest among supposedly self-evident moral principles we can confidently expect that the intuitive principles will reign over any proposed supreme principle.

3. Kantianism

Kantianism is the first rival I will discuss. To evaluate it, I'll start with an epistemic appraisal of it. Epistemic appraisal, once more, is a direct comparative assessment of any two propositions in a given context to determine which one, if any, is evident to us. Here we'll determine whether Kant's supreme principle is epistemically preferable to the intuitive principles.

The cornerstone of Kantianism is his supreme principle of morality, the categorical imperative. The most important formulation of this principle is the formula of universal law: "Act only on that maxim through which you can at the same time will that it should become a universal law" (Kant, 1964: 88). Kant believed that this formula was the best one to follow in actual situations[3] and that it could solve any moral problem.[4] He also held that it was utterly indispensable to morality itself, and if we did not subject our wills to this very formula, then duty would be "everywhere an empty delusion and a chimerical concept" (Kant, 1964: 70). Quite fascinatingly, Kant held that "The ordinary reason of mankind . . . agrees with this completely in its practical judgements and always has the aforesaid principle before its eyes" (1964: 70).

So how does this principle fare, epistemically, against the intuitive principles? Interestingly, J. S. Mill, the utilitarian, thought the categorical imperative fared poorly against the intuitive principles. Kantianism, he asserts, lays "down as the common groundwork of those maxims some generality much less obviously authoritative than the maxims themselves, and which has never succeeded in gaining popular acceptance" (Mill, 1957: 5). It is easy to see why Mill thinks Kant's categorical imperative is epistemically less preferable than the moral principles it is purported to imply. Suppose you are in a situation in which telling the truth would be embarrassing to you. As you consider your options, which principle seems to be true to you, "Act only on that maxim through which you can at the same time will that it should become a universal law" or "Lying is wrong"? "Lying is wrong" seems to be something I know, whereas I am not even sure I understand what Kant's principle means.

And thus we arrive at the second problem with Kant's supreme principle. It has long been recognized that, as Mill states, agents following it would not be inconsistent in adopting "the most outrageously immoral rules of conduct" (1957: 6). Among the many examples given of maxims that pass the universality test are "I will hold slaves if I am in a position of sufficient power," "I will deceive when it suits me and I can probably get away with it," and "Keep promises your whole life except one." Such examples show, along with the notorious would-be murderer case, the categorical imperative has many *morally absurd* implications.[5] According to intuitionism, we know they are morally absurd because we know the self-evident principles of morality. If we take the categorical imperative on Kant's terms, as being an effective method for determining what to morally do in any situation, then clearly such universality-test-passing maxims provide *reductiones ad absurdum* for the principle.

But absurdities spawned by natural applications of the categorical imperative are not its last problem. To this day Kantians cannot explain the formula of universal law or how to apply it. In a rigorous study of interpretations of how to apply it, Korsgaard recognizes three: the Logical Contradiction Interpretation, the Teleological Contradiction Interpretation, and the Practical Contradiction Interpretation (1996a: 78). A problem that all three interpretations face, on her view, is natural actions, such as killing. She concludes, "In my view, the Practical Contradiction Interpretation deals with these problems better than the other two, although *not always* with complete success" (Korsgaard, 1996a: 101) (emphasis added). This last clause is very telling. It means that no interpretation of the use of the formula of universal law effectively deals with acts such as killing. In clear contrast, intuitionism holds that "Murder is wrong." In each case in which not murdering is our actual duty, intuitionism gets things right.

There are good reasons for not giving up on Kant entirely. Many voices have recently been raised in support of the formula of humanity of the categorical imperative: "Act in such a way that you always treat humanity, whether in your own person or in the person of any other, never simply as a means, but always at the same time as an end" (Kant, 1964: 96). Though questions linger about what it means for someone to be an end, about what it means to treat someone as an end, as well as questions about whether not treating someone only as means covers every kind of wrongdoing, this formulation is relatively easier to understand. Donagan claims that this principle, in one formulation or another, has been recognized as central to morality for millennia, and agrees that it is to be favored over universality principles.[6] Audi embraces the humanity principle, and believes it and other Kantian notions "can help to develop an intuitionism more systematic than Ross's" (2004: 112). If the principle of humanity is indeed self-evident, it is hard to see on what grounds we could object to its inclusion in intuitionism.

A theory's power is not fully demonstrated by its explaining the facts. Its true power is shown only when it also explains the kernel of truth in other theories, and why they are mistaken. Intuitionism has the same starting-point as Kant's theory. We know what's right.[7] Unfortunately for Kant's theory, the universal law formulation he thought implicit to moral thought is shown to be highly flawed once made explicit. Our account of moral wrong-making helps explain why the formula of universal law often gets things right. Take the matter of lying. "Lying is wrong" is self-evidently true because the universal kind "lying" necessarily implies any instance of it is prima facie wrong. We grasp the self-evident lying principle just as our intelligence grasps that lying necessarily involves telling a believed falsehood. In short, adequately understanding the universal "lying" implies knowing that any of its instances is prima facie wrong.

When we first examine Kant's formula of universal law, we are impressed that we sense that we cannot conceive a universal law of lying. Since "Lying is wrong" is self-evidently true, and evident to us, and is true based on the property "wrongness" necessarily belonging to the universal "lying," this should not come as a surprise. It should be no more surprising than our sensing something is amiss when we try to think that "Blue is not a color" or "2 + 2 = 5." Also, as we attempt Kant's universality test we are implicitly applying Ross's worlds test for intrinsic value. When we think of a world in which everyone lies, the fact that our thought recognizes that such a world contains a great deal of intrinsic bad helps explain why we recoil at the very thought of it. That we can universalize "tell the truth" should not surprise us either. For our sense that truth-telling can be universally practiced is based on our having a firm grasp of the related universal, a moral kind, which is right and good. And thinking of such a truth-telling world with vast intrinsic value accounts for our thinking well of it.

4. New Kantianism

The would-be murderer case had exiled Kantianism for much of the twentieth century. But Kant has recently made a comeback. New Kantians have attempted to save Kant by removing his absolutism, while defending his fundamental doctrines. Kant previously had the reputation of being an absolutist, one who holds that if a given kind of act is wrong, it is wrong without exception. New Kantians acknowledge that Kant's more incautious statements, especially those concerning the would-be murderer case, helped him earn his reputation. New Kantianism may be characterized briefly as Kantianism without the absolutism.

Rescuing Kant has required showing that he permits exceptions. We all know that it is morally permissible to lie when a murderous scoundrel is after your friend. But how is this consistent with Kantianism? Korsgaard shows how. On her account, by taking "lie to a deceiver" as our maxim, we can universalize it without any contradiction (Korsgaard, 1996b: 137). The key to doing this, and the key to New Kantianism, is to understand maxims in such a way that we are morally permitted in exigent circumstances what we would not ordinarily be permitted. Marcus Singer opened the path for this maneuver. The categorical imperative, he says, "cannot be applied to an action taken apart from any determinate context. It must always be applied to an action considered as taking place in certain circumstances, or for a certain purpose. The proof of this is that a reference to the circumstances and purpose of an action is *necessarily* involved in the 'maxim' of the action" (Singer, 1954: 590) (emphasis added). So rescuing Kant requires including the circumstances in the maxim of the actions we consider. All other New Kantians agree with this approach.

The first question is, is this Kant's view? When testing a maxim against the universal law formulation of the categorical imperative, must we include circumstances? There are many points in Kant's exposition of his theory that suggest that we *can* use circumstances in maxims, but there is no statement or indication that we *must*. In this case, as in others, Kant's way of speaking does not aid his cause. In his exposition he includes a number of things in maxims, some of which are questionable from the standpoint of his theory: occasions, intentions, circumstances, the epistemic state of the agent, motives, cost-benefit-based predictions, and actions.

Kant's writing often suggests that he holds what may be called the "open view of maxims," that any action-rule that can be put in sentence form can count as a maxim. Clearly, New Kantianism presupposes the open view of maxims. The chief problem with the open view is that it is employed by anti-Kantians to show the theory is absurd. And if the open view is the correct way to understand maxim formulation, then maxims such as "I will hold slaves if I am in a position of sufficient power" do show that Kantianism is morally absurd. So New Kantian reliance on the open view of maxims exposes New Kantians to the following dilemma. Kant can either be rescued from absolutism or from absurdity, but not both.

Here is why. If New Kantians are to save Kant from absolutism, then they must hold the open view of maxims. However, if they hold the open view, then Kant's theory is reduced to absurdity, as anti-Kantians have shown. Therefore, (C1), if they are to save Kant from absolutism, then Kant is reduced to absurdity. On the other hand, if New Kantians are to save Kant from absurdity, then they must give up the open view of maxims. If they give up the open view of maxims, then Kant cannot be saved from absolutism. Therefore, (C2) if they are to save Kant from absurdity, then Kant cannot be saved from absolutism. Combining (C1) and (C2), we conclude: Kantians can either save Kant from absolutism or absurdity, but not both.

But what is the alternative to the open view of maxims? What I call the "restricted view" of maxims is more consistent with Kant's entire theory, and it removes the threat posed by anti-Kantians. A maxim, on this view, includes an action, its components, and nothing else. A whole action is describable using common terms such as "walk," "throw," and "lie." The components of actions captured by maxims are intentions and motives. Kant's universality test initially tests the whole action. So the maxim "lie" would immediately fail the test.[8] The intention with which we lie would be irrelevant, so a maxim such as "lie to a deceiver" immediately is ruled out. But the converse does not hold. Just because a whole action such as "walk" initially passes the universality test does not mean it completely does. For if our intention is "step on the homeless man" then it will not pass the test. Finally, Kant holds that a nonuniversalizable motive can undermine an otherwise passable maxim.[9]

Absolutism is not the only of Kant's central doctrines New Kantians have abandoned. Kant held that the formula of universal law provides an effective method for solving any moral problem.[10] Use of this formula by New Kantians has been labeled the "CI-procedure," which, as Millgram points out, "is not technically a procedure or algorithm" (2003: 552).[11] What remains of Kant's universality test, however, is practical consistency. Conducting the CI-procedure, and, by doing so, discovering maxims that would be self-frustrating if universalized will result in our doing what is moral.[12]

What makes New Kantianism attractive is it is closer than Kantianism to our intuitive moral beliefs. But its moral explanations eliminate these gains. New Kantian explanations home in on an accidental property of moral action that if immoral action is ubiquitous, it will frustrate our own actions. What is left unexplained is how such a nonmoral property explains any moral property. From the intuitionist standpoint, employing the CI-procedure is epistemically unnecessary. We know that lying is wrong, so devising an elaborate apparatus of decision won't fortify that knowledge in any way. Nevertheless, we do welcome the New Kantians' interest in bringing circumstantial considerations into moral thinking. What may be called their "circumstantial imperative" brings Kantianism closer to intuitionism. And intuitionists cannot but consider that progress.

5. Utilitarianism

The intuitionist case against utilitarianism begins with an epistemic appraisal of the two theories' principles. Ross does this by consulting "what we really think" about morality (1930: 39), in actual moral situations. Suppose you find it inconvenient today to keep a promise you made last week. Realizing you should keep it, you think "it is wrong to break a promise," and regard that as sufficient reason not to. Ross compares this ordinary moral belief to the principle of utility in its generic form: "maximize good." When we consider breaking a promise to be wrong, the thought that it will not maximize good plays no role in persuading us to keep it.[13] And in fact when we are tempted to break a promise we often think of ways in which it would do the most good. Excuse making is often a utilitarian enterprise. So in such a situation, "breaking promises is wrong" is what we really think rather than "it will not maximize good."[14]

In an actual moral situation, the intuitionist belief for why we should do what is right is epistemically preferable to that of the utilitarian. Such comparative appraisal should be repeated for all of the intuitionist moral principles, "Harming others is wrong," "Lying is wrong," and so on, in the context of the relevant moral situations. The result will be that, any intuitionist principle will be found to be epistemically preferable to the principle of utility. Each intuitionist principle is evident to us in its corresponding kind of moral situation, while the principle of utility is never thus evident to us, except in situations where maximizing good is our actual duty.

As I mentioned previously, Mill epistemically appraised Kantianism against the intuitionist principles, and found Kantianism to be wanting. Interestingly, Mill does admit that intuitionist principles are epistemically preferable to the principle of utility (1957: 34), but thinks this a function of the way society has educated people. However, Mill seems also to think that we have implicit knowledge of the utility principle (1957: 6). That suggests that at some point it will seem as evident to us as the intuitive principles. It hasn't happened yet. And there is no evidence that it will.

The second mark against utilitarianism is based on implications of the utility principle. Many particular utilitarian prescriptions are morally absurd. To see, consider Case 1 in which Jones has two options: to lie or to not lie. The good produced can be any selected by a particular utilitarian theory: pleasure, well-being, or preference-satisfaction.

Case 1

Option A	*Option B*
Jones lies—produces 1,001 units of good	Jones does not lie—produces 1,000 units of good

Which choice is moral, Option A or B?[15] Option B, not lying, seems the moral choice. But suppose we adhere to utilitarianism. By employing the utilitarian principle, "maximize good," it appears the moral choice is Option A. The utilitarian would agree that Option B is what we normally think of as moral. But since the principle of utility accounts for what is moral, we shouldn't put much stock in what we normally think. Instead, since Option A would produce 1 more unit of good than Option B, the utilitarian is absurdly committed to Option A as the moral choice. Intuitionism claims we know that choosing Option A is morally absurd because it is self-evidently true that lying is wrong.

Here intuitionism relies once more on what we really think about morality to bolster the case against utilitarianism. We believe "Lying is wrong" in such situations with more confidence than we believe "it's wrong to produce less than maximal good." And so the previous point concerning the epistemic preferability of the intuitive principles supports the second point, that utilitarianism has absurd implications. The morally absurd implications of utilitarianism have long been recognized. The power of certain absurd counterexample intuitions continue to haunt utilitarianism, and have done more damage to it than a dozen arguments against it.[16]

What, it might be asked, are the implications of committing to intuitionism? Do any particular intuitionist absurdities arise? Intuitionist moral principles directly capture what is morally relevant and *only* what is morally relevant in each moral situation. For example, we believe we ought to keep our promises. Where keeping our promise is our actual duty, following the principle would simply mean keeping our promise, and no more. Thus intuitionist moral principles contain nothing morally extraneous that would generate morally absurd implications. That is why intuitionism, unlike utilitarianism, has no outstanding counterexamples against it.

6. Utilitarianism and action-guidance

Utilitarianism and intuitionism have long argued over which theory is better able to guide agents in moral situations. Historically, utilitarians have considered their principle as both an account of right action and as a decision procedure. They have expressly claimed that its ability to decide what to do in the face of conflicting obligations shows its superiority to intuitionism, which is asserted to have no "umpire" to decide such cases.[17] Because intuitionism, having only plural independent moral principles, eschews a single criterion of right action, it has been declared inadequate for action-guidance. Call this the "impracticable pluralism" objection.

Well, what are intuitionism's action-guiding capabilities? Intuitionism claims that we agents can recognize when we have one or more prima facie duty in a situation. When there is a conflict of prima facie duties our task is to determine which of them is most stringent, thus enabling us to do our actual duty. Ross addressed the impracticable pluralism objection by noting that utilitarianism is no better off in this respect. Ideal utilitarianism must contend with *plural goods* as hedonistic utilitarianism has *plural ways* of being pleased and displeased to grapple with (Ross, 1930: 23). Thus, if intuitionism has an impracticable pluralism problem, so does utilitarianism.

The action-guiding dispute is no longer prominent, because a 1971 paper by R. Eugene Bales seems to have settled it. Bales defended utilitarianism against several practicability objections that are spawned by the theory's action-guiding function. Bales states, "a systematic confusion runs throughout all such arguments" (1971: 257). The confusion of which he speaks is that the acceptance of the utilitarian "account of right-making characteristics somehow commits one *a priori* to a particular decision-making procedure" (Bales, 1971: 263). Everybody, including all utilitarians, were guilty of this confusion.[18] Bales' way of evading practicability objections is to assert that the principle of utility need not be action-guiding. This soon became the utilitarian consensus position.[19]

Utilitarians have essentially bowed out of the action-guiding dispute. While we should not put too much weight on the original intentions of utilitarians, it is significant that the only way for utilitarianism to survive as a theory is to give up the practical half of its program, one of its major selling points. So on the matter of which theory has principles by which to guide us, there is actually no contest. As a matter of fact, we *are* guided by "Lying is wrong," "Keeping promises is required," and so on. Even utilitarians recommend following the content of the intuitionist principles, while often considering them as merely "rules of thumb." Why? Because we can actually act on them.[20]

7. Utilitarianism and moral explanation

Despite these flaws in utilitarianism it seems to have one advantage over intuitionism. It has seemed to have explanatory promise where intuitionism has not. Utilitarian moral explanations advertise a number of attractive features. They are unified. They most often use one kind of value. And the chief explanatory factor—pleasure, well-being, or preference-satisfaction—is empirically accessible. All such features apparently give utilitarianism the edge over intuitionism in the explanation department. On the other side, intuitionism has seemed afflicted with explanatory impotence. Hopefully the intuitionist explanations in previous chapters have shown that at least this charge against intuitionism is mistaken.

But up to now it is understandable that utilitarianism seems stronger than intuitionism on moral explanation. The main reason things appear so is because intuitionism has tried to make do with the "right" alone. Having just reconnected intuitionism with the good, matters now appear differently. One result is that intuitionism and utilitarianism appear to have the same level of explanatory force. I must stress that "appear" is the operative word here. It has merely appeared to many that utilitarianism has explanatory power because it asserts that the good can explain the right, where early analytic intuitionism denied that possibility. My account of intuitionist moral explanation is that the right is truly explicable by good structured by moral kinds. Including the moral good in this way gives intuitionism greater explanatory force than utilitarianism.

I have made the case for intrinsically morally good actions. Including them has transformed the intuitionist-utilitarian debate. The principle "maximize good" takes on a wholly different meaning once all right actions are considered to be intrinsically good. One result is that the principle "maximize good," when considered alone, is not clearly and necessarily a utilitarian principle.

To see this, consider Case 2 involving Jones. In this case let us assign more nonmoral good in Option 1 than we did in Case 1. As before, the good that is being considered is any preferred by a particular utilitarian theory:

Case 2

Option 1	*Option 2*
Jones lies—produces 3,000 units of good	Jones does not lie—produces 1,000 units of good

In this situation, as in the previous one, Jones does not lie in Option 2. The difference in this case is that lying in Option 1 produces much greater value. Three thousand units of good are produced in Option 1 and Option 2 produces only 1,000 units of good. So choosing Option 1 produces three times the good as the second option.

Our response to this case is bound to be different from the first. We are likely to be less confident that Option 1 is obviously wrong. Although some of us will stick to Option 2, because Jones does what we normally regard as moral, some of us will judge that Option 1 is correct. Others will at least waver in their judgment. In considering Case 2, we will think about situations in which lying might produce much good. Perhaps a friend has asked for Jones's opinion on her new multicolored jacket. We might reason that by lying, Jones makes her happy, no one is hurt, and it is only a minor moral infraction.

The reason why Option 2 appears morally dubious is because utilitarians, as well as early analytic intuitionists, restricted the good involved to *nonmoral goods*, such as pleasure. Now, since there is a strong case for a distinct moral good, the exact same situation receives an entirely different evaluation, just by including the goodness of such actions. This time in evaluating Case 2, we will include the moral good, as well as the moral bad, along with the nonmoral goods. Option 1 now includes the intrinsic moral badness of lying. Option 2 includes the intrinsic good of not lying.

Case 2: Modified Intuitionism

Option 1	*Option 2*
Jones lies—produces 1,500 units of good	Jones does not lie—produces 2,000 units of good

A modified intuitionist assessment of Case 2 shows that "Maximize good" provides an entirely different evaluation of the same case, which results from including intrinsic moral values. Taking such values into account, the "maximize good" principle apparently explains why we should often do what is morally right, even if the alternative produces more nonmoral good.

If utilitarianism is right about the explanatory sufficiency of the "maximize good" principle, and if there is an intrinsic moral good, then intuitionism is explanatorily superior to utilitarianism. Once we interpret the "maximize good" principle intuitionistically, we have the conditions under which it won't often lead us astray, telling us to do what is amoral or even immoral. Also, from that perspective, we can see that utilitarianism, by excluding the moral good, often prescribes actions that produce *less than* the maximal good. That is, utilitarianism violates its own principle.

I am not arguing that the "maximize good" principle should be considered the supreme principle of morality. We have witnessed several pitfalls that its utilitarian interpretation has encountered. And given its current association in our minds with a nonmoral good, it is probably safer for now not to act on it exclusively. But despite being potentially hazardous for everyday use, "maximize good" will be useful for dealing with extreme situations. When something very horribly bad is bound to happen to many people if you do not lie, then by all means lie.[21] Since Ross, intuitionism and utilitarianism have agreed that producing the most good is moral. The difference is the "maximize good" principle is, for intuitionism, a prima facie duty like all the others, subject to being overridden by another principle, whereas utilitarians elevate it to a level of undisputed normative supremacy. The inclusion of the intrinsically morally good changes both sides of the discussion. If intrinsic moral goodness is embraced, the ways in which such intrinsic moral goods should be evaluated alongside the traditional nonmoral goods will have to be worked out.

An intuitionist interpretation of the "maximize good" principle as a supreme moral principle, although previously proposed, is problematic.[22] The principle does not contain information sufficient to guide us. In actual moral situations, we most often learn what is maximally good by knowing what is right. Lastly, often the maximal good is brought about by prudent action, not moral action, and so regarding the "maximize good" principle as a supreme principle of morality only confuses things.

Most utilitarians are unlikely to accept intrinsic moral goodness into their ontologies. But if we consider the principle "maximize good," anyone who is not already psychologically committed to utilitarianism, and who accepts that morally right actions are also morally good, will have to agree that the principle often favors intuitionist evaluations of moral cases. This forces the utilitarians to commit to some value-specific formulation of the principle, such as "always maximize pleasure." But this only deepens the ditch for utilitarianism. For clearly, such a principle is even weaker in an epistemic appraisal with the principles of intuitionism.

8. Virtue ethics

Virtue has recently received the respect it deserves in ethics. Initially, the central thrust of virtue ethics was clear: replace morality with virtue, moral action with virtuous agents. At the time it was revolutionary and was widely rejected for being so. More recently, however, virtue ethics has taken a curious turn, a *moral turn*. At the forefront of moralized virtue ethics are what may be called "exemplarist" moral theories. An exemplarist moral theory attempts to explain moral rightness by means of an exemplary agent, or by the virtues of such an exemplar. And where predecessors have shunned moral principles of any sort, recent virtue ethicists have offered not just moral principles, but what can be regarded as supreme principles of morality.

Supreme principles of morality in virtue ethics? That doesn't sound right. Well, let's take a look at Hursthouse's theory, for hers is the purest form of exemplarism. She offers what she considers the "first premise of an account of right action": "An action is right iff it is what a virtuous agent would characteristically . . . do in the circumstances" (Hursthouse, 1999: 28). Her theory is not the only one with "first premises." There are "first premises of act utilitarianism and deontology" as well (Hursthouse, 1999: 28). The first premise of utilitarianism is the principle of utility. Hursthouse claims that her first premise provides action-guidance and "can be regarded as generating a number of moral rules or principles" (1999: 17). So to review, Hursthouse's first premise aims to explain morally right action, is action-guiding, and can generate a number of moral rules. It is comparable to the principle of utility. It sure sounds like a supreme principle to me.[23]

The rules that Hursthouse's *exemplar principle* generates are virtue rules such as "Do not do what is dishonest." Such virtue rules in turn explain why we must not tell lies (Hursthouse, 1999: 39). Thus, Hursthouse's supreme principle appears capable of generating and explaining the intuitive principles we have been all along discussing.

I would like to leave Hursthouse's theory for the moment to examine the idea of an exemplar rule generally. Any exemplar principle can quickly be shown to be problematic. The question, "Why (morally) ought one to do *a*?" is ultimately answered by exemplarism with: because the exemplar, *Ex*, would do it. Suppose Jones follows this rule. Jones does not harm another person because the exemplar would not. But now suppose that the exemplar is in a situation similar to Jones's. Why should the exemplar not harm someone? If the proper rule to appeal to is the exemplar rule, then a curious result ensues. The exemplar must do *a* because, were *Ex* in a similar situation, *Ex* would do *a*. But now *Ex is* in a similar situation. So it follows that *Ex* ought to do *a* because *Ex* would do *a*. Where we expected an explanation, we instead find a sheer vacuity.

The virtue ethicist has a ready response to this result. "The exemplar has a reason to do *a*: flourishing." It is true that *Ex* would have the reason of flourishing to do *a*. And so flourishing might be thought to answer our previous question, "Why would *Ex* do *a*?" Fine. But a little reflection will show that flourishing will not free the exemplar rule from vacuousness. For the flourishing that would give *Ex* reason to *a* would be *Ex*'s flourishing, not my flourishing or yours. So the exemplarist must claim that I should do as *Ex* does for the sake of *Ex*'s flourishing. If, however, what is really meant is that I should do *a* ultimately for reason of my own flourishing, then *Ex* does not play the explanatory role we were told it does. In that case, we are left with the exemplar *Ex* only serving in an action-guiding role, and having only a loosely related part in explaining why anyone should *a*. Now it becomes clear why an exemplar principle should be introduced in the first place. A time-honored criticism of Aristotle's ethics was that flourishing cannot plausibly explain morality. The criticism is right. Flourishing cannot explain morality, although I do not think it's fair to regard this idea as Aristotle's moral theory.[24]

The fundamental flaw of exemplarism is it breaks down when it comes to explaining the morality of the exemplar's actions. Now let's test the moral principles offered by the main exemplarists, Hursthouse and Swanton. A study of two characters will help us to do so. The first one is Adams, a struggling entrepreneur. Adams displays a great deal of fortitude in starting up a company. So what she does is virtuous. However, there is nothing morally binding Adams to the whole undertaking. If she decides to close shop, she will have done nothing immoral.

Robinson presents a different kind of case. He is a cowardly right-doer. Robinson seriously considered doing a favor for Taylor, a shady character. Taylor asked Robinson to carry a package with unspecified contents on a flight to Bogata, to give it to a man with a blue hat in his hotel lobby, then return with another package the man was to give him. Robinson never had a scruple about delivering the package for Taylor. In fact, the idea of doing something that would likely break the law greatly excited him. So why did he decline to do it? His cowardice allowed him to panic and forced him to do the right thing. His action was morally right, but definitely not virtuous.

Now, consider the following virtue principle, V: *An action is right if and only if it is virtuous.* This appears to be the principle underlying the exemplar principle just discussed, as well as other virtue principles. Depending on how "virtuous" is understood, three particular principles can come out of V:

V^1: An action is right if and only if it is what the exemplar would do.

V^2: An action is right if and only if it is what is expressed by a particular virtue.

V^3: An action is right if and only if it hits the target of a particular virtue.

V^1 comes from taking "virtuous" to mean "what the exemplar would do." V^2 comes from taking "virtuous" to mean "what is expressed by a particular virtue." V^3 comes from taking "virtuous" to mean "hits the target of a particular virtue." Hursthouse, as we have seen, holds a version of V^1, Swanton a version of V^3.[25]

The vice of V (and its first two offshoots) is that it falls apart on both its necessary and sufficient conditions. A more perspicuous formulation of V is "In order for an action to be morally right, it is necessary and sufficient that it be virtuous." The sufficient condition in V is "being virtuous is sufficient for an action to be right." That is, if an action is virtuous then it is morally right. Adams exhibits a great deal of fortitude in setting up a company. There is nothing moral, either right or wrong, about Adams doing so. Thus we have a counterexample to V's sufficient condition. The necessary condition in V may be expressed as "being virtuous is necessary for an action to be right." So if an action is not virtuous, then it is not right. By refusing to break the law, what Robinson did was right but not virtuous, thus undermining V's necessary condition.

Swanton's "target principle" (V^3) might be thought to escape this problem.[26] But notice, it appears to because it detaches the action completely from virtue and relies solely on what the virtue *aims at*. Even though the separation from virtue has made for a more plausible moral theory, for the theory to be virtue-ethical virtue itself must be the primary concept in explaining what makes actions morally right.[27] And this theory makes virtue seem to be only accidentally related to right action. But does this theory explain the rightness of actions? I would say that it does not. For it seems that all the target principle shows is that certain virtues *aim at* what is morally right. That is true and is only disputed by certain virtue ethicists. But the fact that an archer aims at a target does nothing to explain the target. Likewise, simply because some virtues aim at morality does nothing to explain morality.

A kind of exemplar rule, "An action is right if and only if it would likely be done by the exemplar," is clearly intuitively plausible. It is also true. But just because it is true does not mean it explains moral rightness. To see why, consider two possible explanations for one moral proposition: Stealing is wrong, represented by p. Explanation 1 for p is that the exemplar would not likely steal. Explanation 2 for p is that stealing tends to produce less than maximal utility than the alternative option. Just because Explanation 1 is true and p is true does not mean that Explanation 1 explains p. Why? Because Explanation 2 is true as well, yet it is not clear that it explains p. It is true that both stealing is wrong and the exemplary person would probably not steal. But such agreement in truth value between these apparently related propositions does not imply that one explains the other. Likewise, no anti-utilitarian would deny that moral actions tend to maximize utility. But they will deny that an action's maximizing tendencies explain its morality.

In 1912, H. A. Prichard stated that, "an obligation can no more be based on or derived from a virtue than a virtue can be derived from an obligation" (1912: 33). From our examination, I can't see that exemplarism has done anything to budge, let alone overturn, Prichard's statement. How *could* an obligation be based on a virtue?

So what is virtue's place in ethics? A virtue *theory* need not be a comprehensive ethics like the moral philosophy of old. A comprehensive systematic ethics requires both morality and virtue. Otherwise, how to explain the complex notion of virtuous action? A division of labor between moral theory and virtue theory results. Where appropriate, areteic concepts can go to work to explain certain moral phenomena, such as moral motivation. And for its part, moral theory can explain other moral phenomena, such as the content of morality.[28] Coming together, moral theory and virtue theory could forge a systematic ethics, one that could explain and guide moral action.

9. Criteria of right action

Supreme principles do not and cannot function as their advocates claim. The intuitionist orientation toward each supreme principle theory stems from the point from which we began. We know what's right. Such knowledge is what each rival theory draws from to make its case. And such knowledge also shows us just where intuitionism's rivals are absurd.

However, the practical value of any plausible criterion of right action is undeniable. Included among such principles are the principle of utility, the categorical imperative, in both formulas mentioned, the exemplar principle, and the golden rule. In a moral situation, each one of these principles can direct our minds away from thoughts that can interfere with moral thinking, and aid us in thinking objectively about the situation. For example, suppose I am questioning whether I really promised to help you move to a new dwelling this Saturday, my day off. You understood me to do so. If I ask, "Am I treating this person as I would want to be treated?," my thinking can gain great clarity. If I determine that I would not want to be so treated, I will decide it is right in this instance to help you move. From the intuitionist standpoint, my reflecting on the golden rule has helped me to think objectively about whether my original assertion to you was a promise. Having decided it could naturally be interpreted as one tells me all I need to guide my action.

What, after all, has driven the quest for a supreme principle? A few things. The belief that a desideratum of a moral theory is to provide *distinct* epistemic backing for any intuitive moral principle or action, that the only legitimate structure of epistemic justification is the binary one, and finally that in order to justify or explain a particular intuitive principle we must turn to a supreme principle upon which we can act. We have already revealed problems with the first two supreme principle rationales. Concerning the third, there is no reason to assume that an explanation for a particular moral principle must itself be a moral principle. An explanation of a moral principle can be a theory that makes no claim to guide action, such as the theory of moral kinds.

10. The incorporation project

Whether a moral principle is to be counted as intuitionist is an open-ended matter. There are two requisites for any principle to count as one of the intuitive principles. It must be self-evidently true, and it must not be assumed to be a supreme principle. Although many moral principles are widely enough believed to be considered "commonsense morality," there is no requirement that most people believe a moral principle for it to count as intuitionistic. Also, intuitionists have no undying allegiance to a particular set of proffered moral principles, such as Ross's, just because they were introduced by a prominent intuitionist.

Intuitionism embraces any self-evident moral principle, even those from theories opposed to it. Ross claimed that "Doing the most good is right" is a self-evident moral principle. He was unabashed by the fact that it closely resembles the principle of utility. The difference between Ross's principle and the principle of utility is found in one word: "always." Ross's principle lacks it, while it is essential to utilitarianism. Since there are times when it would be wrong to maximize the nonmoral good, Ross's principle is epistemically preferable to the principle of utility. Another strong candidate for inclusion is Kant's principle of humanity: "Act in such a way that you always treat humanity, whether in your own person or in the person of any other, never simply as a means, but always at the same time as an end." Audi argues that this principle is self-evident, and so should be included among other traditional intuitionist principles. The fact that it appears to be a principle of higher generality, and wider scope, only means that it can be used to illuminate more specific intuitionist principles.[29]

A strategy emerges from these reflections. Intuitionism must incorporate any moral principle that is self-evident. This is not to say inclusion of a new moral principle should proceed with haste. Testing the intuitiveness and theoretical adequacy of a moral principle should be conducted continually. However, in order to effectively do this we must abandon a traditional framework for ethical theorizing. The overarching aim is to find the moral truth. Given that, we cannot be overly concerned about how ethicists previously have seen fit to do this. More specifically, we cannot place too much weight on the common practice in ethics of "school positioning." School positioning is the practice of dividing the ethics landscape into rival camps, making sure that the statements of the original theorists are forever assigned to their respective camps, and resisting any attempts to form theories that appear to mix claims from the different "schools."

Correct classification is vitally important in philosophy. But our main classificatory enterprise is to categorize things, not theories. Ethics is too serious a business to allow overzealous taxonomists to dictate the terms of inquiry. The fact that Kant formulated an important moral principle is of secondary theoretical importance, however historically important it might be. Its being self-evident, if it is, is what really matters. As the incorporation project proceeds there are likely to be protests from other ethicists. But once enough ethicists see that rivals to intuitionism carry too many demerits, see that ethical truth is potentially near at hand, and see the many ways in which intuitionism opens up new avenues of inquiry, then resistance to the incorporation project will lessen. When that occurs, our efforts at taxonomy will be fruitfully directed at classifying and investigating kinds of actions, rather than kinds of theories.

11. Chapter summary

Intuitionism and its normative rivals agree that morality is an objective matter. Intuitionism differs from the rest in focusing on the moral propositions with the greatest epistemic weight, the intuitive principles. Also, intuitionism, at least on my account, looks into the nature of the acts referenced by these principles for why they are right or wrong. Other normative ethical theories look outward for justification or explanation. Kantianism looks toward reason itself for answers. Utilitarianism scans the overall consequences for moral enlightenment. Virtue ethics of the exemplarist sort seeks out the exemplar for guidance. But all the while each normative rival employs and bases its case on the intuitive principles. Epistemic appraisal shows each rival to be wanting. Also, each supreme principle breaks down when confronted with counterexample intuitions. Nor is the proper use of any supreme principle settled, even among its adherents. None of this is to say that criteria of right action are useless. In practical situations considering the rival principles I cover here can help us to objectively identify what is right.

Further reading

Two outstanding introductions to normative ethics are Kagan's *Normative Ethics* (1998) and Timmons' *Moral Theory: An Introduction* (2002). Kagan's approach is analytical, in that it examines, combines, and compares key ethical concepts to evaluate different theories. Timmons directly examines different schools of thought.

CHAPTER EIGHT

Practical and ultimate moral issues

Introduction

Defending and explaining the theory of intuitionism has been the aim of this book. I have not attempted a comprehensive, systematic work on the matter, only a brief case for it. In many respects I have concentrated on the middle range of issues in ethics. There are two directions in which this book has been thus far incomplete: the practical direction and the ultimate direction.

Without touching upon practice, intuitionism is incomplete. To know what we ought morally to do we must know what is right. So the most pressing practical matter is the content of morality. Exactly what moral principles does intuitionism endorse? This chapter explores the matter. Intuitionism has often been criticized for being unable to guide action, for not having a decision procedure. I argue that intuitionism's open approach to deliberation is actually a strength. Next, I will ask what reason intuitionism gives us to be moral and what motivates people to do what is right. I will answer both questions from the standpoint that we do, in fact, have moral knowledge.

Finally, I briefly address the ultimate issues of ethics, the other direction in which this book has been incomplete. How is it that the universe contains morality? Is intuitionism, with its timeless moral truths, not ruled out by evolution? Lastly, is God necessary for there to be objective morality?

1. Which principles?

Someone familiar with writings of different intuitionists would ask, "*which list* of principles is right?" Throughout this book I have mentioned several intuitive moral principles: it is wrong to lie, harming others is wrong, keeping promises is required, and several others. I acknowledge the incompleteness of the list, and make no attempt now to complete it. Rather, I will provide the lists given by other intuitionists, and say how I think they ought to be treated.

It is natural to start with Ross's self-evident principles, for his are most frequently examined. One problem accompanies discussing Ross's list. It is not clear what it is a list of. A careful reading of the passages in which he seems to list his prima facie duties affords two interpretations of the list's purpose. The most common interpretation is that he is simply listing the fundamental moral *duties*, an interpretation Ross seems to hold. Alternatively, he may be presenting *categories* of duties.

What he states is, "Of *prima facie* duties I suggest, without claiming completeness or finality for it, the following division" (Ross, 1930: 20). Unfortunately, this quote, along with others, supports both interpretations. But four considerations incline me toward the categories interpretation, whether Ross intended that view. First, one clear purpose in stating his division is to lay out "all the ways in which *prima facie* duties arise" (Ross, 1930: 27). Second, Ross states, there are "duties that may be summed up under the title of 'not injuring others'" (1930: 21), what we have discussed as the duty not to harm. In this, as in all other categories of duty, Ross speaks of them in the plural: duties of justice, duties of gratitude, and so on. Third, in the midst of discussing the duty not to harm, Ross says: "The recognition of this duty of nonmaleficence is the first step on the way to the recognition of the duty of beneficence; and that accounts for the prominence of the commands 'thou shalt not kill,' 'thou shalt not commit adultery,' 'thou shalt not steal,' 'thou shalt not bear false witness,' in so early a code as the Decalogue" (1930: 22). Each of these commands seems to be self-evident and to be based on kinds of acts that are by their very nature wrong. Lastly, remember that Ross claims that there are a number of moral relations besides that of being a possible beneficiary of one's action: creditor-debtor, wife-husband, child-parent, friend-friend, and so on. Well, "each of these relations is the foundation of a *prima facie* duty" (Ross, 1930: 19). Each is presented in this passage as being on the same level as the promise relations. Since Ross holds that the promise principle is self-evident, all the duties based on these other moral relations should also be self-evident.

I now give Ross's division, followed by the duties given by contemporary intuitionists:

Ross

1 Duties of reparation.

2 Duties of fidelity.

3 Duties of gratitude.

4 Duties of justice.

5 Duties of beneficence.

6 Duties of self-improvement.

7 Duties of nonmaleficence.

Audi[1]

1 We should not injure or harm people.

2 We should not lie.

3 We should keep our promises.

4 We should not treat people unjustly and should contribute to rectifying injustice and to preventing future injustice.

5 We should make amends for our wrongdoing.

6 We should contribute to the good of other people.

7 We should express gratitude in a way that befits good things done for us by other people.

8 We should develop or at least sustain our distinctively human capacities.

9 We should contribute to increasing or at least preserving the freedom of persons.

10 We should, in the manner of our relations with other people, treat them respectfully.

Shafer-Landau provides examples of self-evident moral propositions, not a fundamental list. Huemer also only provides examples of general moral intuitions. But their selections are significant, as we will see.[2]

Shafer-Landau

1 It is wrong to take pleasure in another's pain.

2 It is wrong to taunt and threaten the vulnerable.

3 It is wrong to prosecute and punish those known to be innocent.

4 It is wrong to sell another's secrets solely for personal gain.

Huemer

1 Enjoyment is better than suffering.

2 If A is better than B and B is better than C, then A is better than C.

3 It is unjust to punish a person for a crime he did not commit.

4 Courage, benevolence, and honesty are virtues.

5 If a person has a right to do something, then no person has a right to forcibly prevent him from doing that thing.

We notice immediately the intuitive principles differ widely from intuitionist to intuitionist. Ross apparently gives us only categories of duties. Audi's principles tell us what we *should* do. Shafer-Landau's inform us of what is wrong. And Huemer's principles are various, some making abstract claims of comparative value, one telling us what is unjust, another identifying virtues, and still another telling us what we have no right to do.

The discrepant lists raise various questions. The core one is, what are the intuitionist principles? Next, on what basis should we accept or reject any supposed principle? Are the intuitionist principles all on the same level? Or are some lower-order, others higher-order, principles?

Unfortunately, we can't sort all this out here. But previously discussed points should guide us when undertaking the task. On my account, what we know are that certain actions are right and that others are wrong. So principles that inform us of what is right and what is wrong are preferred to those stating "oughts." The theory of moral kinds holds that each action that is wrong is wrong by its very nature. This suggests that there are many self-evident principles. Although murdering, assaulting, and raping all involve harming another, each has a distinctive nature, and each involves harming another in a distinctive way. So "Murder is wrong," "Assaulting is wrong," and "Rape is wrong" are all self-evident on my view. They cannot be reduced to or fully explained by "Harming others is wrong." This indicates that the intuitive principles will be expansive and include many principles not discussed in this book. Although right and wrong are the main practical moral issue, self-evident value principles must be included as well. With these few guidelines the above lists should be gathered together, divided by category, and sorted out. Then we can eliminate those that are redundant or for which we do not find strong enough intuitions.

2. Moral decisions

A moral theory must have something to say about moral decision. Intuitionism's theory of moral decision has often been criticized for not providing moral guidance. It does not tell us *how* to decide what's right. Intuitionism has been faulted for not having a "decision procedure," equipment other moral theories claim to have. Thus, intuitionism is practically incomplete. Although this incompleteness is often considered a flaw of intuitionism, I will argue that it is a virtue of the theory.

A false picture of intuitionism on moral decisions has emerged. It depicts an agent who is facing a tough moral decision. This agent finds that, say, the prima facie duty principle "Harming others is wrong" is in conflict with the prima facie duty "Helping others in need is right." Then, with no aid of a supreme principle, he must decide, by considering which principle is more of a duty here, which principle represents his actual duty. This picture is not false because moral principles are involved. It is false merely because it misleads as to the way they are involved.

An agent in an actual moral situation need not be aware of moral principles being involved at all. Rather, he recognizes and guides himself by *kinds* of actions. He recognizes that, in this case, it appears to him that one course of action, because it would harm someone, would be wrong. The other course of action, because it would help others in need, would be right. By thinking about the situation and about the kinds of acts being contemplated, the agent must try to determine the morally best course of action. Moral decision, then, involves agents thinking *with* the intuitive principles, not about them.

Intuitionism is practically incomplete. But not because of its tenets. It is incomplete because it is a moral theory, and all moral theories are practically incomplete. Leveling the charge of practical incompleteness against intuitionism assumes that moral theory *can* provide a procedure for deciding difficult moral quandaries. Moral theorists have long believed that deciding what's right requires a supreme moral principle. Such views are *deliberatively closed*: they hold that their supreme principle is necessary and sufficient for acting morally. Without it, it is suggested, we are at best making good moral guesses. At worst we are flying blindly through moral hazards. But rival theories like Kantianism and utilitarianism do not have decision procedures in any helpful sense, and, where action is concerned, they both often fall back on the intuitive principles, probably because we can actually act on them.[3] So once again, intuitionism's rivals are living off of their promises, but this time it is not explanatory promise but *practicability promise*—the promise of effectively guiding our actions.

Intuitionism has been criticized for lacking a decision procedure. It would be more proper to say that intuitionism has no supreme principle, and leave it at that. Unlike its rivals, intuitionism does not make a promise for facilitating moral decision on which it cannot deliver. Moral reasons, or moral principles, are neither necessary nor sufficient reasons, or principles, for acting morally. So it is a virtue, not a defect, of intuitionism that it is a *deliberatively open* moral theory.

Moral reasons are not necessary for one to act morally. Take the moral rule "do not lie." At first glance, it seems that in order for me to not lie to you, I must follow the rule not to lie, or I must act on the moral reason not to lie. But none of that is necessary. By not talking to you at all, I don't lie to you. Likewise, by not promising you anything, I do not break any promise. And if I avoid you altogether, then I don't harm you. In each of these cases, I don't wrong you without relating to moral reasons or rules in any way. You cannot even say that I am "following the rule without intentionally following it."

Morality is also not sufficient for one to act morally. Suppose Johnson has sincerely vowed to uphold his marital vows. He has never thought of cheating on his wife. One day, as he drops his wife at the airport, they get in a horribly heated argument. Afterwards, he drives to the house of his attractive colleague, Robinson, for dinner, a meeting of which his wife is aware. Although Johnson has never entertained the idea of intimate congress with Robinson, she has. On this night on which Johnson is especially vulnerable, Robinson works her charms, fine food and wine, soft lighting and enthralling music. Robinson's campaign is ultimately effective.

Several responses to the story suggest themselves. Johnson ought to have avoided the dinner. He should have exercised greater will power. Or he ought to have headed off Robinson's maneuvers as they began to take effect. All good suggestions. But none of these "ought's" is a moral one, although following them would have had a moral result.

3. Moral risk

There is moral risk in every action we take.[4] But don't we sometimes know exactly what's right? Recall that we are certain only of the intuitive principles, when considered alone. In actual situations we often have at best rational belief of what course of action is right. This claim alone is enough to establish the ubiquity of moral risk. For Ross, however, the main consideration that justifies his claim is consequences. Our acts have many consequences of which we cannot be aware. Some benefit others in unexpected ways, and others harm others just as unexpectedly.

The fact of moral risk puts an additional burden on us. It is difficult enough to act on what we think to be right. But we must also find ways of reducing moral risk. Ethicists characteristically think that reducing or eliminating moral risk can be done through moral considerations alone. This thought, it seems to me, partly accounts for the quest for a foolproof decision procedure. It has been argued that Kant's moral theory, with its categorical imperative reigning supreme, aimed to eliminate moral luck.[5] Whether or not that is correct, thinking that the way to manage moral risk is by moral principles is a mistake. Principles and procedures for assessing and reducing risk are not plausibly moral in content. It seems that something else besides morality is needed here.

Good judgment is certainly needed in such cases. But ethicists have not expended nearly as much energy on explaining what good judgment is, or how to develop it, as they have on identifying challenges to it, like moral luck. Consider some of the ways in which applying intuitionist principles to particular situations poses difficulties. In our own lives, it seems, the difficult moral situations are not, as many ethicists assume, most often ones in which the problem confronting us is of the sort "Should I lie in this case?" Often, the problem we face is "Is this a lie?," "Would this be a breach of faith?," or "Would this be a wrongful harm?" In other words, one of our greatest challenges has to do with *identifying* whether an action we consider is the *kind* of action that is wrong to do.[6]

Such situations don't give us the information we need to act morally. Our moral information is vague and incomplete. And there is no mechanical procedure to improve or increase our information in order to know what to do. It is often mistakenly assumed that the vagueness or incompleteness of such situational factors can be made precise or complete through moral theory. Furthermore, it is assumed that the increased precision and completeness of information will be found, not in the world, but in a supreme principle grasped by the mind. But this cannot work, and here is why. If I cannot even say for sure that by doing *a* that I am lying, what maxim could I possibly formulate to put to Kant's universality test? Neither can I be sure that I am employing a secondary principle such as "Do not lie," which is implied by the utility principle. The point is that if it is unclear that the "Do not lie" principle covers this case, then any supreme principle that is supposed to imply it would not be of any help here. To remedy such situations it seems that something entirely other than moral considerations is needed.

Moral discernment is necessary for deciding what's right. But it is not enough. What is vitally crucial for agents to handle present and anticipated moral difficulties is prudence. Developing greater will power to deal with situations such as Johnson's, and for tempting situations generally, is a matter of prudence. Heading off a tempting situation before it overwhelms us is also highly prudent. What is necessary for us to reduce moral risks as much as possible is prudence. And in order to deal with moral situations in which the information we have is lacking, only prudence can see us through. In brief we need *moral prudence* to determine what action is right and, equally critically, to succeed in doing what's right.

4. Between thought and action

Even if we are sure that we know what's right, doing the right thing is uncertain. Between thought and action there are many hazards we face. Though identifying what is right can give us the end of our action, we also require effective means to act rightly. So prudent action is necessary to acting morally, even if we could have perfect moral information, which clearly we cannot.

Ross's theory provides tools for addressing this problem. They may be found in a brief but suggestive discussion of what he calls "consequential duties" (Ross, 1930: 22). Here I interpret and draw out some implications of his discussion in view of prudential considerations. For Ross, "primary duties" are those that are the proper moral *end* of our actions. Consequential duties are the *means* to achieving such moral ends. These are not additional categories of duties, just moral ends and their related means. To see the differences and relations between primary and consequential duties, consider the matter of harming others. The primary duty is to not harm others. Ross considers two consequential duties that may serve this primary duty. An agent might have to deal with one, the other, or both in order to not harm another. We may have to resist an inclination to harm others. Or we may have to resist an inclination to satisfy ourselves in a situation in which doing so incidentally harms someone else. "Resist your inclination to harm another" is one consequential duty; "Resist your inclination to satisfy yourself" is the other consequential duty.

Neither consequential duty is an actual duty. But in an actual moral situation, following a consequential duty will have the effect of doing one's duty. Thus consequential duties serve primary duties. It must be emphasized that particular consequential duties are only so because of a primary duty they may serve. Without the duty not to harm others, "Resist your inclination to harm another" is not a consequential duty. Quite importantly, consequential duties arise not only because of a primary duty at hand, but also because of the situation, as well as one's particular character and psychology. Consider a single situation in which Jones is vulnerable to harm. Taylor, an angry person, will have to heed the consequential duty to resist harming Jones. Wilson, on the other hand, is quite selfish. In the particular situation in which the action he is inclined to do will likely harm Jones, he will have to resist his inclination to satisfy himself in order not to harm Jones.

Both agents in this case have the same primary duty: not to harm Jones. Consequential duties, in contrast, in highly similar situations, can differ between agents. This informs us that consequential duties are a matter of prudence. One thing that separates morality from prudence is that what is moral is the same for all. What is prudent for you, in contrast, is not necessarily prudent for me. Since what is a consequential duty for you is not necessarily a consequential duty for me, consequential duties are prudential matters. Supporting this is the fact that failing in one's consequential duty is not necessarily violating a primary duty. Wilson, for example, may succumb to his inclination to satisfy himself, but manage to change his course of action before Jones is harmed.

Returning to the Johnson case will allow us to flesh this out. His primary duty is to remain faithful to his wife. He's aware of this duty and is committed wholeheartedly to abiding by it. In our story, Johnson fails in his duty because of moral weakness. As we all recognize, Johnson could have been saved the trouble of having to grapple with his moral weakness if only he had followed the prudential principle, "Avoid trouble." Where the prospect of a tempting moral situation lurks, our consequential duty is to avoid the situation. Once in the situation, Johnson is given more than one opportunity to meet his primary duty. In any situation we encounter, it is prudent to "Be aware of one's situation," including one's responses to what is happening. Johnson has failed his consequential duty to head things off when there are signs that Robinson is seducing him. Lastly, when Johnson realizes what is going on, he fails his consequential duty to resist his inclination to copulate with Robinson. To sum up Johnson's case, the main thing he failed in was remaining faithful to his wife, his primary duty.

But his imprudence allowed him to fail each consequential duty as it arose.

We now may see how prudence equips us to handle situations of vague or incomplete moral information. We have all been told things in private. Sometimes we are sworn to secrecy. Other times we are not sure, as we have been given no explicit instructions of concealment. In such cases, once more, the question is not whether we should break a confidence. It is whether there is a confidence to keep at all. The moral risk is obvious for such situations. But no moral principle can aid us in reducing it. Although the problem is moral, the means by which to solve it isn't.

The morally prudential principle, "When you think an act might be morally wrong, play it safe and act as if it is" is what best guides us here. The uncertain moral danger of breaking a confidence implies a consequential duty of playing it safe and acting as if the information you received was given in confidence. We are also to play it safe when we are not sure whether what we are about to say is a lie, and the same goes for cases in which we think a course of action might break a promise. Playing it safe is a consequential duty for vague or uncertain situations in which not breaking a confidence, not telling a lie or keeping a promise is the primary duty.

5. The prudence dependency thesis

Moral weakness, according to Hare, is the central difficulty of the moral life.[7] I unhesitatingly agree. Unfortunately, ethics has ignored this supremely important matter. And ethics has neglected to study what Ross calls consequential duties, the means we actually have to employ to succeed in doing right. What accounts for these neglects is the fixation of contemporary ethics on morality. Its predominant foundational concern is to determine whether moral acts, moral agents, or good moral consequences is the subject matter of ethics.

But as I have pointed out, there are assessment problems, risk management problems, and implementation problems of doing what is morally right, which are outside the purview of morality. These issues point to areas in which the moral "oughts" *underdetermine* what we ought to do. Because such problems confront us in our actual moral life, no deliberatively closed moral system is equipped to deal with them. While it is true that Ross did not identify prudence as the missing piece of the moral decision puzzle, investigating his perspicacious insights into moral risk and consequential duties will move ethics in the right direction. The deliberatively open structure of intuitionism naturally fits it to receive the wide-ranging, manifold, and effective support of prudence.

We can agree that where moral decision is concerned intuitionism has been missing something. But that something, a systemic, integrated inclusion of prudence, has been missing from every contemporary moral theory. Since prudence supports morality in action, relating them so that prudence can give agents the effective practical leverage over moral problems requires we consider matters from the agent's perspective. The insight that ties together the two supreme normative authorities, morality and prudence, is the "prudence dependency thesis," *one cannot be a moral person without being prudent.*[8]

6. Moral knowledge again

Moral knowledge is the chief ethics issue. Intuitionism is distinctive in claiming straightway that we know what's right. The conviction responsible for the content and structure of this book is that once we accept our moral knowledge, ethics advances by investigating and trying to understand all the implications of having it. Unearthing such implications requires examining what makes moral knowledge possible. The primary explanation of moral knowledge is self-evidence. To determine what exactly we know requires reflecting on how morality seems to us in actual moral contexts.

The alternative, predominant approach to ethics is to begin by doubting our moral knowledge, and ignoring or diminishing the fact that our moral reflections and experiences do result in moral intuitions a great many others share. The strategy is to bracket our moral knowledge, while implicitly assuming what's moral, then trying to justify positions on all topics other than moral knowledge, thinking that somehow, some way, we can see whether we can have moral knowledge. Two areas in which we can see this approach at work are moral motivation and what reason we have to do what is right. These seem like large problems, I claim, only because we are ignoring or downplaying the basic fact that we do have moral knowledge. If, instead, we accept our moral knowledge, then these problems will remain, in that we still need accounts of them, but they will be considered philosophical puzzles, and not hooks upon which the fate of morality hangs.

The problem of moral motivation is a central issue in contemporary ethics. I think it is too central. Michael Smith claims that reconciling moral realism with the problem of moral motivation is "the central organizing problem in contemporary meta-ethics," which he calls "the moral problem" (1994: 11). If this assessment holds today, then one half of the moral problem, the motivation part, signals a misplacement of priorities in metaethics. For as I will argue, possessing moral knowledge alters our perception of its significance.

7. The motivation problem

What theory best explains being motivated to do what is right? Moral motivation is quite often thought to show that intuitionism and other kinds of moral realism are false. Here is how. Intuitionism holds that there are moral facts. We have moral knowledge when we have justified true beliefs of such facts. The content of such beliefs is descriptive. And the content involves either a description of an act being wrong or being right.

The motivation problem argument rests on such claims. There are several forms of it. But here is a simplified version of it (M):

1 Every moral judgment motivates all by itself.

2 Factual judgments cannot motivate all by themselves.

3 Therefore moral judgments are not factual judgments. (Shafer-Landau, 2005: 516)

This sort of argument is put forth by expressivists. They do so because they think that, compared with moral realists, they have a better account of moral motivation. We are motivated by but one thing, on this Humean view: desire. Desire is the only human capacity that can move us to act. Coupled with this view of moral motivation is the expressivists' claim that moral judgments are merely expressions of feeling, not judgments about the world. So there are no moral facts. The argument from moral motivation achieves two aims. It puts intuitionists on the defensive concerning motivation and concludes with the expressivist position on moral judgment.

To defend intuitionism, I need only reveal flaws in one of the above premises. But both premises are vulnerable. Take the first one. The behavior of some people should make us pause in endorsing the first premise. They make moral judgments, but are unmotivated by them. They say, "Sure, adultery is wrong, but I'll do it anyway." Such people are called "amoralists." Consider the lyrics of a popular 1970's song by Luther Ingram about a man involved in an extramarital affair, "If Loving You Is Wrong I Don't Wanna Be Right":

If loving you is wrong, I don't wanna be right.

If being right means being without you,

I'd rather live a wrong doing life.

Aside from the musical merits of the song, it was not popular because it described an impossible combination of motives and facts. It tells a story about the sort of thing that happens. Taking amoralists into account, it seems the first premise of argument (M) is false.

The second premise is equally problematic. Is it possible that a factual judgment can motivate us to act, with desire playing no role? Yes. There are cases in which all a person's desires are pulling him in one direction, while his judgment of his duty pulls him in the opposite direction, and he acts on his duty. Shafer-Landau describes what actors in such a situation are thinking: "I wanted to give in, yield to my desires. I didn't because I thought it would be wrong to do so. I didn't *want* to x (stand in front of that bullet, accept the blame, remain chaste) but duty called. I knew what had to be done, and did it, desires . . . be damned" (2003: 123).

The claim that moral facts cannot motivate us is based on a pattern of error we have previously seen. It is true that knowing facts about material states of affairs cannot alone motivate us. We need an additional independent motive that matches such facts to move us. But just because material facts cannot motivate us to act does not imply that mixed nonnatural-natural factual moral judgments cannot move us to act. Once again, morality is different from every-thing else. The opponent of intuitionism begins with material facts, and gets us to agree that such facts cannot be intrinsically motivat-ing. But we need a separate argument to show that facts of the kind we are investigating—nonnatural-natural moral facts—cannot do so. And no one to date has produced such an argument.

But there is a more fundamental problem with the argument from moral motivation: its originators, the expressivists. Theories in ethics, as everywhere else, ought to be compared as wholes. The contemporary practice of fighting out the finer points of the-ory in journal articles often obscures this requirement of reason. Expressivism says that it satisfactorily explains our motive to act morally but insists that there is no morality. Intuitionism says there is morality, we know what's right, but challenges the underlying claim of expressivism that desire is the only way we can be moti-vated to act. I ask now, which theory is more coherent?

Our moral knowledge also helps us to grapple with a related question, why should we be moral at all? This is often considered a pressing question. It is put most clearly by asking if what is right and what is in your interest conflict, why do what is right? Such conflicts undoubtedly arise at many points. The crucial case to con-sider is where one can benefit by doing wrong, and get away with it. Intuitionism holds that the right act contains reasons *in itself* to do it. Such acts are right and good. Beyond that, the basic point that you *know* what's right gives very good external reasons to act morally. Given our moral knowledge, we should do what's right in each case. People who do wrong and know they are doing wrong regret it. Regret diminishes happiness. So those who knowingly do wrong will either lower their intellectual integrity, by denying what they know, or be less happy. Either way, the external reasons to do right are to protect some personal good.

8. The ultimate issues

Moral theory has some limits that frustrate our desire to know all the answers. There are a number of things about intuition-ism, especially about the form I have argued for, which only raise further questions. At length I've defended the notion that there are self-evident moral propositions. I have argued for nonnatural moral properties and moral grounds. Good and right exist, but not in the way spatiotemporal objects do. More, I claimed that there are abstract universal kinds, such as lying, murdering, and so on, which our minds grasp. Directly grasping these kinds can afford a priori moral knowledge.

The big questions intuitionism raises are many. How did non-natural facts get here? How can we possibly have a priori moral knowledge? Does that mean this knowledge is innate? How is this whole account of morality consistent with what we know about our evolutionary history? Does intuitionism require the existence of God to be true? These are ultimate moral questions.

Although their magnitude is such that I cannot answer them here, I will briefly address them. We do not know how the universe emerged. Based on its laws, physics can tell us how events unfolded up to a certain point. But physics necessarily has a number of limitations. It cannot tell us of every conceivable object whether it does or does not exist. Taking into account the state of physics at a given time, it can only tell us whether something purported to exist has physical existence. So it is of no help in determining whether there are moral kinds. The question concerning a priori knowledge can only be answered by considering claimed instances of a priori knowledge, and debating their status with philosophical arguments. No other discipline can decide the matter. The matter of innate moral knowledge is only partly within the purview of philosophy. Empirical psychological research is required to find out if we have such knowledge. What we are learning, however, seems to suggest that we do.[9]

Does evolutionary theory undermine the case for intuitionism? I don't think so. And if you have been persuaded by my case for intuitionism you should agree. However, let us consider one objection from evolution against it. The objection is that there is no evolutionary reason for humans to know objective moral truths based on moral kinds because doing so cannot be said to have any survival value for the species. Therefore, humans do not know such truths. If reproductive fitness is to be the touchstone for all human knowledge then the following question makes just as much sense:

[W]hy do we have the ability to see stars? After all, our evolutionary ancestors presumably would have done just as well if they only saw things on Earth. Of course, this is a silly question. We can see the stars because we have vision, which is useful for seeing things on Earth, and once you have vision, you wind up seeing whatever is there sending light in your direction, whether it is a useful thing to see or not. Likewise, once you have intelligence, you wind up apprehending the sorts of things that can be known by reason, whether they are useful to know or not. (Huemer, 2005: 216)

Among the things we humans apprehend are moral kinds and their several corresponding self-evident moral truths.

Does intuitionism require the existence of God? Intuitionism can be true whether or not God exists. It can likewise be false under either condition. It might be argued that the existence of God is necessary to explain nonnatural moral facts. But theists insist that God's existence is necessary to explain the existence of anything and everything—the universe, matter, energy, animals, and everything else—and explains each thing's existence adequately. A theist who thinks nonnatural moral properties, just by existing, require God to explain them would simply be working out an implication of his world view. However, theists who single out nonnatural moral realism as especially requiring the existence of God, as making no sense without Him, are unwittingly joining hands with moral nihilists. They agree with them that moral facts are just too queer to exist in the universe without God. One reason to advance this claim is that moral facts require further explanation. They cannot just be brute facts having no external reason. This line of argument is not one such theists are well positioned to make. For they believe that God exists, but that God cannot Himself be explained. God on such a view is a brute fact. So in this one respect, theism and nontheistic moral realism are explanatorily on par, while disagreeing on the point at which explanation ends.[10]

However, the fact of objective morality in the universe tells us something. The universe contains information that it would be wrong to do certain things, right to do others. It is certainly a curious feature of the universe. But just because the intuitionist form in which this information is presented is through objective mind-independent nonnatural entities does not decide the matter of whether their existence indicates a deity who created them. For theists would argue that any objectivist morality, including naturalism, reveals and requires the handiwork of God.

9. Chapter summary

Contemporary intuitionists have concentrated efforts on laying the metaethical groundwork for intuitionism. As a result, discussion of what the principles of intuitionism are has not been a priority. My view is that the intuitive principles are many and various, and should reflect the primary importance of moral kinds in grounding and knowing morality. Humans actually do act on the intuitive principles. And our moral deliberations indicate that the deliberatively open intuitive principles actually make wise moral decisions possible. Moral risk and moral weakness require that our moral decisions are supported by prudent judgment and action. Ross's consequential duties allow us to see how moral risks can be lessened through prudence. Simply knowing what is right gives us reason to do what is right, and suggests that the problem of moral motivation is less of a problem than has been thought. Finally, intuitionism is not undermined by evolution, nor does it in itself support theism.

Further reading

Two defenses of Rossian principles pluralism are McNaughton's "An unconnected heap of duties?" (1996) and Gaut's "Rag-bags, disputes and moral pluralism" (1999).

Conclusion

At this point my case for the claim that (a) you know what's right should be plain. The whole of this book provides it. Our real thoughts about what's right, our experience of morality in our lives, and the persistence of our core moral beliefs are best explained by the self-evidence of the intuitive moral principles.

The case for intuitions of self-evident propositions is strong. Most contemporary ethicists already agree that intuitions are indispensable for ethical inquiry. Contemporary intuitionists have effectively revealed many misunderstandings of the concept of self-evidence. And I have shown that the assumptions against self-evidence are not well justified.

The fact of moral disagreement has long appeared to undermine intuitionism. But even today we have no clearly stated and structured moral disagreement argument. My intuitionist account of moral disagreement is based on the fact that each party to a genuine moral disagreement has some justification for their position. However, one kind of moral disagreement I anticipate continuing is expert moral disagreement. Intuitionism will continue to be at a disadvantage as long as its opponents feel they can ignore or epistemically downgrade what intuitionism claims is data central to moral theory: what we really think about morality.

While intuitionism is often plain in its content, the account I favor is metaphysically expansive. A nonnatural account of moral facts requires a nonnatural theory of moral relations and moral kinds, as well as nonnatural right. No objectivist moral theory can do without moral relations. And moral kinds are the main instruments of moral explanation. Once we include the intrinsic moral good in our account, we are poised to provide moral explanations that closely reflect what we really think, and overcome the most serious objections to nonnatural moral realism, including those stemming from moral supervenience.

One concern about intuitionism I have yet to address. Intuitionism, with its reliance on what we really morally think, leaves nothing for ethicists to do. Given my investigation of intuitionism, and especially given the open questions concerning the correct list of intuitive principles, the nature of moral kinds, the adequate explanation of moral relations, I think we can all agree that on this point there is no cause for concern.

NOTES

Introduction

1 Cf. Annette Baier, 1985: 207–8.

1 Thinking about morality

1 W. D. Ross (1930) makes wide use of "what we really think" about morality. For example, he uses this consideration to determine what is the meaning of "right" (8), what moral reasons we have for acting (17), whether there are conflicts of duties (28), and to refute utilitarianism (39).

2 However, not all intuitionists base their case on self-evident truths. Elizabeth Tropman avoids reliance on them (2009). Huemer appears to take an agnostic stance on them, 2005: 106.

3 Epistemic appraisal helps determine what we really think through contrasts. This simple method contributed to the triumph of early analytic philosophy and was used effectively in ethics by W. D. Ross (see Chapter 2, Section 2). In Chapter 3, Section 4, I explain it at length.

4 I am not suggesting that there is agreement among intuitionists about what the fundamental moral principles are. There is not. I take up this issue in Chapter 8, Section 1.

5 Thus intuitionism explains why (i) there is no satisfactory way to resolve some moral disagreements at this time.

6 There are several different theories called "intuitionism" in ethics (see Stratton-Lake, 2002b for discussion). I mean by "intuitionism" the theory just defined, which has been and continues to be the main one discussed in ethics.

7 Ross (1930) makes these points on pages 29 and 32, respectively.

8 See Chisholm, 1976: 178.

9 "*Prima facie*" means "apparent." In first coining this term Ross seems to have had the practical epistemological aspect of prima facie duties foremost in mind. However, Ross himself was aware of the shortcomings of the term "*prima facie* duty*," and he agonized about providing a proper substitute (1930: 19–20).

There has been much subsequent controversy about the term "*prima facie*
duty" due to its etymological roots. It is wisest to recognize that Ross
proposed a technical philosophical term, and that debating the most
appropriate term based on its etymology is about as philosophically fruitful
as worrying about how misleading the term "utilitarianism" is because
its principle is not of much practical utility, as most utilitarians now
acknowledge. See Chapter 7, Section 6.

10 Ross says we have at best "probable opinion" of actual duties in *all* cases. I
think "rational belief" better captures for us what he was getting at. But I
disagree with Ross by holding that we sometimes do have moral knowledge
in particular cases. Some extreme examples will show this. An arsonist
burns down a well-populated apartment building. A woman leaves her baby
to die in a dumpster. A man sells a dozen kidnapped women into slavery.
Unless there is some catastrophic event, such as the detonation of a nuclear
bomb in a large city, that will be prevented by performing these actions, we
know they are wrong.

11 This and the previous several points show that intuitionism agrees with
the common view that (b) not everything is black and white concerning
particular moral situations and (c) sometimes it is morally permissible to,
say, break a promise.

12 This was (k) in our 12 points.

2 The story of contemporary intuitionism

1 For a bibliography of intuitionist work, see Stratton-Lake, 2002a. For
discussion of earlier work of naturalist moral realists and of nonnaturalist
moral realists, see Little, 1994a and 1994b, respectively.

2 The first two of these characteristics are similar to those that Soames
ascribes to analytic philosophy (Soames, 2003: xi). I add the third.

3 I divide intuitionists by period by the designations "traditional," "early
analytic," and "contemporary." For background on the just mentioned
traditional intuitionists, see Sidgwick, 1902: chapter 4. Major early
analytic intuitionists are Prichard, Ross, and Ewing. Major contemporary
intuitionists are Audi, Shafer-Landau, and Huemer.

4 For the case that Aquinas is the first intuitionist, see Audi (2004: 203).

5 In the *Republic*, Plato has Socrates overturn an account of justice by
appealing to our intuitions through a counterexample (Nelson, 1990: 283).
Aristotle has a plural set of fundamental moral principles, each of which we
may interpret as being self-evidently true (1107a10).

6 Prichard, 1912: 25.

7 Ibid.: 30.

8 I investigate moral relations in Chapter 5.

9 I will argue in Chapter 6 that this was a monumental blunder, a theoretical decision which has cost deontological theories dearly to this day.

10 So intuitionism agrees with the common view that (f) there is no way to prove that, say, lying is wrong. However, some intuitionists now challenge this claim. See Chapter 3, Section 3.

11 For example, Hurka gives Ross credit for the "Frege-Geach" objection to noncognitivism (Hurka, 2011: 3).

12 Russell uses this approach to undermine idealism and universal skepticism in his *Our Knowledge of the External World* (1914: 17–18, 73–4). Moore uses it to reject eliminationist and reductionist accounts of matter in his "Some judgments of perception" (1922: 228).

13 Soames points out Moore's inconsistent treatment of morality (Soames, 2003: 70). Moore is an epistemological intuitionist, but the resultant theory has a consequentialist structure.

14 Ewing, 1959: 126.

15 Utilitarians, for example, employ the notion of prima facie duty in their exposition of utilitarianism. See Bykvist, 2010: 10. However, moral particularists would be in that class of the few exceptions.

16 Arrington, 1989: 7.

17 Strawson was undeterred from taking this line of argument by Ross's pointing out that R. B. Perry had previously made a similar mistake on the same basis. Ross states, "Here he seems to be stressing too much the analogy which Professor Moore has alleged to exist between goodness and yellowness. The analogy exists only in respect of the indefinability of both. It is not argued that in other respects the two qualities are on all fours" (1930: 87). See also Ewing, 1947: 51.

18 Quine, 1951.

19 See, for example, Nielsen (1972), Hare (1981: 164), Shaw (1999: 182), and Bykvist (2010: 114). Smart, however, acknowledges that in some cases, this action could be utilitarianly correct (Smart, 1973: 70–1).

20 Kant, 1993b.

21 See especially Korsgaard's "The right to lie: Kant on dealing with evil" (1996b) and more recently, Cholbi (2009).

22 Darwall et al., 1992: 123.

23 Arrington, 1989: 5.

24 Cf. Audi, 1996: 106.

25 See, for example, Ross, 1930: 32.

26 To be fair to Mackie, this is not the whole of his argument from "relativity." He also provides an explanation for disagreement that supplements his

posing of the problem. In Chapter 4, I will return to the matter to discuss explanations of disagreement.

27 Incidentally, this little counterexample shows how baseless "experimental ethics" attempts to undermine intuitionism have been. Experimental ethicists believe that because people's intuitions differ on cases such as the trolley scenario, intuitionism is wrong (see Appiah, 2008: chapter 3). Given the even greater empirical evidence of disagreement about elementary mathematical truths, they are committed to holding that we do not have basic mathematical knowledge.

28 Cf. Huemer, 2005: 11.

29 These examples are from Huemer, 2005: 134–5.

30 See Huemer, 2005: 137–9.

31 Huemer (2005: 130) points out that no one making the argument from disagreement uses cases of obvious wrongdoing.

3 Moral knowledge

1 This is not to say that a nonrationalist form of intuitionism is impossible. See Audi, 2004: 232.

2 See Laurence BonJour (1998), Jerrold Katz (1998), and Christopher Peacocke (2003).

3 See BonJour, 2010: 84.

4 In 1963, Edmund Gettier showed that these three conditions are not sufficient for knowledge. Since then many epistemologists have been seeking a fourth condition which would complete the account of knowledge.

5 For example, Ross was well aware that we really do not think that "Getting pleasure for ourselves is a duty." However, he recognized that since "Maximizing the good is right" and "Pleasure is good" are both self-evident, our strong intuition against the duty of getting pleasure for ourselves is mistaken (1930: 24–6).

6 See Audi, 2004: chapter 2. Stratton-Lake (2002b: 21) and Shafer-Landau (2003: 248) seem to agree with this point. It is somewhat ironic that intuitionists should aim to show that intuitionism is capable of moral proofs. For it is one area where virtually everyone has come to agree the intuitionists were right: there are no moral proofs.

7 See Butchvarov, 1989: 62.

8 Audi rightly argues that self-evident principles more general than the intuitive principles we are discussing can give them epistemic support. See Chapter 7, Section 10.

9 Thus intuitionism holds that (f) there is no way to prove that, for instance, harming others is wrong.

10 See Chapter 2, Section 2.

11 Ross (1930: 17) makes this point concerning promise-keeping.

12 "Epistemic appraisal" and "epistemic preference" are Chisholm's terms. See Chisholm (1966) and Chisholm (1977: chapter 1).

13 See Schaffer and Knobe, forthcoming.

14 Some have recently argued that such comparative confidence is more than just a basis for a belief's being justified. Contrastivists assert that such contrasts are essential to knowledge. Contrastivism holds that we never simply know that p, we only ever know that p *in contrast to* q (see Blaauw, 2008). Epistemic justification does often involve contrasting candidates for belief. Perhaps this, along with other propositions, implies contrastivism, perhaps not.

15 See Huemer, 2009: 232.

16 Moore in one place holds that intuitions are propositions (1903: x). Audi holds that intuitions are like beliefs (2004: 32, 36) and that one must believe p as a necessary condition to having an intuition that p (2004: 34).

17 As I discussed in the previous chapter, early analytic intuitionists made no positive claims about intuition-generating mechanisms.

18 The following point was made by Ewing (1947: 26).

19 It is getting things backward to assume we know this because of formal logic. Rather, we know such inferences to be valid by intuition. And such intuitions are the basis for constructing formal systems of logic.

20 Ross (1930: 29–30) and Prichard (1912: 28) have drawn such parallels. Audi distances himself from them (1996: 108, 114).

21 I borrow Audi's terms here but shift them to different objects. Audi recognizes that some kinds of self-evident propositions are easier to grasp than others (2004: 35). Nonetheless, he goes on to claim that the distinction between such different kinds of self-evident propositions is between the *immediately self-evident* and the *mediately self-evident* (2004: 51). Given Audi's insight, and the fact that all self-evident propositions are self-evident, it seems that the immediate/mediate distinction is better moved away from the propositions and placed on the epistemic subjects who experience different degrees of difficulty apprehending different kinds of self-evident propositions. An omniscient deity would not sort propositions into the immediately self-evident and the mediately self-evident. But for us, some are immediately evident, others are mediately evident.

22 But what about variations in social conventions? Consider the Australian aborigine practice that women "could not carry two children." The response to twins was that "One or both twins were killed" (Sumner, 2002: 316). We consider the beliefs behind this practice superstitious. But I would claim that the aborigines were right that murder is wrong and mistaken about the evilness of twins. Not all twins are evil.

23 For more on this topic see my article "Synthetic concerns about intuitionism" (2009).

24 Johnson, 1960.

4 New challenges to intuitionism

1 Garner (1990) claims that moral nihilism's real challenge to realism is to explain how external facts could have authority over us.

2 I say "in discussion" on purpose. People do consult their own intuitive moral beliefs, and trust their authority, when facing their own moral situations. I say "almost" because doubts about the authority of modern science are increasing.

3 Also, recall that a science without intuitions is no science. See Chapter 3, Section 7.

4 See Sinnott-Armstrong, 2006.

5 I won't be examining these theories. For a thorough refutation of them see Huemer (2005: chapters 2 and 3).

6 It is estimated that the average American child sees 16,000 simulated murders on TV before the age 18. See US Senate Committee on the Judiciary. "Children, violence, and the media: a report for parents and policy makers," September 14, 1999.

7 I do not mean to suggest that providing a line of demarcation between the natural and the nonnatural is easy. See Ridge, 2008.

8 See Tropman, 2008: 169.

9 Moore puts forth a similar argument by elimination (1903: 15).

10 This approach draws from Butchvarov (1989: 61–6).

11 "Conceptually necessary" is unhelpful. It would be more precise to say it is analytic (Zangwill, 1995: 253). This would be surprising, for "every moral property supervenes on some set of natural properties" is possibly the worst candidate for an analytic truth ever, whatever the account of analyticity. It is more likely a synthetic a priori truth (ibid.). But the claim by opponents of intuitionism that the moral supervenience thesis is conceptually necessary illustrates that they can hold strong moral intuitions, at least when attacking moral realism.

12 This formulation is paraphrased from Ridge (2007: 335). I alter the language for terminological consistency. The following paragraph owes much to Ridge (2007: 335).

13 Shafer-Landau, 2003: 75.

14 Shafer-Landau presents a similar challenge (2003: 88).

15 This way of undermining Shafer-Landau's theoretical strategy is taken up by Ridge (2007).

16 These are three conditions Ross (1930) claims are necessary for knowing them.

17 In this section I will provide an intuitionist explanation of why (l) moral disagreement is common.

18 Such as physical, psychological, exploitative, deprivations of freedom, and
    social harms (Audi, 2004: 188).

5 The grounds of morality

1 "Intuitionists certainly do not say enough about what the relation is between
    rightness and the ground of rightness" (Stratton-Lake, 2002b: 14).

2 However, an issue related to the grounds of morality has been much
    discussed: agent-relative reasons. Many have thought that "Ross revealed
    our commitment to agent-relative reasons" (Shaver, 2011: 127). This is
    surely an important topic, but my aim is to examine the entities that may be
    said to ground such reasons. They are introduced next.

3 Prichard, 1912: 27–9 and Ross, 1930: 19. Quite recently, Audi, 2011 has
    introduced "fittingness relations" into his system.

4 Although kinds are essential to both Prichard's and Ross's moral
    explanations, they left no hint of what these kinds are like, or of what their
    metaphysical status might be.

5 So in this chapter I begin to answer Audi's question concerning the extent
    to which we can "'factually' specify the grounds of duty—the bases of our
    moral obligations—that are central in the principles of duty" (Audi, 2004:
    115). "Can we say in (non-normative) factual terms what it is to *promise*, or
    for someone to be *injured*, or to *need* our help?" (ibid.).

6 This can be seen concerning both the metaphysical grounding function of
    moral kinds and their role in moral knowledge. The following quotes support
    this. First, Ross says that "*prima facie* duty" is a "way of referring to the
    characteristic . . . which an act has, in virtue of being of a certain *kind* (e.g. the
    keeping of a promise)" (1930: 19) (emphasis added). Second, he states, "That
    an act, *qua* fulfilling a promise, or *qua* effecting a just distribution of good,
    or *qua* returning services rendered, or *qua* promoting the good of others, or
    qua promoting the virtue or insight of the agent, is *prima facie* right, is self-
    evident" (1930: 29) Third: "When we consider a particular act as a lie, or
    as the breaking of a promise, or as a gratuitous infliction of pain, we do not
    need to, and do not, fall back on a remembered general principle; we see the
    individual act to be *by its very nature* wrong" (1939: 173) (emphasis added).

7 Mark Schroeder states that intuitionism "is characterized more by its
    resistance to the answers to explanatory questions in ethical theory, than by
    any positive answers of its own" (2009: 203).

8 This description of Jane's day illustrates how (j) most of our duties are based
    on particular relations we have to other people.

9 I aim only to establish the existence of moral relations, not catalogue them.
    For that reason I will concentrate on moral relations between two agents,
    and leave moral relations to oneself aside.

10 We have to personally be in a moral relation to believe we really have a duty to someone else. That our first-person experience is what indicates to us that we enter moral relations explains why (d) we each feel more confident claiming that, for example, *we* have a duty to keep our promises than claiming that others do.

11 See especially Singer, 1972.

12 For more on these and other necessary features of promise relations, see Reinach, 1983.

13 Adolf Reinach's pioneering ideas concerning transaction kinds were first published in 1913, and first translated into English in 1983.

14 I recommend that you try to figure out what the necessary parts of a promise are. After all, if there is a universal "promise," its structure should be in principle universally accessible.

15 For a fuller argument against promises to oneself, see Hills (2003: 132–4).

16 Reinach, for one, thought this was a requirement of a promise (1983: 28).

17 See Chapter 2, Section 4 for Strawson's use of this argumentative tactic.

18 Searle (1964: 55) has such a theory.

6 The right and the good reconsidered

1 See Johnson, 1953 and 1957 and Audi, 2004: chapter 4.

2 See D'Arcy, 1931–2: 172; Metz, 1939: 300; and Taylor, 1939: 274.

3 Prichard, 1912: 22–3.

4 Ross does, however, correctly note that "right" and "morally good" do not mean the same thing (1930: 3). But that implies nothing about the existence of intrinsically morally good actions.

5 Oliver Johnson provides a similar worlds test argument for moral actions being intrinsically good (1953: 606). However, he neither mentions that it is Ross's method nor that Ross neglects to use his usual worlds test for right actions. Instead Ross inconsistently thinks consideration of a single case is sufficient to show right actions have no intrinsic value: "Suppose for instance that it is right for a man to pay a certain debt, and he pays it. This is in itself no addition to the sum of values in the universe" (1930: 132). If Ross were to use this "single instance" test instead of his worlds test for his four intrinsic values, they would not appear as good.

6 Throughout this discussion I will focus only on actual duties, not prima facie ones.

7 Moore's (1903) theory of organic unities captures this element of my moral explanation. But it is the unities of components of actions that primarily matter, not unities of their consequences.

8 Prichard claims that "The word 'ought' refers to actions and to actions alone" (1912: 24).

9 Ross, 1930: 3. However, he does note "a minor difference" between them (ibid.).

10 A nominalist might counter that F2 is true without abstract objects like 2, without humans, given a true counterfactual statement like "F2 would have been true if humans with a number system would have correctly judged F2 true." This does not eliminate the need for abstract objects, however, because such counterfactuals are best explained by possible worlds, which are best understood to be abstract objects.

11 In his recent account of moral facts, Christopher Kulp, 2011 appears to draw the same parallel.

12 See Chapter 4, Section 6. Shafer-Landau's exhaustion thesis is stated on 2003: 75.

13 Given that Ross holds that ignorance and vice are bad it is curious that he did not see that the badness of the components of actions like Davis's lie would make the whole action bad.

7 Intuitionism's rivals

1 In this chapter I will be showing why (h) supreme principle moral theories, such as utilitarianism or Kantianism, are not initially convincing, and are often not ultimately convincing.

2 See Kant, 1993a: 8 and Bentham, 1988: 4.

3 Kant, 1964: 104.

4 Kant, 1993a: 8.

5 I discussed the would-be murder case in Chapter 2, Section 6.

6 For Donagan's reasons, and for a discussion of its historical antecedents, see Donagan (1977: 57–66).

7 As Kant states, "human reason can, in matters of morality, be easily brought to a high degree of accuracy and precision even in the most ordinary intelligence" (1964: 59).

8 I am assuming for the moment that the universality test is effective.

9 Kant holds that if one preserves her life out of an immediate inclination then "the *maxim* of their action is without moral content" (1964: 65) (emphasis added).

10 Kant, 1993a: 8.

11 He adds, "Rawls 2000, 166, acknowledges this point, as does Nell 1975, 73" (ibid.)

12 Millgram, 2003: 527.

13 I say that the generic utility principle is "maximize good" rather than "maximize good consequences" because it is common now for consequentialists to include the good of the act in its consequences. See Shaw, 2006: 6 and Kagan, 1998: 27.

14 Ross, 1930: 17.

15 Ross uses this argument to show that it is not self-evident that "The right is what produces maximal good" (1930: 34–5). He uses promising, not truth-telling, in his argument. I use truth-telling to show that it makes more sense to follow *any* of the intuitionist principles over the utility principle.

16 A striking example is the "sheriff" case, which I discussed in Chapter 2, Section 6.

17 See Mill, 1957: 33 and Hare, 1981: 39–40.

18 Bales, 1971: 262–4.

19 Recent consequentialists "have nearly unanimously argued that it is a theory for assessing the right option for an agent or an agency to have made, not necessarily a useful theory to be applied in decision making" (Pettit, 1993: xvi).

20 In comparison with following the utility principle, Shaw states, "we are generally less likely to go wrong and more likely to promote good by cleaving to well-established secondary rules," such as telling the truth and keeping our promises (2006: 14). See also Smart, 1973: 42.

21 Thus, (e) there are emergencies in which a cold cost-benefit assessment makes the most moral sense.

22 Oliver Johnson, in his own modified intuitionism, argued that *the moral imperative* of intuitionism should be "Always maximize good" (1957: 195).

23 But see her claims against decision procedures and for uncodifiability. Hursthouse, 1999: 18.

24 Aristotle regards a set of actions and emotional responses as self-evidently and by their very nature wrong (1107a10).

25 Swanton offers a complicated version of V^3: "(1) an action is virtuous in respect V (e.g., benevolent, generous) if and only if it hits the target of (realizes the end of) virtue V (e.g., benevolence, generosity); (2) an action is right if and only if it is overall virtuous" (2001: 34).

26 Swanton's theory seems an impure form of exemplarism. I categorize it thus for two reasons. First, the second component of Swanton's principle is nearly identical to V. Second, it seems the virtues Swanton discusses are virtues of exemplars.

27 Oakley, 1996: 129.

28 Audi (1995) provides a good example of this approach.

29 Audi adds that, "the complexity and partial conceptual independence of the two sets of principles make it possible for explanatory connections to be made in both directions" (2004: 111).

8 Practical and ultimate moral issues

1 Some of Audi's principles are paraphrased.

2 Shafer-Landau's principles are mentioned on 2003: 248, Huemer's on 2005: 102.

3 More ethicists today are apt to take intuitionism's side on this matter than would have been 30 years ago. Virtue ethicists and anti-theorists are largely responsible for this shift of opinion. So on the point of theory guiding action they should be counted among intuitionists' unintentional allies discussed in Chapter 2. See Crisp and Slote (1997) for essays on virtue ethics. See Clarke, 1987 for a discussion of anti-theory.

4 Ross, 1930: 30.

5 See Nagel, 1979: 98.

6 Prichard acknowledged this as a problem and thought that we must sometimes think through what he calls "preliminaries" before we recognize the wrongness of an action (1912: 27–30). Ross notes a related problem: "any act may be correctly described in an indefinite, and in principle infinite, number of ways" (1930: 42).

7 Hare, 1963: 72. Hare distinguishes between moral weakness, which he considers not to be a problem for ethics, and weakness of will, which he does (ibid.).

8 For a fuller treatment of this thesis see my article "Can morality do without prudence?" (2011).

9 In a recent *New York Times* article, May 3, 2010, Paul Bloom, a research psychologist relates, "A growing body of evidence . . . suggests that humans do have a rudimentary moral sense from the very start of life."

10 For a defense of nontheistic nonnaturalism, see Wielenberg (2009).

REFERENCES

Appiah, K. A. (2008), *Experiments in Ethics*. Cambridge, MA: Harvard University Press.

Arrington, R. (1989), *Rationalism, Realism, and Relativism: Perspectives in Contemporary Moral Epistemology*. Ithaca, NY: Cornell University Press.

Audi, R. (1993), "Ethical reflectionism," *Monist*, 76, 295–315.

—. (1995), "Acting from virtue," *Mind*, 104, 449–71.

—. (1996), "Intuitionism, pluralism, and the foundations of ethics," in W. Sinnott-Armstrong and M. Timmons (eds), *Moral Knowledge? New Readings in Moral Epistemology*. Oxford: Oxford University Press, 101–36.

—. (2004), *The Good in the Right: A Theory of Intuition and Intrinsic Value*. Princeton: Princeton University Press.

—. (2011), "Intuitions, intuitionism, and moral judgment," in Jill Graper Hernandez (ed.), *The New Intuitionism*. London: Continuum, 171–98.

Ayer, A. J. (1952), *Language, Truth and Logic*. New York: Dover Publications.

Baier, A. (1985), "Theory and reflective practices," in A. Baier (ed.), *Postures of the Mind: Essays on Mind and Morals*. Minneapolis: University of Minnesota Press, 207–27.

Bales, R. E. (1971), "Act-utilitarianism: account of right-making characteristics or decision-making procedure?," *American Philosophical Quarterly*, 8, 257–65.

Bentham, J. (1988), *The Principles of Morals and Legislation*. Amherst, NY: Prometheus Books.

Blaauw, M. (2008), "Contrastivism in epistemology," *Social Epistemology*, 22, 227–34.

BonJour, L. (1998), *In Defense of Pure Reason: A Rationalist Account of a Priori Justification*. Cambridge: Cambridge University Press.

—. (2010), *Epistemology: Classic Problems and Contemporary Responses*, 2nd edn. Lanham, MD: Rowman and Littlefield Publishers.

Brandt, R. B. (1959), *Ethical Theory*. Englewood Cliffs, NJ: Prentice-Hall.

Butchvarov, P. (1989), *Skepticism in Ethics*. Bloomington, IN: Indiana University Press.

Bykvist, K. (2010), *Utilitarianism: A Guide for the Perplexed*. London: Continuum.

Carson, T. (2005), "Ross and utilitarianism on promise keeping and lying: self-evidence and the data of Ethics," *Philosophical Issues*, 15, Normativity, 140–57.

Chisholm, R. M. (1966), "The principles of epistemic appraisal," in F. C. Dommeyer (ed.), *Current Philosophical Issues*. Springfield, IL: Charles C. Thomas, 87–104.

—. (1973), *The Problem of the Criterion*. Milwaukee: Marquette University Press.

—. (1976), *Person and Object: A Metaphysical Study*. Chicago, IL: Open Court.

—. (1977), *Theory of Knowledge*, 2nd edn. Englewood Cliff, NJ: Prentice-Hall.

Cholbi, M. (2009), "The murderer at the door: what Kant should have said," *Philosophy and Phenomenological Research*, 79, (1), 17–46.

Clarke, S. G. (1987), "Anti-theory in ethics," *American Philosophical Quarterly*, 24, (3), 237–44.

Cohen, M. R. and Nagel, E. (1934), *An Introduction to Logic and Scientific Method*. New York: Harcourt, Brace and World.

Crisp, R. and Slote, M. (1997), *Virtue Ethics*. Oxford: Oxford University Press.

D'Arcy, M. C. (1931–2), "The good and the right," *Proceedings of the Aristotelian Society*, New Series, 32, 171–206.

Darwall, S., Gibbard, A., and Railton, P. (1992), "Toward fin de siecle ethics: some trends," *Philosophical Review*, 101, (1), 115–89.

Donagan, A. (1977), *The Theory of Morality*. Chicago: University of Chicago Press.

Ewing, A. C. (1947), *The Definition of Good*. New York: Macmillan.

—. (1959), *Second Thoughts in Moral Philosophy*. London: Routledge & Kegan Paul.

Garner, R. T. (1990), "On the genuine queerness of moral properties and facts," *Australasian Journal of Philosophy*, 68, (2), 137–46.

Gaut, B. (1999), "Rag-bags, disputes and moral pluralism," *Utilitas*, 11, (1), 37–48.

Gettier, E. L. (1963), "Is justified true belief knowledge?," *Analysis*, 23, (6), 121–3.

Hales, S. D. (2004), "Intuition, revelation, and relativism," *International Journal of Philosophical Studies*, 12, (3), 271–95.

Hare, R. M. (1963), *Freedom and Reason*. Oxford: Clarendon Press.

—. (1981), *Moral Thinking: Its Levels, Methods and Point*. Oxford: Oxford University Press.

Hills, A. (2003), "Duties and duties to the self," *American Philosophical Quarterly*, 40, 131–42.

Huemer, M. (2005), *Ethical Intuitionism*. New York: Palgrave Macmillan.

—. (2009), "Apology of a modest intuitionist," *Philosophy and Phenomenological Research*, 78, (1), 222–36.

Hume, D. (1969), *A Treatise of Human Nature*. London: Penguin Books.

Hurka, T. (2011), Introduction to T. Hurka (ed.), *Underivative Duty: British Moral Philosophers from Sidgwick to Ewing*. Oxford: Oxford University Press.

Hursthouse, R. (1999), *On Virtue Ethics*. Oxford: Oxford University Press.

Johnson, O. A. (1953), "Rightness, moral obligation, and goodness," *Journal of Philosophy*, 50, (20), 597–608.

—. (1957), "Ethical intuitionism—a restatement," *Philosophical Quarterly*, 7, (28), 193–203.

—. (1960), "Denial of the synthetic *a priori*," *Philosophy*, 35, 255–64.

Kagan, S. (1998), *Normative Ethics*. Boulder, CO: Westview Press.

Kant, I. (1964), *Groundwork of the Metaphysic of Morals*, trans. H. J. Paton. New York: Harper.

—. (1993a), *Critique of Practical Reason*, 3rd edn, trans. Lewis White Beck. Upper Saddle River, NJ: Prentice-Hall.

—. (1993b), *Grounding for the Metaphysics of Morals: On a Supposed Right to Lie because of Philanthropic Concerns*, 3rd edn, trans. James W. Ellington. Indianapolis: Hackett.

Kaspar, D. (2009), "Synthetic concerns about intuitionism," *Southwest Philosophy Review*, 25, 119–26.

—. (2011), "Can morality do without prudence?," *Philosophia*, 39, (2), 311–26.

Katz, J. J. (1998), *Realistic Rationalism*. Cambridge, MA: MIT Press.

Korsgaard, C. M. (1996a), "Kant's formula of universal law," in C. M. Korsgaard (ed.), *Creating the Kingdom of Ends*. Cambridge: Cambridge University Press, 77–105.

—. (1996b), "The right to lie: Kant on dealing with evil," in C. M. Korsgaard (ed.), *Creating the Kingdom of Ends*. Cambridge: Cambridge University Press, 133–58.

Kulp, C. B. (2011), "Moral facts and the centrality of intuitions," in Jill Graper Hernandez (ed.), *The New Intuitionism*. London: Continuum, 48–66.

Little, M. (1994a), "Moral realism I: naturalism," *Philosophical Books*, 25, 145–53.

—. (1994b), "Moral realism II: non-naturalism," *Philosophical Books*, 25, 225–33.

Mackie, J. L. (1977), *Ethics: Inventing Right and Wrong*. New York: Penguin.

McCabe, D. L., Treviño, L. K., and Butterfield, K. D. (2001), "Cheating in academic institutions: a decade of research," *Ethics and Behavior*, 11, (3), 219–31.

McCloskey, H. J. (1957), "An examination of restricted utilitarianism," *Philosophical Review*, 66, (4), 466–85.

McLaughlin, B. and Bennett, K. (2005), "Supervenience," *Stanford Encyclopedia of Philosophy*.

McNaughton, D. (1996), "An unconnected heap of duties?," *Philosophical Quarterly*, 46, 433–47.

Metz, R. (1939), "Recent trends in ethical thought," *Philosophy*, 14, 299–312.

Mill, J. S. (1957), *Utilitarianism*. New York: Macmillan.

Miller, A. (2003), *An Introduction to Contemporary Metaethics*. Oxford: Polity.

Millgram, E. (2003), "Does the categorical imperative give rise to a contradiction in the will?," *Philosophical Review*, 112, (4), 525–60.

Moore, G. E. (1903), *Principia Ethica*. Cambridge: Cambridge University Press.

—. (1922), "Some judgments of perception," in G. E. Moore (ed.), *Philosophical Studies*. New York: Harcourt, Brace & Co, 220–52.

Nell, O. (1975), *Acting on Principle: An Essay on Kantian Ethics*. New York: Columbia University Press.

Nelson, M. T. (1990), "Intuitionism and conservatism," *Metaphilosophy*, 21, (3), 282–93.

Nielsen, K. (1972), "Against moral conservativism," *Ethics*, 82, (3), 219–31.

Oakley, J. (1996), "Varieties of virtue ethics," *Ratio*, New Series, 9, 128–52.

Peacocke, C. (2003), *The Realm of Reason*. Oxford: Oxford University Press.

Pettit, P. (1993), Introduction to Philip Pettit (ed.), *Consequentialism*. London: Dartmouth Press.

Posner, R. A. (1999), *The Problematics of Moral and Legal Theory*. Cambridge, MA: Harvard University Press.

Prichard, H. A. (1912), "Does moral philosophy rest on a mistake?," *Mind*, 21, 21–37.

Quine, W. V. O. (1951), "Two dogmas of empiricism," *Philosophical Review*, 60, (1), 20–43.

Rawls, J. (1971), *A Theory of Justice*. Cambridge, MA: Harvard University Press.

—. (2000), *Lectures on the History of Moral Philosophy*, ed. Barbara Herman. Cambridge, MA: Harvard University Press.

Reinach, A. (1983), "The a priori foundations of the civil law," trans. J. F. Crosby. *Aletheia*, 3, 2–142. Originally published (1913) "Die apriorischen grundlagen des bügerlichen rechts." *Jahrbuch für Philosophie und phänomenologische Forschung*, 1, 685–847.

Ridge, M. (2007), "Anti-reductionism and supervenience," *Journal of Moral Philosophy*, 4, (3), 330–48.

—. (2008), "Moral non-naturalism," *Stanford Encyclopedia of Philosophy*.

Ross, W. D. (1930), *The Right and the Good*. Oxford: Clarendon Press.

—. (1939), *Foundations of Ethics*. Oxford: Clarendon Press.

Russell, B. (1914), *Our Knowledge of the External World*. London: Allen and Unwin.

Schaffer, J. and Knobe, J. (forthcoming), "Contrastive knowledge surveyed," *Nous*.

Schroeder, M. (2009), "Huemer's Clarkeanism," *Philosophy and Phenomenological Research*, 78, (1), 197–204.

Searle, J. R. (1964), "How to derive 'ought' from 'is,'" *Philosophical Review*, 73, 43–58.

Shafer-Landau, R. (2003), *Moral Realism: A Defence*. Oxford: Clarendon Press.

—. (2005), "Ethical subjectivism," in Joel Feinberg and Russ Shafer-Landau (eds), *Reason and Responsibility*, 12th edn. Belmont, CA: Wadsworth/Thomson, 510–21.

Shaver, R. (2011), "The birth of deontology," in Thomas Hurka (ed.), *Underivative Duty: British Moral Philosophers from Sidgwick to Ewing*. Oxford: Oxford University Press, 126–45.

Shaw, W. H. (1999), *Contemporary Ethics: Taking Account of Utilitarianism*. Malden, MA: Blackwell Publishers.

—. (2006), "The consequentialist perspective," in James Dreier (ed.), *Contemporary Debates in Moral Theory*. Oxford: Blackwell Publishing, 5–20.

Sidgwick, H. (1902), *Outlines of the History of Ethics*. London: Macmillan.

Singer, M. G. (1954), "The categorical imperative," *Philosophical Review*, 63, 577–91.

Singer, P. (1972), "Famine, affluence and morality," *Philosophy and Public Affairs*, 1, (3), 229–43.

Sinnott-Armstrong, W. (2006), *Moral Skepticisms*. Oxford: Oxford University Press.

Smart, J. J. C. (1973), "An outline of a system of utilitarian ethics," in J. J. C. Smart and Bernard Williams (eds), *Utilitarianism: For and Against*. Cambridge: Cambridge University Press.

Smith, B. (1992), "An essay on material necessity," *Return of the a priori* (Canadian Journal of Philosophy, Supplementary Volume 18), 301–22.

Smith, M. (1994), *The Moral Problem*. Oxford: Blackwell Publishing.

Soames, S. (2003), *Philosophical Analysis in the Twentieth Century, Volume 1: The Dawn of Analysis*. Princeton: Princeton University Press.

Stratton-Lake, P. (2002a), Bibliography in W. D. Ross, *The Right and the Good*, ed. P. Stratton-Lake. Oxford: Clarendon Press, li–lviii.

—. (2002b), Introduction to P. Stratton-Lake (ed.), *Ethical Intuitionism: Re-evaluations*. Oxford: Clarendon Press, 1–28.

Strawson, P. F. (1949), "Ethical intuitionism," *Philosophy*, 24, 23–33.

Sumner, W. G. (2002), *Folkways: A Study of Mores, Manners, Customs and Morals*. Mineola, NY: Dover Publications.

Swanton, C. (2001), "A virtue ethical account of right action," *Ethics*, 112, 35–52.

Taylor, A. E. (1939), "The right and the good," *Mind*, 48, 273–301.

Timmons, M. (2002), *Moral Theory: An Introduction*. Lanham, MD: Rowman and Littlefield Publishers.

Tropman, E. (2008), "Naturalism and the new moral intuitionism," *Journal of Philosophical Research*, 33, 163–84.

—. (2009), "Renewing moral intuitionism," *Journal of Moral Philosophy*, 6, 440–63.

Väyrynen, P. (2008), "Some good and bad news for ethical intuitionism," *Philosophical Quarterly*, 58, 489–511.

Wielenberg, E. J. (2009), "In defense of non-natural, non-theistic moral realism," *Faith and Philosophy*, 26, (1), 23–41.

Zangwill, N. (1995), "Moral supervenience," in Peter French, Theodore Uehling, Howard Wettstein (eds), *Midwest Studies in Philosophy*, 20, Moral Concepts. Notre Dame, IN: University of Notre Dame Press, 240–62.

INDEX